Financial Literacy for Millennials

Financial Literacy for Millennials

A Practical Guide to Managing
Your Financial Life for Teens,
College Students, and
Young Adults

Andrew O. Smith

PRAEGER™

An Imprint of ABC-CLIO, LLC
Santa Barbara, California • Denver, Colorado

Library of Congress Cataloging-in-Publication Data

Names: Smith, Andrew O., 1962– author.
Title: Financial literacy for millennials : a practical guide to managing your financial life for teens, college students, and young adults / Andrew O. Smith.
Description: Santa Barbara : Praeger, 2016. | Includes index.
Identifiers: LCCN 2016015425 | ISBN 9781440834028 (hardcopy : alk. paper) | ISBN 9781440834035 (ebook)
Subjects: LCSH: Finance, Personal.
Classification: LCC HG179 .S5384 2016 | DDC 332.024—dc23
LC record available at https://lccn.loc.gov/2016015425

ISBN: 978-1-4408-3402-8
EISBN: 978-1-4408-3403-5

20 19 18 17 16   1 2 3 4 5

This book is also available as an eBook.

Praeger
An Imprint of ABC-CLIO, LLC

ABC-CLIO, LLC
130 Cremona Drive, P.O. Box 1911
Santa Barbara, California 93116-1911
www.abc-clio.com

This book is printed on acid-free paper ∞

Manufactured in the United States of America

Contents

Acknowledgments

This book started as a letter.

A relative asked me to spend some time talking about money with his daughter, a doctor who was newly married to another doctor. They turned out to be the perfect objects of a personal-finance education: intelligent, responsible, successful, and high earners. Unfortunately, like many intelligent people with good incomes, they were too busy to learn how to be smart about their money, and they weren't particularly interested in doing so, either. Over a lifetime of following the financial press and marveling every time I would read about a financial scam or some sophisticated investment fraud, I noticed that doctors were often among the victims. Then it made sense: they had lots of money but spent little time learning how to handle it properly.

After several unsuccessful attempts to engage the young doctors in a conversation about their finances, I decided to write them a letter. Over a few weeks, I considered the important things that young people should know about money, some of which I had learned through education and training, others that had come to me naturally through my experiences advising others, and some I had learned the hard way. The result was a 10-page letter setting out a basic course in financial literacy for young adults. This letter led to a series of conversations with the young couple, and from all evidence it appears to have done them good. It didn't turn them into readers of the *Wall Street Journal*, fans of *Mad Money*, or subscribers to *Kiplinger* magazine, but it did make them think about their life goals, how money would figure into achieving them, and why they should take personal finance more seriously.

I benefitted greatly from the extensive comments given me by the primary readers of this book in draft form: Jeff Henderson, Ragan Memmott, David Roberts, and Sally Zuckert. I was also helped by comments from Bernie Ostrowski and Hope Wolman, who reviewed small sections of the book. Thank you all. I thank my agent, Steve Hutson, and the people at Praeger/ABC-CLIO for recognizing the importance of this topic and for having confidence in my ability to make a useful addition to the literature. I am grateful to my family for supporting my writing efforts over an extended period of time and for tolerating the impacts on our family life. Most of all I thank my great-grandparents, who had the courage and wisdom to immigrate to the United States, allowing me the great privilege to be a citizen of this country and adopt the financial habits of thrift, skepticism, and self-reliance that are the natural inheritance of all New Englanders.

PROLOGUE

A Tale of Two Teens

Wendy was a fairly typical high school student. She participated in several clubs, was an okay athlete (better than average, but no college scholarship offers), had a few good friends, worked hard in school, and got decent grades. She was pretty sure she wanted to go to college but didn't have any career goals figured out yet. Wendy's parents were divorced. Her dad wasn't in the picture, but her mom was caring and provided a good home. Her high school offered a mini-class in personal finance, and although Wendy wasn't particularly interested in the topic, her mom persuaded her to take it. Although most of the mini-class didn't seem at all relevant to her, she filed away in the back of her mind some important lessons about managing her financial life.

Wendy loved music and shopping and hanging out with her friends at the mall. Because her mom didn't have a lot of extra money, Wendy babysat for local kids all through high school and got a summer job lifeguarding at the public pool. These jobs gave her spending money for the things she liked, and she was even able to save some of her earnings at the local bank. By the time she was ready to graduate from high school Wendy had almost $2,000 in her bank account. Wendy's mom lived nearly paycheck to paycheck, so she couldn't help Wendy very much with college expenses. Wendy would have to rely on financial aid and loans to pay for college.

Brian was a very popular boy in high school, a leader in student government, a star athlete, and part of a local band with some of his friends. He wasn't that serious about his classes, figuring high school grades didn't matter much and that he had plenty of time to buckle down in college. Despite that attitude, his grades were still okay. Someday Brian wanted to own and operate his own restaurant. He liked food and cooking, so running a restaurant seemed like a great idea. He wasn't quite sure how college figured into the program, but decided he should go. Both of Brian's parents had good jobs, so his family was comfortable financially. When his high school offered an after-school course in personal finance, Brian thought he wouldn't have any need for it, so he chose to hang out with his friends instead.

Brian spent most of his time at sports practices, rehearsing with his band, and playing video games. Even with his team commitments he had plenty of free time, and he liked being able to do what he wanted with it. During a few summers he worked construction for a friend of his dad's, but he didn't like the work. His parents gave him an allowance that covered his spending money, so he didn't worry about having to work during high school. He knew that college was going to be expensive, but he wasn't focused on that part of it: it was hard enough just doing all the applications.

COLLEGE

Wendy spent a lot of time with her high school guidance counselor and decided that a smart move for her would be to start at the local community college. It offered a two-year degree program in nursing, and if she wanted to get more serious about it as a career, she could transfer to a four-year college and work toward her bachelor's degree in nursing. Wendy was a little intimidated by the science classes required even for the two-year degree, but she really liked the idea of helping people, and after researching trends in the economy, discovered that nursing was likely to be a reliable and well-paying career in the years ahead. Best of all, given her limited financial resources, the community college was affordable.

In order to save money, Wendy lived at home during her first two years in college. While she craved the true collegiate experience of living in a dormitory, she realized it didn't make sense for her to spend the extra money. Wendy made new friends, participated in a few campus organizations, and worked part-time and summers in retail for extra money. She was even able to add to her savings account from high school. Wendy really liked her nursing program, so in her second year she applied to transfer to a nearby state university to get a bachelor's degree, which would give her better job opportunities. She convinced her mom it was time to move on campus despite the extra cost, which is where she spent her last two years finishing college. Wendy needed some loans to make it work financially, so by the time she finished college she had $25,000 in debt. After graduation Wendy set aside time to study for her registered nurse exam, submit the state papers for her nursing license, and look for a job.

Brian loved college. He didn't spend a lot of time looking at where to go and ended up at the state university a few hours from his home. He was fine with that, since a lot of his friends were also going there. He wasn't able to keep his band together, but he joined a fraternity, played club sports, went to his fair share of parties, and made many friends. His university offered every course of study he could imagine, but he wasn't sure what he wanted. Brian's academic interests fluctuated: he liked movies so took a few courses in film studies, then tried some psychology courses and a few introductory business classes. His dad suggested that since he wanted to own his own business someday he should take an accounting course, but Brian wasn't interested in something so technical.

Brian's parents thought he should use his summers to explore different job interests, so one summer he worked as an intern at an advertising office. They asked him to do a lot of tasks that Brian thought were beneath him, so that didn't work out. Another summer he worked at a restaurant but didn't care for the grimy work, rude customers, and long hours on his feet, and concluded that his childhood dream of owning a restaurant wasn't really for him. Whatever money he made he spent on going out with his friends—he didn't see any need to save. Because he kept changing majors (he finally decided on sports marketing) it took him five years to graduate, but graduate he did, and his parents were very proud of him. Because his family had above-average income, Brian didn't get a lot of financial aid, but his parents couldn't foot the whole bill. Brian had taken out some loans as he went, and with the cost of an extra year of college he ended up graduating with $45,000 in debt.

EARLY CAREER

Wendy landed her first job as a nurse at a large local hospital affiliated with a major university. Since this was her first real job, she had a lot to learn about the nursing profession (school only takes you so far) and the practicalities of a work environment. Nursing paid well, but Wendy wanted to be careful so she chose to rent a low-cost studio apartment on the bus line that went directly to the hospital, avoiding the need for a car. The hospital offered a retirement plan where it matched (up to a point) whatever Wendy contributed, so even though retirement barely entered her mind, she loved the idea of "free money" from her employer. Wendy was very practical with her spending, eating at home most of the time, saving up for her vacations, building an emergency fund, never carrying a balance on her seldom-used credit cards, paying down her college loans, and investing anything left over in stock market index funds.

Wendy had settled into her life as an independent single adult. She had enough friends and dated occasionally, planning someday to get married but in no particular hurry. Her employer gave her increasing responsibility and regular pay raises, and after a few years Wendy took a job at another hospital that allowed her to work in pediatrics—she loved kids. She moved to a different apartment near her new job, and even though she could afford a bigger place and even a car, she chose a modest one-bedroom apartment and still used the bus to get to and from work. Wendy kept adding to her high school savings account, which she used as an emergency fund, and continued to build her investments using index funds. Both of Wendy's employers since college were nonprofit organizations, and she discovered that after ten years from graduating, the remaining balance on her federal student loans was forgiven. At age 32, Wendy had become debt free!

After finishing college Brian moved back home. He had sent out a few resumes his senior year, but with all the graduation activities he had put off a serious job search. He really wanted to work for a professional sports team, but none of the responses he received were encouraging. After a few months his parents pushed him to get a job, so he worked part-time for a caterer. It wasn't enough pay to get his own apartment, and although he loved his parents, he chafed at living under their roof. About a year after graduation Brian accepted a job offer to sell mortgages for a national finance company. They put him through an intensive training program, but after he finished and started in his new sales role, Brian decided he didn't like it. So went a three-year odyssey of changing jobs, changing industries, and living at home with his parents. He wasn't miserable, but it wasn't what he wanted, either.

Finally, Brian landed a job that he liked, selling restaurant equipment. He was pretty good at it, using his natural likability, good people skills, and interest in food to become a star performer. Almost overnight he started earning a good income from all the sales commissions, so he moved into a fancy apartment (finally out of the house), filled it with new furniture, and was loving life again. He had to borrow on his credit cards to buy all the new stuff for his apartment, but he was sure he could afford it now. The college loans had ballooned during the first three years after graduation because he hadn't paid anything on them, but now he was able to start making regular payments. Brian didn't focus on all the benefit programs his new employer provided or see the need to put any money aside for retirement; he could worry about that later. Finally, he was living on his own!

FAMILY

Many of Wendy's friends were getting married. She went to numerous weddings, was a bridesmaid at a few, and was genuinely happy that her friends had found their mates. Despite her generally active social life, it hadn't yet happened for her. Her fortieth birthday was still a few years away, but she could hear her biological clock ticking. On the career front things were going well: she had moved into a role with a specialized rehabilitation unit at a nearby children's hospital that paid substantially more than her previous job, gave her regular hours, and presented interesting challenges as a nursing professional. With the extra income she finally bought herself a used car, since now she had to drive to work, but she stayed in her modest one-bedroom apartment. She treated herself to a nice vacation every year, even taking her mom to Europe for her 70th birthday. Wendy continued with her modest living and steady savings habits: her bank savings account, retirement fund, and stock market index-fund investments had all grown nicely as a result.

One of Wendy's continuing interests was reading novels, and she had been in a book club since shortly after she finished college. She took an immediate interest in a new member of her book club named Scott, a man who had recently moved to town to teach at a local college. He was a few years older, had been married and then divorced without children, and seemed to reciprocate her interest. After a few dates it was pretty clear they both were falling in love, and a year later they married and combined their households into a two-bedroom apartment near Scott's campus. It wasn't fancy, but it allowed them to have a home office for Scott that doubled as a guest room. They both wanted children and got right on it; at age 39 Wendy was married and pregnant. The lives that Wendy and Scott had previously known were about to change dramatically.

Brian continued with his success as a restaurant equipment salesman. He developed such a good track record that he was hired by the leading distributor in his city. He owned an exotic sports car, took lavish vacations, had closets full of fashionable clothes, and bought himself a newly-constructed condominium in an exclusive neighborhood when he turned 35 years old. He liked to play the lottery—someone had to win, right? He got a big bonus one year and went all in on a green energy investment he heard about, unfortunately that went bust. Brian seemed to spend as much money as he made. His college loan debt was falling but at a slow pace; his credit card debt had mushroomed; and now he had a big mortgage payment. Because Brian had no savings, he had to borrow the condo down payment from his parents, and he was sure he could pay it back. Things were generally going really well for him.

On the social front Brian had always been popular with the girls, and as a young adult he dated frequently. Brian used several online dating apps, but he hadn't found anyone special. He hadn't really felt like settling down when he was younger, but now the single life was starting to feel empty. At a weekend barbecue one summer he met Allison, the sister of one of his old fraternity brothers, and although she was much younger they found they had a lot in common. They dated exclusively for three years before Brian, after strong encouragement from Allison, proposed. After a year of planning and a huge wedding (mostly paid for by Brian), they married. Allison moved into Brian's place, and they settled into married life together. Brian was about to turn 40.

MID-CAREER

Wendy and Scott were very excited to become new parents, and were surprised, but pleased, when they learned they were having twins. After the babies arrived the parents were continually exhausted, but life with the twins was exhilarating. Wendy had planned carefully so she could take off work for an entire year to be with her newborns, relying on her employer's generous parental leave policy, savings, and Scott's income. Then she went back to work part-time. Scott's college had a terrific day care center, so he took the kids over there on the days Wendy worked. They stayed in this groove until the twins were ready for all-day kindergarten, at which time Wendy returned to work full-time. Soon after that, Scott was granted tenure at his college, so the growing family felt secure.

Although Scott was well-educated and intelligent, he left the family finances to Wendy, who continued to read books on personal finance, watch Suze Orman on public television, and pay attention to online articles about money and investing. When the twins were born she and Scott hired a local attorney to draft wills that included guardianship provisions. Wendy also insisted they both have living wills and health-care proxies, just in case. Both of their employers offered some life insurance, but Wendy made sure they bought additional term life insurance. And while they continued to save as much as they could for retirement, they also created a 529 college savings fund for the twins. Wendy and Scott had each been good savers before they married, and together they had saved enough for a down payment on a three-bedroom house a few blocks from their current apartment, just the right size for their growing family. Wendy made sure they got a good mortgage.

Brian and Allison enjoyed life as a married couple, but Allison struggled to find a career that interested her, holding a series of different administrative jobs but never doing the same thing for too long. Brian kept advancing in his equipment sales career, now working exclusively with high-end restaurants and corporate cafeterias. Brian wasn't sure he wanted to have children, but Allison was adamant about it. Before long, they had two children a few years apart. This prompted a move from the fancy down-town apartment to a big house in the suburbs and the purchase of a new minivan. The net proceeds from the sale of the condo were just enough to cover the down payment on the new house, and now they had a bigger mortgage on top of all the extra expenses of two children. Brian remained the sole breadwinner.

As the children grew older Brian and Allison drifted apart. Allison loved being a mom but sometimes felt trapped at home. Brian resented not being the focus of his wife's attention and wished she had other interests besides the kids. He also didn't feel his hard work was appreciated, and wished his wife were more careful about spending. At the end of every month they never seemed to have any money left over. They both missed being able to go out with their friends and blamed each other for it. Their love life cooled. Things got so bad that Allison insisted they go to marriage counseling, which Brian did reluctantly, but their relationship didn't improve. Sadly, when the kids were ages 8 and 5, Brian and Allison decided to divorce. Brian moved into an apartment, leaving Allison in the big house with the children.

CRISES

Wendy and Scott both continued with their careers while remaining involved parents. Nursing had turned out to be an excellent profession for Wendy, and so had teaching for Scott, with good job security, benefits, and regular, if modest, financial advancement. The twins were now in high school and starting to think about college. The family's careful saving, disciplined spending habits, and prudent investing had enabled them to build up a substantial amount of money in the 529 college plans for the twins, so while they knew college was going to be costly, they felt able to help their kids manage it. Their retirement funds were also in good shape, and because Wendy had been paying extra on the house payment each month, their mortgage was shrinking rapidly. They never carried balances on their credit cards. As Wendy and Scott entered their mid-fifties, their life together was on solid financial ground.

Then something terrible happened. Scott was biking home from campus one rainy evening at dusk, lost control of his bicycle on the slippery road, and skidded into a tree. Even though he was wearing his helmet the force of impact was so great that he was seriously injured. After being hospitalized for several weeks Scott returned home and faced many months of rehabilitation. Although the family health insurance paid for much of Scott's care, Wendy decided to take a leave of absence from work so she could provide the extra care Scott needed. Fortunately,

Scott and Wendy both had purchased the optional disability insurance their employers offered, despite its relatively high cost, so Scott's income was replaced by this insurance while he was recovering. Although Wendy wasn't paid for her own time off to care for him, their emergency fund came in handy to help out while she was on leave. After six months Scott was able to return to work full-time, and the family had come through this calamity without suffering financial ruin.

Brian was entirely unprepared for being divorced. Because Allison had never earned much money, Brian was required to pay child support and alimony until the children turned 18. He was still responsible for the mortgage on the house that his ex-wife and children occupied, with the new burden of his own apartment to pay for. His only comforts were work, where he continued to be a top performer, and his regular visits with his children. After a few years he started to regain his confidence about life, even slowly getting back into the dating scene. Despite his above-average income money was tighter than ever, so when a friend offered Brian an opportunity to get in on the ground floor of a sure-fire Internet stock, Brian borrowed everything he could to make the investment.

Brian had never paid much attention to the economy, but some of his colleagues at the equipment distributor said a recession was coming and moved into other businesses. After a while the economy did, in fact, start to slow down, and it quickly grew much worse. People stopped eating out at expensive restaurants, corporations cut back on their dining services, and soon Brian had no customers. His employer had no choice but to lay Brian off. Worse, Brian's credit card debts had escalated, and he still had his college loans and the big mortgage on the house. His sure-thing Internet stock had crashed, but he still owed the money for it. Brian had no savings he could tap, and his parents were retired on a fixed income, unable to help him. Brian's financial life had collapsed. He got some advice from a friend whose financial judgment he trusted, met with an attorney, and filed for bankruptcy.

MATURITY

As Wendy celebrated her 60th birthday, she felt a quiet satisfaction with her life. She and Scott had a strong marriage despite the occasional disagreement, they found comfort and companionship with their many friends, and they had the freedom and resources to travel several times a year. The twins were away at college, thriving, about to become independent adults themselves. They video chatted regularly. Wendy's mom wasn't well, so Wendy spent increasing amounts of time looking after her, including taking over her financial affairs. Work continued to fulfill Wendy professionally. She didn't have any interest in early retirement, unlike some of her colleagues. She spent more time volunteering at her church and took up stamping as a hobby. Her kids taught her how to use Facebook, but she didn't quite get the appeal.

Financially, Wendy and Scott were in solid shape. With financial aid grants and the 529 plans Wendy and Scott had started when the twins were babies, all the college expenses were paid: the children were going to leave college debt-free, perhaps the greatest gift any parent can give a child. The mortgage on the house would be paid off later that year, ten years ahead of schedule due to Wendy's extra monthly payments. Wendy and Scott both owned retirement plans that had grown handsomely, despite the ups and downs of the stock market, from their regular contributions they had invested in index funds. At whatever point she decided to stop working, Wendy's retirement would be secure. Her lifelong attention to careful financial planning was about to provide her security when she needed it.

Brian's bankruptcy was a rough process, emotionally and financially. He got one break: because he had been unemployed for over four months before he filed for bankruptcy, his income was low enough that he was able to qualify for a Chapter 7 liquidation. When it was all over the big house was gone, but so were most of his debts. The bankruptcy didn't get him out of the support payments to his wife and kids, and he still had to pay off his old college loans. He was able to keep some of the equity in the house, which he used to buy a smaller house for Allison and the kids, as the divorce agreement required. He would have been able to keep any retirement plan he owned after the bankruptcy, but unfortunately Brian had never started one. Still, Brian was ready for a fresh start.

During the bankruptcy Brian downsized to a small, low-cost apartment and actively sought a new job. A business associate from Brian's early days owned the regional franchise rights to a new fast-food restaurant chain that had just entered the local market, and needed someone to visit each new location to make sure the equipment was installed properly. The job paid a lot less than what Brian had been making before, but in this economy Brian was grateful to have any job at all. He was still paying on Allison's mortgage, now thankfully smaller, as well as his college loans, but the mountain of debt had become manageable. The bankruptcy process required Brian to take a credit counseling course, which he didn't get much out of, but the trauma of bankruptcy taught him that he needed to pay more attention to his financial future, which, as Brian entered his 58th year, still looked pretty bleak.

RETIREMENT

Wendy kept working into her mid 70s, largely because she enjoyed the good she was doing for her young patients. A few years earlier her mom had passed away, and Wendy herself had transitioned to an administrative position that was easier on her joints, which had started to ache a bit after long days on her feet. Scott, too, continued to work into his 70s. Together, they decided it was time to retire from their long, successful careers while they were still healthy. Because they had deferred their Social Security checks until actual retirement, their combined annual payments covered almost their entire living expenses. Wendy worked with a financial advisor and decided that she and Scott should modify their investments to provide more income for their retirement years. They considered moving to a smaller home but decided it wasn't worth the all the costs of selling their house and moving.

The twins had started families of their own. Now that Wendy and Scott were retired it would be easier to visit their children more often. It was exciting for the couple to be part of their grandchildren's lives, and they were comfortable enough to help contribute to the 529 college savings plans that the twins had set up. Wendy didn't want to overstay her welcome, however, so she and Scott enjoyed lots of other travel as well. They both maintained an active schedule with friends, hobbies, culture, and volunteer work. After a lifetime of working hard and making smart money decisions, Wendy and Scott approached their retirement years together with the freedom and confidence that financial security provides.

Brian was hoping he could fix his financial life, but it wasn't entirely in his control. Brian's alimony and child support payments to Allison had finally stopped, and she was required to take over the mortgage payments. But now he wanted to help out with the kids' college tuition. They qualified for a lot of financial aid, largely because none of Brian's income was counted in the aid calculation. But as much as Brian wanted to help them, he simply couldn't. He felt like a failed parent because he couldn't help his kids with the cost of college, but he was advised by a financial expert that he needed to worry about himself first. Gone were the fancy cars, flashy clothes, and spendthrift ways. Brian had to use every extra penny he earned to pay off his remaining debts and build some savings for retirement. Brian saw many of his friends stop working and spend their time playing golf, eating out, and traveling the world. Unfortunately, his own retirement would be far off.

Brian never achieved his childhood dream of owning his own business, but at least he now had a job. The restaurant chain he worked for expanded, but there were few opportunities to advance. His once-athletic body was starting to fail him. He developed chronic back pain and had several other ailments that made his constant traveling for work difficult. He wanted to retire at age 65 but knew he didn't have enough money for that. So he kept working until his body couldn't take it anymore, when he was 70 years old. He would collect a monthly check from Social Security and could rely on Medicare for his medical insurance, but he had built up only a small retirement fund since the bankruptcy. He didn't own his own home, and with the rent payment and regular medical bills to pay, every month it was touch and go with his money. Brian was hoping he wouldn't have to go to his kids and ask for help, as that would be embarrassing. But if he encountered just one unpleasant surprise, he would have nowhere else to go. This wasn't at all the life he had hoped for when he started out as a young adult.

YOUR FINANCIAL PATH

Financially, do you want to be more like Wendy or more like Brian?

Wendy didn't begin adulthood with a passion for personal finance, but early on she saw the value in it. At every stage in her life she worked hard to make good decisions about money. She controlled her spending, saved as much as she could, invested intelligently but cautiously, and devoted energy to managing her financial life. She made a lot of smart financial moves, such as beginning her higher education at a community college, starting early with her retirement fund, making sure there were life insurance and disability insurance just in case, paying extra on her mortgage to accelerate paying it off, and taking advantage of the loan forgiveness feature of her college loans. Like everyone, Wendy faced some difficult times, in her case the temporary disability of her husband, but the strength of her financial planning prepared her to rebound and ultimately prosper, both emotionally and financially.

Brian, too, began with little interest in managing his financial life, and he barely paid attention to his personal finances as a young adult. He was a big spender, never saved, and failed to plan for his future. At every turn he seemed to make bad financial decisions: he never developed a career plan, used credit cards recklessly, bought more house than he needed, ignored his retirement, made risky investments, and didn't prepare for having children. When a financial crisis hit—in Brian's case, divorce and losing his job—he was utterly unprepared and had no choice but bankruptcy. After that, Brian was forced to live within his means and make efforts to improve his financial life, which is what he should have done as a young adult. Brian wasn't able to turn things around, as it was too little too late. He retired in near poverty, with little freedom to enjoy his leisure time, and he faced financial insecurity throughout his final years of life.

If you absorb the lessons of this book, make good choices about your money, and pay attention to financial matters throughout your life, you can be like Wendy. If you avoid learning about your financial world, make financial decisions based on impulse, and fail to take financial planning seriously, you could end up like Brian—or worse. You control your own financial future. Read on, and you'll be prepared.

ONE

Financial Planning

Most people can quickly list dozens of things they want to buy, places they want to visit, and activities they want to do. It doesn't take much effort to think of something you want. But coming up with a sound plan for how to get it takes some thought. Consider the following:

You're in high school and want a new dress for the prom. How will you buy it?

You're a college student and want to take a camping trip with a group of your friends after graduation. How much will it cost, and how will you pay for it?

You're a young adult living at home with your parents but want to get your own apartment instead. What do you need to do?

These are only a few situations where a financial plan will help you achieve the things you want. There are many more challenges that will confront you financially as you move through life, and they'll be considerably more complex. Buying a house, having children, changing jobs—all are big decisions that impact your financial life.

Some people aren't good at planning. They like to live in the moment and figure that things will take care of themselves. If the future is so uncertain, why bother making plans that will have to change anyway? This may be true, but it doesn't mean you shouldn't have a financial plan.

Why? We live in a society where almost everything you need to be physically comfortable and secure requires money. Even your spiritual health requires money—if you go to church, think about who pays the salaries of the pastors. This doesn't mean that your life should be all about money—far from it. What they say about money not buying happiness is true. Not having money, however, can contribute to misery.

A financial plan is all about what you want to do with money, how to achieve your goals, and how to protect the things you buy with your money. It can be about big dreams you have for the future, or it can be about small needs you must meet right now.

MONEY

Money. Everybody needs it, we all certainly seem to want more of it, and people spend a lot of time talking about it. But what is it, actually? If you think that money is a way to get the things you want in life, you're on the right track. You give money to somebody and they give you something in return. If you want milk at the supermarket, you give the clerk a few dollars, and you get the milk. If you want a place to live, you give the landlord a check every month, and you get to stay in the apartment. If you want to see a Taylor Swift concert, you give Ticketmaster your money, and you get a seat at the show. Money is simply a way to get the things you want and need. We call this using money as a *medium of exchange*. This means money has value in the things it can get you when you trade it for goods or services.

Money can play a different role, as well, before you trade it for something you want. Your money has a value to you even if you don't spend it. In the United States we use money called "dollars," and we track its value by the number of dollars we may have. In this sense, money is storing the value for us to use at a later time—when we trade it for goods or services. We consider this use of money a *store of value*. Economists also describe another use for money: as a *unit of account*. This means that we use money to record and measure the value of things: measuring someone's income, a country's output, or a company's debts.

In the past, people didn't use money. They traded directly with each other in what was known as the *barter system*: I'll give you wheat if you give me meat; this person will repair your shoes if you mend her clothing. In small, simple communities, this system worked well. We even barter today, informally: I'll help you with your homework if you clean up the kitchen; your friend will drive you to the game if you proofread her paper.

Early forms of money were often made of precious metals. During the first years of our country's independence, the United States adopted the *gold standard*, where paper money could be converted into gold at a fixed rate. People thought this was a good idea because it gave money a physical and defined form, as well as confidence that the paper money was worth something more. The United States abandoned then readopted the gold standard numerous times in its history in response to various economic crises or the influence of fashionable economic policies. By 1976, the United States had abandoned the gold standard once and for all, and the rest of the world has followed suit. The paper currency we use today is called *fiat* money, meaning it isn't backed up by anything physical such as precious metals.

All the combined money in the economy is called the *money supply*, and there are different ways to measure it. It's easy to see that dollar bills in your wallet and coins in your pocket are money, as is the value of any bank accounts you may own.

Other forms of money aren't so easy to see, however, because they're hidden in the banking system: all the money banks keep in their vaults and certain transactions between banks also add to the money supply.

Our money supply is important. The narrowest measure of the money supply tracked by our government counts it at around $3 trillion, supporting an economy of around $18 trillion.[1] When the relationship between the money supply and the size of the economy changes, employment and economic growth can feel the effect. In addition, some people believe there's a relationship between money supply and inflation: if the money supply isn't managed carefully, inflation can get out of control.

INFLATION

Since the recession of 2008–09, the public has heard little about inflation. Nevertheless, for much of U.S. economic history, inflation has been an important concept. *Inflation* means a general increase in the price of things we buy. You probably have noticed that most things get a little bit more expensive every year. College tuition, health care, automobiles, restaurant meals, subway fares, and rent are just a few of the things that tend to cost more each year or two.

On the other hand, the costs of cell phone service, electronics, clothing, and toys have all fallen in price in recent years. Some things we buy change prices frequently: energy costs and groceries are the best examples. So it's sometimes hard to tell if prices overall are rising or falling.

Why should you care about inflation? Inflation erodes your purchasing power and requires constant attention in order to evaluate changing prices. You might have a great financial plan, but substantial inflation will disrupt every element of that plan. In an inflationary environment the money you earn won't go as far, your assumptions about what you can afford won't hold up, your expenses will change unpredictably, interest rates will typically rise, and business activity often contracts, leading to lower job growth. Every seller in the economy must constantly change prices, so they tend to devote resources to price management instead of the actual production of goods and services.

Government and private economists spend a lot of time studying inflation. They've developed measures to determine if, throughout the entire economy, prices on average are rising or falling. One common measure is the *Consumer Price Index*, which quantifies the change in cost of a group of items typically purchased by most people on a regular basis. Another measure of inflation is the *GDP Deflator*, which examines the price of everything produced in the economy and compares it to the price of all those things in a previous year.

An inflation rate of 1–2 percent seems to be what most economists think is an appropriate level. If inflation is higher, businesses and consumers must constantly implement and evaluate price changes, and wages are slow to keep up. At a lower rate, the economy risks falling into *deflation*, which is a general decrease in the level of prices throughout the economy. While the United States historically came through its deflationary periods pretty well, today deflation is associated with low or negative growth and serious damage to the economy.

Over a long period of time, even a low rate of inflation can make a major difference in prices. Let's say your grocery bill costs $100 per week at the start of 2017, and it will increase at 2 percent per year (inflation) for the same groceries over the next 10 years. At the start of 2027, those same groceries will cost you about $122 (the extra $2 is from compounding, explained later in this book). So you'll need $122 in 2027 to buy the same groceries you bought in 2017 for only $100. If you only are able to spend $100 in 2027, you won't be able to get as much food. That's inflation: you get less for your money.

If we're in 2027 and referring to the money we use at that time, we call the $122 "nominal" dollars. If we want to compare the 2027 price level with 2017 in this case, we can say that the "real" value of the grocery money is $100 in 2017 dollars. "Real dollars" will always refer to a base level year, in this example 2017. If you ever hear or read about "real" versus "nominal" prices, people are talking about inflation, and all they're doing is comparing two different time periods. From a personal finance point of view, stable prices (low or no inflation) are a good thing. You don't have to constantly assess new prices, worry about the loss of purchasing power of your money, or strive for an increase in your income merely to keep up with the higher prices.

PERSONAL RESPONSIBILITY

The first thing to know about your financial life as you move toward independent adulthood is that someone else won't take care of it for you. Most parents take care of their children's financial needs, but that doesn't last forever. If you're very lucky, you may have a family with enough resources to set you up so you'll have few financial worries as an adult, but even so, you'd better know how to handle it. Rich or poor, everybody needs to take charge of their own financial lives.

You make hundreds of decisions every day, and many involve money. You need to have the ability to make good decisions about money, just as you need to make good decisions about whom to become friends with, how you treat your family members, and what to do when you make a mistake. Good decision making is important, but so is taking ownership of your decisions regardless of how they turn out. We're each responsible for our own actions, and this is never more true than when it comes to money.

Whether you have a lot of money or very little, you must be aware that everyone around you is trying to get it from you. It may be as innocent as McDonald's tempting you to buy their hamburgers, Walmart competing to sell you their groceries, or an insurance company offering you their "minimum coverage." Or someone may try to take your money from you by fraud or deception, offering a once-in-a-lifetime deal that you feel you can't pass up. No matter what, your decisions about money will determine the condition of your financial life.

And that's the point: these will be *your* decisions about *your* money that will affect *your* financial future. Yes, it's possible to blame someone else when something goes wrong, but in most cases you'll have to live with the results your decisions. Taking personal responsibility for the decisions in your life takes many forms, but it starts with how you handle your money.

LIFE GOALS

It's unrealistic to expect teens to know what they want to do with the rest of their lives. It may even be a challenge for many 30-year-olds to know what direction to take next with their lives. That's okay. Nobody has to have a life plan, if that means a set of clearly defined objectives to be met by a certain age. But it's important to have a sense of the possible life goals out there that you might take an interest in later on. Recurring themes become apparent for those who want to lead meaningful, productive, and fulfilling lives:

Education: It's really hard to be a good citizen without a solid education. It's even harder to keep up with the changing world or to have a successful career without it. Education is valuable in its own right, but it's also a tool to help you achieve other life goals. Without a good education your life options will be limited. Attaining a high level of education or training is an important life goal for many people.

Career: A career is simply a series of jobs that you mostly intended. There's a lot of randomness in the job market or in running your own business, but you can control it to some extent by developing certain skills and obtaining experience in a particular field. Having a sense of where jobs are headed can help you make a good career choice. Many people derive great satisfaction from the work they do.

Relationships: Whether you remain single your entire life, marry your highschool sweetheart, or have serial partners, a committed relationship with another person can bring support, comfort, and meaning. Love can't always be planned for, but successful relationships require work, commitment, and understanding. Personal relationships of all forms will be a big part of your life.

Family: The nature of family life today is diverse and unpredictable. Many people choose to have children, to others parenthood comes by surprise, and some prefer to remain childless. Many families care for extended relatives, both younger and older than those who provide the support. Raising children and caring for other family members will become life goals for many people.

Material Comforts: Some people seek spiritual heights and emotional contentment, others desire large homes, fancy cars, and expensive jewelry, but most of us just want to be comfortable and secure. Many people want to own their own homes, often the single most important financial commitment you can make. Understanding what you want in this department will help drive your plan.

Charity and Service: One of the greatest satisfactions in life is helping other people—giving of your time, energy, talents, love, and sometimes money. People have different levels of interest in performing charity or devoting energy to service, but it's one of the defining features of being a human being. The ability to help others can be an important goal in your life.

Travel and Entertainment: Everybody likes to have fun, right? Maybe it will take the form of becoming a great cook, or assembling an awesome music collection, or visiting every state in the country. Maybe you want to travel overseas and visit spiritual retreats to study under master gurus. Perhaps you simply like to go to the movies a lot. Once you identify the special pleasures you want out of life, they can become goals.

Retirement: For most people, there will come a time to cease their "work" years and enter their "retirement" years. Some people want to work their entire lives, and certain careers lend themselves more easily to that than others. Since this is a book for those at the beginning of their financial lives, not the end of it, retirement thoughts will naturally be far away. Just know it's coming, and how you live that part of life will ultimately be among your goals.

EXPERTS

Many experts work professionally as financial advisors, financial service providers, and financial planners. Perhaps someday such an expert can help you. For now, however, professional help is probably unnecessary. Still, it's important for you to know that these experts exist, what they do, and how you might use them should the need arise.

Just about anyone can call themselves a financial advisor or planner, but an *investment advisor* must have a license. A license or a title doesn't indicate much about the knowledge or abilities of the person with the license. Various organizations certify financial advisors through a combination of education, testing, and experience requirements. The federal government also offers certifying examinations for investment professionals. One of the more prominent designations is Certified Financial Planner, but there are scores of such titles. Keep in mind that many people who call themselves a financial planner or investment advisor are actually commissioned sales people trying to sell you a stock, an insurance policy, or another financial service. There's nothing wrong with making stock market investments, and insurance policies can be an important part of a financial plan. The problem is that when the advisor has a financial interest in your purchase of whatever she's selling, you may not be getting the most objective recommendation or the appropriate product for your needs.

Fortunately, there are numerous professionals available to assist you with your financial needs who work on a fee-for-service basis, and they won't have that built-in conflict of interest of getting compensated only when they sell you something. You pay them a fee, and they help you develop a plan. New online services that focus on investments, such as Wealthfront and Betterment (sometimes called "robo-advisors"), offer low-cost planning tools as an alternative to using financial planners for those without complex finances. If you're at the start of your financial life and read this book carefully, you'll have everything you need to develop your own plan without outside advice. If you inherit a fortune, win the lottery, or become a millionaire at a young age, that's when you should start looking for a fee-only financial planner.

ELEMENTS OF A FINANCIAL PLAN

A financial plan is an organized strategy for the elements of your financial life. Each chapter of this book, for example, could serve as a single element in a financial plan. Putting your financial plan in writing is a good idea: forcing yourself to craft a document can help you refine and define what you really want and need. Finally, a financial plan is the result of a process, the process of analyzing and organizing your financial life. Whether simple or complex, a financial plan will usually cover these basic elements:

Spending. How much money do you regularly spend to maintain your current lifestyle? Will there be any changes soon that increase or decrease your monetary needs? Many people create a budget to identify and control where their money goes.

Income: Even if you're a student living at home, you have an income: whatever money you get from your parents, plus whatever money you earn from any jobs. You can also view an asset (for example, a bicycle you own) as something that can become income if you sell it. An important reason to work and have a career is to generate income.

Savings: You should always consider saving some of your money. There are many reasons to save and many ways to do so. How much and how well you save your money is a critical factor in any financial plan.

Debt: Credit cards, home mortgages, student loans, and what you owe your friends and family members are all different forms of debt. Whether you need to use debt, how much of it to use, and in what forms and under what terms, are all elements of a financial plan.

Security: We use insurance to protect ourselves from the risk of financial losses. We can protect our health, our property, and even our lives using insurance products. Older people also protect themselves using wills, trusts, and other legal documents.

KEEPING TRACK

As you move through life you might wonder how you're doing with your financial plan and seek a way to keep score. One mechanism that can help is a *personal balance sheet*. A simple way to create a personal balance sheet is to divide a piece

Table 1.1   Personal Balance Sheet at Age 27 as of August 31, 2016

Things I Own (Assets)		Things I Owe (Debts)	
Laptop	$600	MasterCard balance	$422
iPhone	$400	Student loan 1	$6,890
Apartment furniture	$2,000	Student loan 2	$12,573
Music collection	$500		
Clothes	$1,000		
Checking account	$1,855		
Savings account	$4,606		
Work retirement plan	$29,243		
Security deposits	$1,600		
TOTAL ASSETS:	$41,804	TOTAL DEBTS:	$19,885
FINANCIAL NET WORTH:	$21,919		

Source: Author's analysis.

of paper in half by drawing a line in the center of the page from top to bottom. On the left side of the paper write down everything you *own* and make an estimate of its current value, then total it up. On the right side of the paper write down everything you *owe* and put some numbers to each item there, then total that up. At the bottom of the page, subtract what you owe from what you own: this is your financial *net worth*.

For a teen, this kind of exercise might be simple: you don't own very much and don't owe anybody much, either. So the personal balance sheet of a teen might include a cell phone, clothing, and maybe a bank savings account that, taken together, are worth about $1,000, offset against a $25 debt to a brother. This teen's net worth would be $975. As you go through life, however, your financial situation will become more complicated, and the balance sheet will include more things you own and debts you owe. Table 1.1 shows the personal balance sheet for a hypothetical young adult who has been out of college for five years. Her financial net worth will keep growing as she earns money from her job to pay off student loans and build her savings. Tracking your financial net worth as you move through life is one way to watch how your financial condition is improving, but of course it only measures the condition of your finances. Your value as a person is immeasurable.

GIVING BACK

Charity and service are life goals for many people, and you may already be involved in such activities today. For example, many high schools have imposed a "service learning" requirement for graduation, where students work with local charities or otherwise help out in the community. Colleges offer opportunities to volunteer in underserved neighborhoods. Churches organize missions to disaster areas to help with relief efforts. Young people can arrange blood drives, collect canned goods for food banks, volunteer at soup kitchens and homeless shelters, or visit assisted living facilities. There are many ways people give back to their communities and help improve the lives of the less fortunate. Importantly, as much as people give of their time and energy, they can also give of their money.

Why should you do this? One benefit of performing charity work or donating money to a worthy cause is that you'll feel good doing so. Helping another person will give you an immediate sense of worth and accomplishment because of the good you just did. Acts of charity can also be part of a religious or cultural tradition, such as giving money at church, putting coins in a charity box, or making efforts to improve the world around you. As a young person you'll probably have more time and energy available than spare money, so maybe most of your charity efforts will be hands-on for a while. Still, you should get in the habit of making small contributions to organizations that help the needy or afflicted, whether it's for the United Way, Red Cross, Salvation Army, cancer research, the local food bank, or your church. As your income grows you'll be able to make larger gifts and have a more significant impact on people's lives. Acts of charity are their own reward.

A BALANCED LIFE

While it's true that life can be difficult without money, it's a mistake to think that money should be at the center of your life. One hundred years ago a majority of Americans lived below what we'd consider the poverty level today, and conveniences we take for granted, like flush toilets and electric refrigerators, were rare. Life was hard, but most people had family they could count on, a belief in something higher than their own lives, and they participated in a community of friends and neighbors that gave them purpose and satisfaction.

This book is about your financial life, and absorbing its lessons will allow you to achieve many of your goals, now and in the future. Its purpose, however, is to improve the nonfinancial aspects of your life that give you joy and meaning. Focusing on your personal finances to the exclusion of your other interests is a mistake and gets the cause and effect reversed. Having a solid financial plan will help you have a good life, but never lose sight of the fact that a financial plan is a pathway to take you somewhere else. It's not a destination; it's a way to improve the journey.

NOTE

1. Board of Governors of the Federal Reserve System, Federal Reserve Statistical Release, "Money Stock Measures," Table 1, data for M1, November 27, 2015; U.S. Department of Commerce, Bureau of Economic Analysis, National Economic Accounts, "Gross Domestic Product," current dollar and real GDP tables, November 24, 2015.

TWO

Careers

It may seem overwhelming to consider a career when you're still a student or just getting settled into your first real job. Some people know from early childhood that they want to work in a specific field when they become adults, whether it's as an auto mechanic or ballet dancer, working for a professional sports team or for a charity serving homeless people. Not everybody finds their calling as a young person, however, and even if you're set on a particular career path at age 15 or 20, it doesn't always work out. It's important for you to have a sense of what it takes to work in certain jobs as you make decisions about education and training. It's also important to have the knowledge and skills to change direction as circumstances require.

A person entering the workforce today will likely change jobs numerous times before reaching retirement age. Some people may work for the same employer their entire careers, although this is rare. Others may work in the same field but change employers: for example, a nursing assistant who's employed by a number of different hospitals or medical offices as she moves or seeks career advancement. Some people will have several very different jobs, perhaps starting in construction, then becoming a truck driver, maybe later working as a warehouse supervisor. Decisions you make as a young person can position you for the job and career options you want, or they may limit you in ways that affect your personal and financial well-being.

CAREER PATHS

A career is a series of jobs in the same occupation, or a variety of jobs within the same industry or even at the same company. Let's say you become a refrigeration technician and work for different appliance service companies during your working life, or perhaps you train as a teacher and work for several schools before you retire. Those are occupation-based careers as a technician and teacher. Maybe you get a job in the public works department of a local government, then move from accounting clerk to program manager to project supervisor; or you start as a cashier at Walmart, move to Banana Republic as a store manager, and end up as a merchandise buyer for Macy's. These are industry-based careers in government and retail. It's hard to predict the exact path of your career, but you can make purposeful decisions that will take your career in the direction you want.

The youngest members of the Baby Boom generation (born 1957–1964) who are currently in the prime of their careers have averaged about 12 different jobs so far over their working lives.[1] While there's a popular perception that today's young people will be more-frequent job hoppers than their predecessors, so far the millennial generation looks a little *less likely* to switch jobs than previous generations.[2] The overall average job tenure in the United States is about four and a half years today, and people change jobs more frequently at the beginning of their careers.[3] Careers of tomorrow will involve a large number of job changes over a working life; unfortunately, young people wildly underestimate how often they'll change jobs and may be unprepared for the many different work environments they'll face. Developing a plan to navigate a world with frequent job changes is critical for young adults.

HUMAN CAPITAL, EDUCATION, AND TRAINING

As you work, you'll develop knowledge, experience, professional networks, and skills that relate to the job you're doing, and you'll become more productive—and more valuable as an employee—as a result. You're developing your *human capital*, and human capital is valuable. If you're in an occupation-based career, the human capital you develop will largely transfer across employers, so you can expect to generally "move up" as you change jobs—obtain an increase in your job responsibility and compensation. If you're in an industry-based occupation, your human capital—your value as an employee—will also typically increase as your career advances, so long as you stay within that industry. If you change industries, much of what you learned in your previous jobs may not be useful in a new industry. The worst career path is to change occupations *and* industries as you change jobs, for example, moving from a salesperson in retail, to a purchasing agent in manufacturing, to providing tech support in education. People in career paths like this may find it difficult to increase their income because the knowledge, experience, professional networks, and skills they developed in each previous job—the human capital— won't easily transfer to new jobs.

The first investment you make in your human capital will be in education and training. A typical high school graduate has already developed an impressive set of useful work skills: she can read, write, knows arithmetic, has learned to work in groups, and can get along with different types of people. That's a good start, but to be ready for the workforce you need additional education or training. Generally, *training* refers to learning specific occupation-related skills, such as how to become a court stenographer, style hair, or repair machinery and equipment. *Education* usually refers to learning broad topics of knowledge that can have applicability to several occupations or prepare you to work in many industries. For example, completing a college liberal arts education will develop analytical thinking and communication skills; learning accounting will be useful in many types of business jobs; mastering a foreign language can facilitate a job in international commerce. Some of your education may have no obvious connection to a job or career, but will help you become a more informed and interesting person; that's okay, too.

While going to college has a great long-term payoff (see Chapter 5), college may not make sense for everyone. What does make sense, however, is that everyone should choose a career path and develop the knowledge and skills necessary to be successful in that career. This can mean vocational school or community college where you learn job skills for a specific career. It can also mean apprenticeship, where you work in an occupation (usually starting at a low wage) and learn from those who have already mastered the craft, developing the skills to command a higher wage. As you advance through life, career-related education and training shouldn't stop. Those who continue to improve their skills and knowledge through advanced education and training usually see career and job benefits. Almost every field offers training and continuing education, whether for an auto mechanic learning about the latest diagnostic technology or a doctor learning about the effectiveness of a new medicine.

Not all 17- or 18-year-olds know how they want to spend the 50 years or so following high school that will constitute their working years. Even so, two things can help prepare you as you refine your career direction. First, develop some skills that will have practical application to several types of jobs, such as taking a course in marketing, learning how to develop a website, or becoming skilled at basic bookkeeping. This will make you an attractive employee and give you flexibility as you move across jobs early in your career. Second, think about the industries or business sectors that are interesting to you and try to focus on one or two that are related, even if you're not quite sure about what occupation you want. Experience in and background knowledge about an industry can ultimately lead to valuable expertise.

THE LABOR MARKET

Employers hire workers because employees bring value to the organization where they work. That value must be higher than the cost of employment, or there's no reason to employ that person, and this is as true of the nonprofit and government sectors as it is of the for-profit sector. If you're a salesperson and you sell services that bring in $100,000 of revenue, can your employer pay you $50,000 and cover other costs of running the business so that the business is profitable? Measuring the value of an employee can sometimes be very difficult: how much "output" does a teacher produce? How should an employer value that work?

As for all products and services you purchase as a consumer, there's a market for the demand and supply of labor. Workers of all kinds—whether it's someone cutting the grass in your yard or the mayor of your city, a call-center worker or the chief executive of a major corporation—are competing in a market for their services. It's not one market, of course: there aren't that many employers for chief executives, and chief executives don't compete against gardeners for jobs. Still, many potential employers will compete to attract the best talent to their organizations. These employers create the demand for labor. In addition, many workers can perform the jobs that these employers are offering, and these workers will compete against each other for the available openings. These workers create the supply of labor. The interaction of these supply and demand forces results in the establishment of a market rate for the value of a person's labor.

At the end of the day, all organizations have to "make money" to stay in business. In the government and nonprofit worlds, making money means keeping expenses no greater than revenues from taxes, bond issues, contributions, grants, or any products and services they sell. In the private sector, making money means earning a profit, so that after paying all the expenses of running an organization, money is left over to pay a return on the capital used to fund the business. Again, in both cases, each worker in these organizations must provide more value to the organization than it costs to keep that person employed—otherwise there's no reason for the organization to employ that worker. This is why it's important to build your human capital through education, training, experience, and continued learning throughout your career.

LIFETIME INCOME

A theory about how people spend money over their lifetimes, called the "permanent income hypothesis," says people base their current spending decisions on how much money they expect to earn over their entire lifetimes, not just on their current or short-term incomes. This means people will borrow to spend more when their incomes are low (as young people) and accumulate savings by spending less when their incomes are high (as older people). It also implies that short-term spikes or drops in income won't change spending patterns very much. Economists have been debating this theory since its inception (the consensus is that the theory is directionally correct), but we don't have to be economists to use this theory to gain important insights into our own behavior. It helps explain why it's okay to borrow to pay for college or a house (we earn more money as we age, so we can pay it all back), and why people save for retirement (our income falls after we stop working, so we need other sources of money).

Unfortunately, there's great uncertainty about what your lifetime income will be. A small change in your annual income will add up to a big number after 45 or 50 years of working. Furthermore, the career you choose may pay substantially better or worse several decades from now, or it may not even exist. For example, before the widespread advent of computers 30 years ago, there were thousands of people working in the United States to connect individual telephone calls, something that today is almost entirely automated. Still, we can say with some confidence that you'll earn more money as you age and progress in your career and less money after you retire. You can probably afford to take on some debt for legitimate reasons while you're young (college, a house), so long as you have good reason to expect your income will be stable or increasing as you get older.

The most important determinant of your lifetime income is the job or career path you choose. Every job has a range of *wages* (an hourly rate of pay times the hours actually worked) or *salary* (an annual rate of pay not tied directly to hours worked). Wages and salaries reflect several factors: the job's difficulty, the demand for what the job produces, how many jobs there are of this type, how many people want these jobs, and the education, training, and experience required to do the job well. As you acquire greater proficiency and experience in your occupation, your job will usually pay more (because you're more valuable to your employer). Industries that are growing and profitable usually pay more than industries that are shrinking or unprofitable, so broad economic forces will also affect your lifetime income. Doctors earn a lot of money because the job is in a growing field that requires intelligence, a commitment to working long and unpredictable hours, years of higher education, and additional years of apprenticeship before a doctor is considered fully-trained. Retail clerks earn relatively low wages because the jobs are in an industry threatened by the Internet, can be learned quickly, use skills that many people already have, and require no advanced education or training.

JOB SATISFACTION

Money isn't the only thing involved in starting and developing a successful career. You'll spend a large portion of your waking hours at work; many of your social relationships will be connected to your occupation; and a great deal of your psychological well-being will be tied to how you feel about your job. It's important to have a strong interest in the occupation, industry, or potential employers you're considering: if you really like what you do, you'll feel good about your work and do it well. It's also important to have an aptitude for your work: if you're great with computers and decide to make that your career, you'll have a good chance at long-term success in, for example, the software industry or as a systems analyst. Do what you're good at, and do what you like (ideally, the two will match up).

What about the practical factors? Do jobs in the field or industry you're considering involve a lot of travel, demand long hours on a regular basis, or frequently require meeting tight deadlines? Some people really want to be in a demanding environment, especially early in their careers: it's exciting, you learn a lot, and it often provides a great sense of accomplishment. Other people, however, may have strong interests outside of work and see their paying job or career as secondary to these other interests. You may be shy, reluctant to confront others, or work better alone—all perfectly fine characteristics but not ideally suited to every career path. Not everybody wants or works well in a pressure-filled, fast-paced work environment, while some people need that energy to thrive.

You also need to consider some important psychological factors. Will you feel your work is meaningful, has a higher purpose, is making the world a better place, or contributes to a goal you believe in? Objectives such as these often motivate people to work in government, at social service agencies, or at nongovernmental organizations with a social mission. Even in the for-profit world, workers want to feel valued, have autonomy, be able to contribute, and earn respect from their peers. Some job environments will deliver on those psychological needs better than others. Unfortunately, you can't always tell in advance whether a particular career, industry, or employer provides such an environment, but at least you can be on the lookout.

Finally, your first few jobs will look a lot different than your last few. A typical career path shows progressively increasing responsibility, pay, and recognition. Whether staying in the same occupation or moving across an industry, there will be moves sideways and moves that advance. larger employers, people to manage under you, increased administrative duties, more customer interaction, and greater influence in big decisions. So it's useful, at the start of your career, to get a sense of how an occupation evolves with seniority and experience, or how people progress in a particular industry.

Here's one example: many people who train as chemists reach a plateau in their careers where, if they want further advancement, they must move out of the laboratory to become managers of other chemists. What if you really like being a chemist, and don't like directing other people's work? Here's another example: as attorneys move through their careers in large firms, their jobs become more about marketing to clients and less about performing legal work—but what if you don't like selling to people, or really enjoy the legal craft? Learning about how careers evolve and giving some thought to how that fits with your interests and personality will help you make good career decisions, at the start and all along the way.

COMPENSATION AND OVERTIME

For any job opening, an employer will offer a specified pay or pay range determined from experience (what the employer has historically paid to fill this job) or, if it's a new position, based on the employer's estimate of what a similar job is paying. Just as you're seeking a job that fits you, the employer has in mind the qualifications of the person to fill that position, whether they're years of work experience, specified minimum education or training, industry knowledge, or personal factors ("willing to work nights and weekends," for example). There will also be geographical differences in pay to account for varying costs of living and local market conditions.

Employers in the United States use many different systems to pay their employees. Some salespeople work on commission: they receive as pay a defined percentage of the selling price of what they sell. Restaurant servers, hair stylists, and massage therapists receive a large portion of their pay in customer tips. The pay of many farm workers depends on the amount of crop they gather (called a "piece rate"). The two most common systems of payment, however, are based on an hourly rate of pay, commonly called an hourly *wage*, and an annual rate of pay, commonly called a *salary*. There are laws that define the *minimum wage* an employer must pay and require a 50 percent higher rate of pay for overtime work, defined as more than

40 hours worked in one week (and some employers voluntarily pay more than 50 percent premium for overtime). Overtime pay isn't required for work on nights, weekends, or holidays but may be offered by an employer. Minimum pay laws and mandated overtime rules apply to some but not the majority of salaried workers, who constitute about 40 percent of U.S. workers today.

Laws governing the minimum wage and overtime exist at the city, state, and federal level; they're complicated and have many exceptions. For example, young workers and those receiving tips can have a much lower minimum wage. Workers on small farms, at seasonal amusement parks, and fishermen aren't covered at all for either minimum wage or overtime. Federal overtime rules don't apply to most transportation workers, live-in domestic workers, agricultural workers, and most commissioned sales people. There are different overtime rules for public safety workers (police, fire) and nursing home employees. Being paid hourly or salaried doesn't matter; if your salary is under a certain level you're automatically entitled to overtime, and above that level, it depends.[4] The biggest exception to the overtime rules is for executive, professional, supervisory, managerial, and administrative workers—most so-called "white collar" jobs are *not* entitled to overtime. It's important for salaried workers to understand their employers' expectations in terms of schedule, number of hours of work each week, night and weekend work, and work outside the office.

NEGOTIATING PAY AND BENEFITS

The relationship between an employer and an employee throughout the United States is one of pure freedom of association. You're free to work for whomever you choose, for however long you choose. The "two-week's notice" that people commonly give an employer when they quit is purely custom: you can walk out the door of your employer at any time, for any reason, without any advance notice at all. Pretty great, isn't it? Unfortunately, the other side of that coin is that an employer can terminate your job for any reason, at any time, and also without any advance notice. We call this relationship *at-will employment*, and it's the general rule almost everywhere in the United States. The good news for employees is that employers don't usually fire people without legitimate reasons, employers often have policies offering some job protections, and there are laws that prevent certain types of discrimination in the workplace. At-will employment can also be changed by agreement, so asking for a letter from your employer that sets out the terms of your employment is a good practice.

Seeking a job can be a very stressful experience, and the job search process itself is beyond the scope of this book. Once you've landed a job offer, it's time to consider the terms of employment, starting with the rate of pay. Your offer will indicate a specified amount, whether it's $32,000 annually or $12.50 per hour. Keep in mind the employer usually has a range of pay it's considering for this position, and you were offered one number within that range (and not usually at the top). You can ask for more: "I am really excited about coming to work for you, but I was hoping to start at $34,000 instead of $32,000—will that be possible?" Most organizations have a policy on how frequently they review your pay, for example every 12 or 15 months, but you can ask for an early review: "While I would prefer to start at a higher rate of pay, can you consider a review for an increase after six months?" During your periodic reviews is a good time to tout your successes and ask for an increase in pay. If you have a reasonable basis for an increase, most employers won't be offended by your request, even if it's large: "I see from a recent magazine article that the average pay for my occupation is $5,000 more than my pay here; I think my performance warrants putting me at least at the national average."

Nail down a start date: you may need some time before you begin, while your employer might need you to start immediately. Employers often offer money to help you move (relocation assistance); if you're local you might ask for a payment in lieu of relocation assistance to help improve your current living space. Pay can include signing bonuses, sales incentives, annual bonuses, and targeted awards for goals like safety or innovations: ask about them. Vacation time, sick days, and personal days (often lumped together and called "paid time off" or PTO) are also valuable to you—asking for an extra week or two of PTO is fine, especially if you're coming from another job. Find out what annual holidays are paid in addition to PTO. Employers typically can't make exceptions to the major benefits they offer—retirement plans and insurance for health, dental, and vision—but you should understand what you're getting, and if an employer doesn't offer these plans, it's fair to ask for higher pay to compensate. Often an employer will give you a document describing all of these benefits, but it's smart to seek this information *before* you start your job.

No employer wants to hire a person who's just in it for the money or who appears greedy. At the same time, if the employer has offered you a job, you know the employer wants you. A positive approach to negotiation is to thank the employer for the job offer, say that you're excited at the prospect of joining the team, and add that you have just a few questions about the job you'd like to discuss with someone in the human resources department. If there's no human resources department, then ask to discuss this with the person who offered you the job, preferably in person. Your questions should be polite and asked without any sense of entitlement. At the end of the conversation ask that the employer consider your requests and get back to you in writing as soon as possible. Thank the person for meeting with you.

CAREERS TO CONSIDER

There are many publications that project the best jobs of the future, and typically these focus on specific occupations. For example, the U.S. Bureau of Labor Statistics routinely publishes and updates the Occupational Outlook Handbook with data on projected job growth and income levels for many occupations (www.bls.gov/ooh), along with other useful information about careers. But be wary: a lot can happen on the way to your career, and these projections aren't guarantees. You'll find that the fastest-growing jobs on a percentage basis tend to be in specialties where there are few jobs, and the occupations with the largest number of projected openings tend to be at the low end of the pay scale. Don't just think about the prospects of a particular occupation, but also consider the industries that may employ these specific occupations. Working as an electrician in the movie industry has different prospects than working in the power industry.

It's also helpful to consider the demographic and economic trends we face today. The United States has an aging population, making businesses and occupations catering to older people attractive, such as in health care. The world also faces increasing global interaction, so those people with skills in foreign languages and international commerce will have advantages. The technology content of business activity keeps increasing, making high-tech businesses and professions an attractive career choice. Governments—local, state, and national—employ people in virtually every occupation but provide a different career experience than private-sector

Table 2.1   Median Annual Pay by Occupation

All Workers	$36,200
Accountants and Auditors	$67,190
Actuaries	$97,070
Administrative Assistants	$36,500
Air Traffic Controllers	$122,950
Ambulance Drivers	$23,740
Audiologists	$74,890
Chemical Plant Operators	$59,320
College Teachers	$72,470
Construction Laborers	$30,890
Customer Service Representatives	$31,720
Financial Clerks	$37,040
High School Teachers	$57,200
Home Appliance Technicians	$36,200
Home Health Aides	$21,920
Interpreters and Translators	$44,190
Logistics Coordinators	$74,260
Maids and Housekeepers	$22,990
Optometrists	$103,900
Paralegals and Legal Assistants	$48,810
Pharmacists	$121,500
Pediatricians	$170,300
Railroad Workers	$55,180
Registered Nurses	$67,490
Restaurant Cooks	$21,720
Retail Salespersons	$22,040

Source: U.S. Department of Labor, Bureau of Labor Statistics, Occupational Outlook Handbook, data for 2015.

employers. Typically, government jobs offer greater job security and higher non-cash benefits; there's debate about whether there are systematic differences in annual pay. The nonprofit sector in the U.S. has been expanding and now constitutes about 10 percent of the workforce, resulting from the growth of foundations and other nongovernmental organizations with a social purpose. Importantly for college students, federal college loan programs offer forgiveness programs for workers in government and nonprofit organizations. Table 2.1 shows the median pay for a variety of occupations (half of the workers earn more, half earn less).

EXPERIENTIAL WORK

Some jobs will be a disaster. That's okay: you'll learn what you don't like or what you're not good at. If you need to move on, think about it carefully, and if you're sure, tell your employer. It's a courtesy to give your employer reasonable notice before quitting, but sometimes that's not possible, and the day you give notice could be your last. Regardless of the circumstances, don't burn any bridges: leaving on good terms may help you later, since everyone you met during that job experience is a potential future colleague, employer, or recommender.

Sometimes you might take a job because it offers training for the future. Some young people enter the military to serve their country, but also because they want to test themselves, develop leadership skills, and learn a trade. It doesn't offer great pay or comfortable work conditions, but it's a way to earn valuable experience for later in life. Some low-paying manual labor positions in construction, manufacturing, and food service are background experiences for people who want to be their own boss and own a business in one of those fields. Jobs off the beaten path—such as working in the merchant marine or leading wilderness trips—offer adventure, teach resourcefulness, and can even lead to a rewarding career.

INTERNSHIPS, MENTORS, AND REFERENCES

An *internship* is a short-term job designed to give a young person exposure to a career or organization. Often these take place in the summer but can also be incorporated into the school year for high school and college students. Internships can be unpaid or offer some compensation. A well-run internship program should have specific goals to educate the intern about the organization and its work and should allow the intern to work in or be exposed to different parts of the organization. Many organizations don't offer formal internships but will arrange one for the persistent. A popular form of internship is *shadowing*, where a young person simply follows an experienced worker throughout her work day. It's not a simple task to operate a good internship program: someone must organize an intern's job assignments, supervise the intern, give her direction, training, and feedback, and move the intern throughout the organization. An intern, conversely, has the duty to make the internship as meaningful as possible through active and attentive participation. Internships are low-risk ways to test your interest in an occupation or industry.

A *mentor* is a person whose career, life experience, and character you admire, and who's willing to maintain a relationship to guide you personally and professionally. It's hard to establish a career on your own, especially if you have few role models for what a successful career looks like. A mentor can discuss challenges and opportunities, offer advice, and serve as a safe outlet to vent frustration. A mentor should be a person whose interests and occupation are related to your own, who has sufficient seniority and accomplishment to serve as a guide, and who has personal qualities you desire for yourself. Teachers can serve as good mentors, especially early in your life, but often the best mentors come from the workplace; you may have more than one mentor as you move along in your career. Most mentorships are informal, although some organizations will assign mentors to young employees. You'll be surprised at how often someone who's far along in a successful career is willing to give back and help guide you in yours, but you have to ask. It can take years to find a good mentor and develop a trusting relationship, but having this kind of advisor can serve you well throughout your career.

As you change jobs during your career, prospective employers will likely ask for personal or professional *references*. Employers do this to test the accuracy of your job application or resume and to learn about your qualities as an employee from someone who knows you. The best references are from people with whom you've worked who will communicate directly with your potential employer—a former colleague or supervisor, the more senior the better, as long as they know you well. References can also take the form of generic letters that can be used repeatedly over many years. A mentor can be a great reference. Early in your career you may have to rely on former teachers or other adults who know your personality and character, or people you meet through an internship. As you develop relationships through your jobs, try to identify one or two people at each workplace who might later serve as a reference, and before you move along from one employer to another, ask these people if they'll serve as a reference for you. These references will come in handy throughout your career.

NOTES

1. U.S. Department of Labor, Bureau of Labor Statistics, "Number of Jobs Held, Labor Market Activity, and Earnings Growth Among the Youngest Baby Boomers: Results from a Longitudinal Survey," March 31, 2015.

2. U.S. Council of Economic Advisers, "15 Economic Facts About Millennials," Fact 11, October 2014.

3. U.S. Department of Labor, Bureau of Labor Statistics, "Employee Tenure in 2014," September 18, 2014.

4. In 2016 the U.S. Department of Labor issued new rules under which all covered salaried workers earning below $47,476 per year are entitled to overtime pay, up from $23,660 set in 2004. These rules also index the salary limit for inflation, so every three years the number will change. See 81 Federal Register 32391-32552 (May 23, 2016).

THREE

Business and Entrepreneurship

Businesses are everywhere. Virtually everything you look at or connect to on the Internet is generated by a business. Nearly everything you buy at any store, in person or online, is supplied by a business. Most of the people you know with jobs are employed by businesses. So even if you aren't interested in business, you won't be able to escape it. Just about every facet of your life, and the lives of your family and friends, will be governed or influenced by the world of business. So it's definitely useful to develop a basic idea of what business is all about.

A business is simply an organization that provides a product or service. Google is a business that provides Internet search services and advertising; Trader Joe's is a business that sells specialty foods; and Ernst & Young is a business that delivers accounting services. Governments also provide products and services, but we don't think of government as a business. We pay for government services through taxes, for example, to provide police and fire protection, education, and roadways. Businesses also provide fire prevention, security, highways, and schools; the difference is that with a business we pay for the products and services in a voluntary market transaction using money. Sometimes people refer to the world of business as the "private sector" and the world of government as the "public sector."

Some private-sector organizations aren't considered businesses even though they provide products and services on a paid basis just as any business would. These are the NGO, education, and health care sectors. An NGO is a *nongovernmental organization* that provides services similar to what governments sometimes do, such as a charity, foundation, or research firm, almost always operated on a not-for-profit basis. Some NGOs consider themselves *social enterprises*, using business methods to create a social impact. Health care and education are services provided both by government and the private sector, together representing over 25 percent of our total economy. These organizations are really businesses, but they aren't often talked about that way.

BUSINESS ORGANIZATION

The simplest form of business is a *sole proprietorship*, where an individual goes into business for herself, by herself. That doesn't mean you can't hire employees and grow, it just means that there's one person who owns the business. Usually people choose this form of *business organization* for small operations that aren't very complicated: individual cleaning services, tutors, artisans, personal trainers, and gardeners, for example. A sole proprietorship can operate under the individual's name ("Ellen Smith Plumbing") or it can use a "doing business as" (DBA) name instead ("Glitter-Glow Nail Salon"). People sometimes use the term *self-employed* or *freelancer* to mean the same thing as a sole proprietorship.

Unless you take specific steps to form another type of business, the business will be deemed a sole proprietorship under the law. There's no financial distinction between the person and the business: the business debts are the person's debts, the business's assets are the person's assets, and the business's tax return will be part of the individual's tax return. Simplicity is the only virtue of a sole proprietorship: the lack of separation between the person and the business has no legal or financial benefit whatsoever, and can cause harm if either the person or the business gets into trouble—neither can be protected from the problems of the other. Also, as a sole proprietor it can be very hard to get personal loans, such as a home mortgage.

Where two or more people join together to form and operate a business you have a *general partnership*. Partnerships were popular among law and accounting firms, investment banks, and merchants in the nineteenth and twentieth centuries until legal reforms created something more suitable. Partnerships are easy to form, very flexible, and don't typically require any state registration. But unlike a sole proprietorship, a partnership must file with the federal tax authorities to get a *taxpayer identification number* (TIN). Most partnerships are created by a partnership agreement that describes how decisions will be made, how much money each will contribute, how the profits will be shared, and other financial matters—partnerships don't have to be equal. As with a sole proprietorship, there's no separation between the business and its owners: each partner is totally responsible for all liabilities of the business, and personal assets can be used to satisfy debts of the partnership business. If a business organized as a partnership fails, so do the individual partners.

The concept of *limited liability* arose to protect owners and investors from unlimited loss in the event of a business collapse; shielding personal assets from a business failure promotes investment in businesses. This concept led to *limited partnerships*, where there's at least one *general partner* who's responsible for the operation of the partnership, and one or more *limited partners*, who are merely investors with little or no role in the partnership's operation. This business form has become very popular for real estate investments, film syndicates, and big construction projects, but it can be used for any type of business. The general partner has unlimited liability for the debts of the partnership, while the limited partners can lose only their investments. A limited partnership must create formal documents that all of the partners agree to, must register with the state government, and must also obtain a TIN from the federal government.

It's the corporation, however, that has become the most well-known form of limited-liability business organization in the United States. A *corporation* operates as a distinct legal entity under state law and is considered its own "person" that can enter into contracts, borrow or raise money, and sue or be sued in court. These actions have no direct impact on its owners, who are shareholders, or its executive managers, who are employees. The corporate form of business offers limited liability to investors, since owners can't be held liable for the debts of the corporation. Promoters register a corporation with the state and create formal documents, called *articles of incorporation* and *corporate bylaws*, which set out the way the corporation will operate, typically through a board of directors elected by the shareholders.

A recent and popular form of business is the *limited liability company* (LLC), which, while not technically a corporation, has many of the same features. Promoters of an LLC will register it with the state and create official documents, primarily the *operating agreement*, that sets out how the business will run, who will be its owners (called members), and who will serve as its executives (called managers). Corporations and LLCs both must obtain TINs from the federal government, but there are important differences between them, including potential tax treatment. Anyone who would otherwise operate a business as a sole proprietorship is almost always better off forming an LLC instead.

THE LANGUAGE OF BUSINESS

Can you imagine going through life without being able to read? *Literacy* is such a basic requirement to lead a meaningful and productive life that we all know we'd be doomed without it. *Numeracy*, or the ability to use mathematics in everyday life, is also extremely important: analyzing your bank account, comparing prices at the grocery store, and understanding mortgage interest rates all require a basic competence with numbers. When it comes to your financial life, however, there's probably no more important skill to acquire than a basic understanding of financial accounting. *Accounting* is the organized system for recording and communicating financial transactions for a person, business, or other organization. Fundamentally, it's the language of business, but it's also the language of personal finance and financial literacy. The German philosopher Max Weber is said to have thought that capitalism couldn't work as an economic system unless average people understood accounting. If you have the opportunity to take a course in financial accounting, do it; and if you don't have the opportunity, make one. It may provide you with the most useful financial skills you'll ever learn.

Accounting uses specific terms to reflect financial transactions in defined records and reports, and the entire practice of accounting is governed by rules known as *generally accepted accounting principles* (GAAP). Sometimes the records and reports of a business are referred to as the *books* of that business. An *asset* is anything of value and is recorded on the books at whatever price was paid for the asset, for example, a computer used to create graphics, or land that's owned for a farm. A *liability* is any amount of money that's owed to another party, for example, a loan that a business borrowed from a bank or money that's owed on an unpaid electric bill. The difference between all the assets and all the liabilities of an organization is called *equity*, also sometimes referred to as *net worth*. Assets, liabilities, and equity are recorded on a report called a *balance sheet*.

Accountants use a system called *double entry bookkeeping*, where every item is recorded twice: once to show where the money came from, and once to show where it went. For example, to buy a computer, an accountant would *debit* the books to create an asset called "computer," and *credit* the bank account to reduce its balance after paying for the computer. The use of "debits" and "credits" can be confusing: when you put money in your own bank account, the bank credits your account, but to you, it's a debit.

While a balance sheet is a financial snapshot of the business at any moment in time, the *income statement* reflects how much money the business has made over a period of time. When a business sells something to another party it generates *revenue*—trading a product or service for payment. When a business spends money as part of its operations it incurs an *expense*. When total revenues exceed total expenses the business has made a *profit;* conversely, if expenses exceed revenues the business has operated at a *loss*. All revenue and expense activity is recorded on the income statement, and businesses usually compile an income statement every month for internal use. Public companies publish their financial statements every three months, and every business compiles financial statements for the full year. Debits and credits are also the terms used to record transactions on the income statement: an increase in revenues is a credit, while incurring an expense is a debit.

Most people associate a financial transaction with cash changing hands: we buy something and pay for it at the same time. This is called *cash basis* accounting. In business, however, often several months go by from the time a product or service is sold to the time it's actually paid for. Similarly, a business often incurs an expense—is legally obligated to pay for something—several months before it actually makes payment. This is why businesses use a system called *accrual* accounting to record transactions at the time they occur, instead of when cash changes hands. This is done through the creation of delayed revenue and payment accounts called *accounts receivable* and *accounts payable*. By using accrual accounting, businesses can match up revenues and expenses when they really happen, and give a more accurate picture of financial performance. Another financial report called a *cash flow statement* shows how much cash the business is generating, which is of great interest to business managers and owners.

STARTUPS

These days it seems like everybody wants to run their own business, launch a startup, or become an *entrepreneur*, someone who organizes and creates a new business. This is a great instinct, and there's probably no other country where this ambition is nurtured and supported to the extent that it is in the United States. But it's not for everyone. The vast majority of new businesses fail; they can require grueling work under poor conditions with frequent travel; they can generate long periods of stress and many sleepless nights. On the other hand, being part of a new venture is exhilarating, offers the potential for huge rewards, and will provide excellent work experience—even if the whole thing crashes and burns.

It takes more than a good idea to start a business, but a good idea is a great place to start. It also helps to be part of a team: having at least one or two partners in the venture will bring to bear different skill sets and increase the chance of success. It's useful to have an *elevator speech* that briefly conveys the basic business idea in just 30 seconds, but it's critical to have a business plan. A *business plan* is a document that describes the crucial elements of the business, for example, a 20-page Power-Point. A business plan describes the business and its goals to all potential stakeholders, whether they're suppliers, customers, or potential employees; it can serve as the starting point for discussions about financing; and it can keep the management team on track as it develops the business operation. Here are the basic elements of a business plan:

- **Products and Services**: Describe the product or service the business will supply, identify any unique features, explain why there's a gap in the marketplace and a need for this new product or service, describe the key factors that will make the business successful, and show how the business will deliver on those requirements. Also identify the risks and opportunities the new business will face.

- **Marketing**: Identify the target customers for the product or service, determine what motivates these customers, identify what need the product or service will fill, develop a strategy to build awareness, and create an action plan to convert prospects into customers. Consider pricing, features, advertising, and promotion. It will take more than a website and Twitter feed to make a marketing plan.

- **Competitors**: Identify existing competitors, potential competitors, or emerging technologies that can impact the business. Survey the competitive landscape including points of differentiation, relative strengths and weaknesses, and anticipated reactions of these other businesses to your own entry into the marketplace.

- **Product/Service Delivery**: Describe how the product or service will be created or delivered. If it's a product, will it be sourced, manufactured internally, or made to your specifications under contract? If it's a service, how will it be offered, by whom, and what will be required by the business to make that happen? Address administrative services such as accounting, human resources, technology, and office support.

- **Suppliers and Key Inputs**: Identify key inputs and how they'll be obtained, for example, with internal staff or using outside vendors. Identify supply-chain partners who will provide critical business services or product components, whether it's a server farm in the cloud, parts for an electronic device, or engineering services for design and construction.

- **Distribution and Logistics**: Describe how the products and services will make it all the way to the customer, whether it's providing a personal service directly to consumers or working in the business-to-business space. Consider a viral marketing strategy, using Internet-based transactions, creating an internal sales force, hiring agents, or developing relationships with existing distributors.

- **Financing**: Show your early-stage funding from founders, friends, and family, as well as from credit-card borrowing (which otherwise should be avoided). Identify angel investors, venture capital firms, finance companies, even commercial banks you might contact. Estimate how much money you need, when you need it, and what form it will take (equity, debt, or something more complicated).

- **Management Team**: Describe the key people involved in the venture, their backgrounds, abilities, and intended roles in the new business. Identify what additional, qualified personnel you'll need as the business grows and how you'll attract them.

- **Licensing and Regulation**: Determine what form of licensing or registration with local, state, or federal authorities is necessary, whether it's formation of an LLC, receiving permission to export technology, or getting a license from the government to handle certain materials. Identify any unique rules that will apply beyond general safety, health, environmental, and employment regulations, and how you'll deal with them.

- **Financial Projections**: Develop a five-year financial projection showing the income statement, balance sheet, and cash flows from start-up through the early stages of the business. Contemplate an exit strategy, where early investors cash out by selling their shares to other investors, through an initial public offering of stock, or if the business is sold.

- **Summary**: Create an *executive summary* and a *mission statement*. The mission statement is akin to your elevator speech, a one-or-two sentence encapsulation of the basic business proposition. The executive summary should be a single page that distills each of the business plan sections into a sentence or two each. Put this at the front of the plan, but create it at the end of the process.

FRANCHISES

In a *franchise* business, the *franchisor* creates a business system that typically includes a well-developed business concept, a strong brand backed by national advertising, established supply and vendor relationships, design and real estate location advice, start-up support, and assistance with ongoing business operations.

Sometimes franchisors even provide partial financing. In exchange for supplying a *turn-key business* and the ongoing support, the *franchisee* will pay a *franchise fee* and *royalty* based on sales of the business. Some franchise systems require their franchisees to buy certain supplies from the franchisor or approved vendors, and earn extra income from those sales. While there are substantial costs to become part of a franchise system, a franchise is worth considering for people who want to own a business of their own but don't have a lot of experience in starting up a new operation.

Each franchisee owns her own business: the franchised business isn't owned by the franchisor, and unless the franchisee violates the terms of the agreement (such as running a poor operation that degrades the brand), the franchise remains an independent business operation. There are many examples of successful franchise systems in the United States, including restaurant chains such as McDonald's, Subway, Burger King, KFC, Pizza Hut, Jimmy John's, and Panera (these chains also have stores owned by the franchisor corporation). But there are many other types of business that franchise, such as 7-Eleven (convenience stores), Aaron's (furniture rental), Servpro (cleaning), CrossFit (health clubs), RE/MAX (real estate), and Snap-on (mechanic's tools). A good franchisee who gets in early can build an empire by obtaining rights to an entire region and owning many locations. For example, Larry Feldman was a mid-level government worker who became one of the first Subway franchisees and grew his chain to over 1,500 stores, becoming fantastically wealthy in the process.[1]

SIDE BUSINESSES

If you have free time and want extra earnings, consider a part-time *side business*, something you can do while keeping your primary job. Suppose you're a good accountant: you might do bookkeeping at night and on weekends for private clients. If you like to cook, you could develop a part-time catering business or make desserts for parties. If you're good with software you might design websites or apps part-time, or an artisan can sell art through Etsy. People who are handy with tools often work part-time making household repairs. Pet lovers can walk or watch animals for neighbors who travel. Teachers can supplement their income by tutoring privately. There are many ways to use your interests and talents to start a side business outside your normal work hours at your primary job.

Be cautious before starting a side business, however. Form an LLC for the business, since it's a low-cost way to protect you from liability should something go wrong. Be aware of any rules or regulations that might affect your business, such as sanitation procedures for food vendors or licenses for service providers. Local zoning regulations may prohibit operating a business out of your apartment or house. You'll need some money to get started. And be realistic about how much time you can devote: you don't want a side business to interfere with your regular job. A side business can be a great part of your financial plan, and who knows: it might take off and grow into a new career.

REAL ESTATE

The popularity of real estate as a business opportunity stems from three factors: real estate tends to be readily available, many people find it familiar and easy to understand, and it can be financed through many sources. We're not talking about the get-rich-in-real-estate schemes you may see advertised, but rather the serious consideration of real estate as a business opportunity that can build wealth and create income over the long term, whether as a full-time or part-time venture.

The real estate industry breaks into three main categories of property: residential, commercial, and industrial. Residential real estate includes single-family homes, apartment buildings, and condominiums that can be sold or rented to individuals or families to live in. Commercial real estate includes office buildings, hotels, and shopping centers that are used by businesses for their operations. Industrial real estate includes factories, warehouses, and support facilities used by businesses for production and distribution of goods. People who work in real estate tend to specialize in just one of these areas—a residential real estate expert typically knows little about commercial or industrial real estate, for example.

Financial participation in real estate also breaks into three main categories: you can be a developer, an owner, or a manager of real estate. A developer creates the project from idea to construction, arranges financing, then usually sells when the project is complete. An owner is an investor and typically has a limited role in the operation of the real estate. A manager is the person or entity that leases, maintains, and operates the real estate. Sometimes you can have several of these interests overlap in the same organization.

As a side business, real estate can be attractive to individuals because it requires concentrated effort for a short period of time (to identify and acquire the property), then occasional effort to manage the property after you own it. Suppose you want to buy your first house and decide to buy a duplex (two-family house) that needs some fixing up, after which you'll live in one side and rent out the other. You need to find the property in the neighborhood you want, arrange financing based on your current income and projections from the rental, and develop a renovation plan with a contractor who will do the work at a price you can afford. At this point you're acting as a developer. After you buy the property you're the owner, and if all goes well you'll live in one side of the duplex and find a tenant to live in the other (now you're acting as the manager). Hopefully, as a landlord, you won't be faced with too many plumbing crises, roof leaks, or deadbeat tenants. Rental real estate can be a great business, but it's never as easy as it looks.

SOURCES OF FUNDING

Every business, even a nonprofit organization, needs money to begin and operate, to pay for expenses such as office rent or employee salaries. *Capital* is a general term used to describe money used in a business. One source of capital is *debt financing*, where the organization borrows money to be repaid on a fixed schedule in the future and pays regular interest to the lender while the loan is outstanding. Any person or entity with money can make a loan, but business loans are typically offered by specialized financial companies that know how to underwrite (assess the risk of not being paid back) and service a commercial loan. Commercial banks, financing companies, insurance companies, and other lenders make loans to businesses. Larger businesses can also borrow by issuing public or private securities (called bonds or debentures) that are sold to multiple lenders at once, often allowing these lenders to trade the debt at any time without affecting the borrower.

Equity financing is money invested by an owner that's meant to be retained by the company indefinitely, and any return to the owner will come from distributions of profit the company might make. Equity investments are represented by shares of *stock* in a corporation and *interests* in partnerships and LLCs. The equity investor can potentially sell her stake in the company to another party. Or, if the shares are publicly traded, she can sell through the stock market. In either case, the company retains the money from the original equity investment. For public companies (traded in stock markets), equity comes from individual investors or pooled investment funds managed by financial institutions, including mutual funds, foundations, endowments, pension funds, life insurance companies, investment banks, and hedge funds. Privately held companies access the same sources of equity directly (not through stock markets) and also raise money from private equity and investment firms that specialize in providing equity financing to privately held companies.

Most startups find their initial capital (or *seed financing*) through *bootstrapping*, meaning that the entrepreneurs scrounge for any money they can find of their own, as well as from personal borrowing and from everyone they know. *Angel investors* are typically wealthy individuals who invest at an early stage of a company's development; several networks of angel investors and intermediaries provide seed money (AngelList, 500 Startups, Y Combinator). Crowd funding platforms (Kickstarter, Indiegogo) are also recent innovations in early stage financing. Venture capital firms (VC) provide equity further along in the business development (the average age of a VC-funded enterprise is about 4 years old); they also offer talent and counseling to make small firms much larger. Then you have private placements of equity—arranged transactions with institutional investors—and initial public offerings of stock to the market (IPOs), at which point a company has matured beyond its start-up phase.

THE ECONOMY

The condition of the economy can have a large impact on the operation of any business. When people talk about "the economy," they mean a constellation of things that relate to money, business, jobs, spending, saving, investment, and production. An economy at its simplest is the system people use in order to produce and consume the goods and services they need to live and enjoy themselves. First, people need organizations that create and distribute goods and services: these are the businesses described in this chapter. Businesses need workers to produce what they sell, in so doing creating jobs, the source from which most people get the money they need to buy things, becoming *consumers*. Ideally, people don't spend everything they earn, so their extra money can become savings, which can in turn be lent to businesses to make investments for the future.

A *good economy* involves high levels of producing, spending, savings, and invest-ment by consumers and businesses, also called *economic activity*, which leads to more jobs, better wages, and profitable businesses. A *bad economy* is characterized by declining economic activity: businesses become unprofitable and sometimes shut down, and people struggle to find jobs to earn a living to support themselves and their families.

By measuring the economic activity in each state, region, and country, policy-makers can become aware of problems and potentially take action to make things better. The most common measure of a country's economic activity is called *Gross Domestic Product* (GDP), which is the value of all the goods and services produced by the people and businesses in that country each year. Some experts argue that GDP is too narrow a measure of a country's output, excluding many subjective factors that people value, such as the quality of the environment or the mood of the residents. The country of Bhutan, for example, has become known for pub-lishing its own Gross National Happiness (GNH) index as a measure of its total output.

Almost every business can be affected by economic factors in another country through suppliers, customers, or the financial system because of international com-merce. The *global economy* refers to all of the individual country economies put together and how those economies relate to each other. What happens in one major economy usually affects other major economies because they trade with each other, have investments in each other's countries, and do business with the same multi-national corporations.

The United States has the largest economy in the world, followed by China, Japan, and Germany.[2] Because the European Union (EU) mostly uses a single cur-rency and coordinates the economies of its 28 member countries, the EU is some-times considered its own economy, and it's about the same size as the United States. The size of the U.S. economy allows many businesses to operate only in this coun-try, and many small businesses never need to consider foreign markets. Still, we're all increasingly tied together by global trade and commerce, and it's hard for one country to isolate itself from what happens in another.

GROWTH AND RECESSION

Our economy produces over $18 trillion worth of goods and services every year (our GDP).[3] That's a lot of stuff. If the economy is stable each year that number will be $18 trillion—neither growing nor shrinking. But nobody likes to just stand still, so policy makers like to see *growth* of 3 percent or better—which means adding in excess of $540 billion each year to the size of the U.S. economy. That growth means producing *additional* goods and services equal to the size of the *entire* economy of a country the size of Poland or Taiwan, every single year. When you have growing economic activity there are typically more jobs, higher wages, and better prospects for most people in the country.

When you have negative growth—we call this a *recession*—the economy actually shrinks. For example, the size of the U.S. economy contracted from GDP of $14.7 trillion in 2008 to $14.4 trillion in 2009, a loss of $300 billion of economic activity.[4] This shrinkage isn't just bad for business, it's bad for people. Recessions are typically associated with pain and suffering in the form of lost jobs, stagnant or lower wages, increased debts owed by governments and households, and strong political disagreements. Some economists see the occasional recession as a natural cycle in the economy, and while painful, these are typically short-lived. Recessions also force businesses to become more efficient, helping the economy in the long run.

One way to achieve growth is to increase productivity. *Productivity* is the amount of output that results from a given level of inputs. For example, if you're a new worker at Chipotle and can produce 15 burritos an hour, this would be one measure of your productivity. As you become more experienced, you might be able to make 20 or ultimately 25 burritos per hour. This is an increase in your productivity, which would hopefully be reflected by an increase in your wages. Since productivity reflects how efficiently we use our resources to produce goods and services, productivity increases can help us become better off economically throughout the entire economy and increase our standard of living.

We sometimes experience a *slow-growth* economy, where output increases at just around 1–2 percent annually. A slow-growth economy is problematic because the U.S. population is increasing. In 2014 the total U.S. population was 318.7 million, and in 2020 it's projected to be 334.5 million, which implies a population growth rate of a little under 1 percent per year.[5] This means our economy has to grow 1 percent every year just to keep up with population growth, or there will be less to go around for each person. With slow growth, it's hard for many people to get ahead.

INTERNATIONAL BUSINESS

There have been two philosophies about trade between different countries over the years. The first philosophy is called *protectionism*: governments should favor producers in the home country and make it difficult for foreign businesses to sell their products and services there. The second philosophy is called *free trade*: governments should promote policies that allow businesses in one country to sell their goods and services throughout the world. If you're involved with a business that operates in international markets, these different national approaches to managing trade will have a big impact on your business and require you to analyze each foreign market individually.

While these philosophies have been debated throughout modern history, experts agree that free trade improves the welfare of the entire world. This is because it allows each country to specialize in the things it has a *comparative advantage* in producing. It makes little sense for countries with little arable land to develop an agricultural sector, or for countries with poor technology infrastructure to develop high-tech industries. Still, there are organized and politically powerful groups in countries throughout the world that seek, sometimes successfully, to implement protectionist policies that favor their industries. A country can charge *duties* or *tariffs* on imports of foreign goods or services, raising their cost and making it harder for foreign companies to sell there. A *free-trade agreement* between countries reduces or eliminates these tariffs on some categories of goods and services.

Each country typically uses a different currency, so when a service is sold from one country to another, there must be a change of currency. For example, if you go to Mexico on vacation and stay in a hotel, you pay for your lodging using the Mexican peso. Since your own money is in U.S. dollars, someone will need to convert your dollars into pesos. This is called a *foreign exchange* transaction, and every business that sells across borders must make these transactions. For consumer transactions banks charge about 3 percent for converting foreign money to the local currency, and other types of money changers can charge up to 10 percent. Business transactions utilize wholesale currency markets at lower fees.

Using one currency helps reduce the costs of foreign trade. For example, many international businesses transact using U.S. dollars, regardless of where they're based, and 18 of the 28 European Union countries use a single currency, the euro. Businesses use a single currency to avoid *foreign exchange risk*: the possibility that the value of holdings in foreign currency will drop when money is converted to the home currency. Businesses can undertake financial transactions called *hedging* to reduce or eliminate this risk. As you can see, however, trading in international markets adds cost and risk to any business operation.

NOTES

1. Drew Harwell, "The Rise and Fall of Subway, the World's Biggest Food Chain," *The Washington Post*, May 30, 2015.

2. World Bank, "GDP (current US$)," 2014 data, country tables accessed November 26, 2015.

3. U.S. Department of Commerce, Bureau of Economic Analysis, "National Income and Product Accounts," November 24, 2015.

4. U.S. Department of Commerce, Bureau of Economic Analysis, National Economic Accounts, "Gross Domestic Product," current dollar and real GDP tables, November 24, 2015.

5. U.S. Census Bureau, "Projections of the Size and Composition of the U.S. Population: 2014–2060," March 2015.

FOUR

Savings and Banking

Having more money than you know what to do with isn't a problem you're facing, right? Young people initially have little control over their money, relying on their parents for support. Then, when they start living independently, it's a big enough challenge just to keep ahead of all the expenses. So having extra money available—money to save instead of spend—sounds like a dream. It doesn't have to be that way: the ability to save should be possible even at an early stage in your life.

Many families teach children about money by giving them a weekly or monthly allowance to cover small occasional expenses and build a history of financial experience. Some young people hold jobs even while they're in school, such as babysitting, lawn care, or working part-time in retail or food service. Collecting a small allowance or working part-time can generate meaningful income and present the opportunity to save. Suppose you're in high school and you receive an allowance of $10 per week. In return, you do chores around the house. Over the course of the year you'll collect $520, so if you manage that over an entire year, then the goal of saving $100, for example, is within reach.

Working part-time commercially can also generate substantial income. Many states have minimum wages above $9 per hour, so even working at the minimum wage 16 hours per week (two full shifts) will generate around $6,000 per year in take-home pay after taxes. This won't be enough money for all the expenses of students paying their way through college, but for many young people who are working for spending money or to supplement parental support, a part-time job can generate useful income. With $6,000 per year coming in from only two shifts of work every week, shouldn't it be possible to put some of that money away as savings?

WHY SAVE?

Saving is simply not spending. What that really means is that you're not spending *today*, so you can have the ability to spend *tomorrow* (and in this case, tomorrow means next month, next year, next decade, etc.). Saving is simply a way to defer your spending, so that you have money down the road when you need it and (if you save wisely) more money than when you started. You want to save for future spending because the future is always uncertain, you may have spending needs arise that are beyond your current income, or your income may decrease for a time and you'll need savings to supplement that lower income. So the first reason to save your money is so you can spend in the future.

A second reason to save money is to help achieve your long-term goals as part of a financial plan. Your life goals will require careful attention to financial planning, so your savings efforts are a critical element to achieve this plan. Typical longer-term goals for young people may include saving for a car, home, college, having children, or starting a business. Furnishing your first apartment or taking a long trip can also require savings. These life goals are more likely to be realized as a result of a regular, careful savings effort.

A third reason to save money is to be ready for emergencies. Maybe your laptop just died and you need a new computer, or the transmission in your car is shot. Your friend is in emotional distress, and you need travel money to go see her. Your apartment is broken into, and you don't have enough insurance to replace all the stolen items. You've had an accident and need to pay some medical expenses. Bad things can happen to good people, and having savings available can help you get through the rough times.

A final reason to save is for the discipline it builds in your life. Becoming a saver is a habit and an element of your character. Saving is evidence that you can exert control over an important part of your life—the natural impulse to spend now for something that gives immediate gratification, in favor of a distant goal that will have more meaning and value. Being a saver requires the power to say "no" today so you can say "yes" in the future. If you're able to regulate your spending and show the restraint necessary to be successful at saving, you'll have developed sufficient self-control to master anything else in life.

HOW TO SAVE

While people develop many unique or personal "tricks" to help them save, they all come down to a common methodology: immediately separate some of your money and move it to a place where you can't easily access and spend it. There's no magic number for how much to save. Social Security collects a total of 12.4 percent for retirement, and the average worker puts about 10 percent of income (including employer contributions) into workplace retirement plans.[1] Since retirement savings alone takes between 10–12 percent of income, a total savings goal of 20 percent of your income is a good rule of thumb.

The first rule is that savings should take place *immediately* upon receiving the income. It's better if you never actually receive the money you intend to save, which is why Social Security and employer retirement plans take the money out of your paycheck before it even gets to you. If your allowance is $10 per week, immediately take $2 and put it away as savings. If you receive a gift of $25 for your birthday, put $5 away at once before considering how to spend the balance. Better yet, put the whole gift away as savings.

The second savings rule is *separation*. Let's say you don't have an employer-based savings plan at work, and your paycheck is immediately deposited into your bank account. You can set up an automatic deduction and move some of your pay into another account. This is important: you don't want to have your regular spending money in the same place as your savings. It can be as simple as just putting some of your income into a savings account, before the temptation to spend can arise. If this separation is automatic, even better.

The third rule of savings is making it *hard to spend*. Money in a piggy bank is hard to spend because in some cases you have to break the bank open in order to get the coins out. A savings account at a different bank from where you have your checking account (while less convenient) will make that money harder to access for routine expenses. Employer-based retirement plans keep the money in separate investment accounts that lack checking access and have penalties for early use. Be aware that human nature makes it hard to resist spending, so you need to create a structure for savings that puts your funds set aside for that purpose out of sight—but never out of mind.

BANKING BASICS

In 2015, there were about 12,500 banking organizations in the United States.[2] This includes the small, single-branch credit union based only in your community, as well as the international giants like JPMorgan Chase and Citigroup, each with thousands of branches throughout the country. There are many different kinds of banks, some of which don't even use the word *bank* in their names, and the way they're organized and regulated can be confusing to those outside the industry. Banks play an important role in our country's finances, and without them our modern economy would come to a standstill.

Banks take many forms: savings and loan associations, credit unions, federal credit unions, community banks, commercial banks, national banks, building societies, mortgage banks, and private banks. There are federal and state charters that give legal authorization for banks to operate. At one point in history, the organizational form made a difference, reflecting a different legal basis, mission, and government regulator. Today, it doesn't much matter to the average consumer what the organization calls itself.

What fundamentally unites all banks is that they take *deposits* from consumers or businesses, and they make *loans* to people and organizations that need to borrow money. Deposit taking occurs when a customer brings her cash or paycheck and leaves it with the bank. The bank will keep this money in an account for the customer to use at a later date. The customer can spend the money through computer-based electronic transactions or by using a *check*. The customer can also withdraw cash from the account at a branch or an automated teller machine (ATM).

Lending occurs when a bank gives money to a customer for a period of time, whether it's a mortgage to buy a house, a loan to buy a car, or a transaction using a credit card. All of these situations involve the bank giving you money now in exchange for your commitment to pay back that money later. This is also called an extension of *credit*, or more commonly a *loan*. The bank will also typically charge you two types of fees to get a loan: a transaction fee, which is a one-time payment for the effort involved in setting up the loan, and an interest fee, which is a continuing cost based on the interest rate and the length of time you leave the loan unpaid.

Most banks choose to have a type of office known as a *branch*. At a branch, the bank will open new accounts, accept deposits, make loans, disperse cash, and handle various other face-to-face financial transactions between a customer and a bank employee (often called a *teller*). Since these branches handle cash, they'll typically have secure vaults where they hold the cash, and possibly special rooms inside the vault as well, where they offer lock boxes to store important documents and valuable items such as jewelry or precious metals.

Physical branches aren't required for a bank to operate, however, and there are many banks that operate exclusively online, such as Ally, Flagstar, and Capital One. Many people who maintain accounts at traditional bricks-and-mortar banks have little need to enter a branch: most transactions don't require a branch, and information about an account can be accessed online or by telephone. This trend has accelerated through the advent of ATMs and smartphones. As ATMs and smartphone apps have become more capable and sophisticated, they've replaced more of the transactions that used to require a teller at a branch.

BANK ACCOUNTS

A *bank account* is a contractual relationship: you deposit money with the bank for safekeeping and to facilitate the use of that money in transactions. The bank, for its part, promises to give you access to that money and to provide the systems that allow you to use your money in many different ways. For example, you can electronically transfer money to the account of another person or business just about anywhere in the world, and that money will "arrive" in a few hours. It takes sophisticated technology and security systems to be able to do that. *Interest* is a payment you earn for the bank's temporary use of your money, also called a *return* on your money. Many bank accounts will earn interest.

A *savings account* is the simplest form of account, as well as the easiest way to maintain a basic savings program. You can deposit money to the account at any time, even linking it to sources of income so that money flows directly into the account, creating that immediate and automatic separation needed for successful savings plans. These accounts typically charge no fees for most transactions, and the bank will pay you interest on your balances. Savings accounts aren't meant to facilitate transactions: you can't make electronic bill payments, use debit cards, write checks, or make frequent cash withdrawals. A savings account is really designed to be just what its name implies: a place to put and save your money.

A *checking account*, on the other hand, is designed specifically to allow you to use your money on a regular basis to pay for the things you need in daily living: it's a *transaction account*. These accounts originated as a way to make payments using the bank draft, or what we call *checks*. A check is a written document instructing the bank to pay a specified amount of money out of your account to the person named on the check. You indicate on the check who gets the money (the *payee*) and how much, then sign the check on the front in order for it to be honored by your bank. The payee must *endorse* the check (sign her name on the back) before it can be processed through the banking system and put into the payee's account. Each check has important identifying information at the bottom printed in magnetic ink character recognition (MICR) code, enabling computers to process checks at high speed. This information includes the bank routing number (a unique identifier for each bank) and your own checking account number.

It can take several days before a check clears through the banking system and the payee can use the money; the banks involved have to make sure the check is legitimate and that there's enough money in your account before it transfers the money to the payee. If your checking account doesn't have enough money to cover the amount of the check, it's not paid, and you'll be charged an *overdraft fee* by your bank. This is called returning a check for non-sufficient funds (the banks use the abbreviation "NSF"). More colloquially, it's called *bouncing a check*. (The term refers to the historical practice of sending the unpaid check back through all the banks that handled it, as if the check were *bouncing* between the banks on its return to the check writer. An unpaid check is also sometimes described as "rubber," as in the bouncy material.)

Using checks at all may soon disappear, as people today increasingly use *debit cards, mobile apps,* and *online payment systems* instead of cash or checks for their spending. A debit card is a plastic card that has your account number and other information embedded into its magnetic strip and chip, and requires you to enter your personal identification number (PIN) for security purposes. When you use a debit card at a merchant that accepts these cards, the payment you authorize by entering your PIN into the terminal will be deducted from your account immediately, just as if you used cash taken from that account. It's almost impossible to overdraw your account using a debit card, since the system keeps track of your balance and declines the transaction if your account doesn't have sufficient funds.

Most banks offer online bill payment systems (sometimes for a fee) that allow you to make routine payments from your account electronically using online software, avoiding the use of checks and allowing recurring payments to be made automatically. Online payment systems also keep your account balance accurate in real time. Banks have rapidly moved such services onto mobile platforms so you can even make these payments on your phone using the bank's payment system or third-party systems such as PayPal, Venmo, and smartphone wallet applications.

You can also obtain cash from your account by using your debit card to make a withdrawal at an ATM or by cashing a check you write to yourself. Checking accounts with normal balances don't pay interest and often charge a monthly fee; if you have high balances the bank may waive all fees and even pay you some interest. It's a good idea to regularly check your account statement online, or when it arrives by mail, to look for bank fees you may not have been aware of and to identify any suspicious or potentially fraudulent activity.

People also use banks to purchase a *certified check, bank check, or cashier's check* (they're all roughly the same thing). These checks are written by the bank itself, and the funds are no longer associated with your account. Sometimes a vendor or merchant will insist that you send one of these forms of bank check instead of a check from your own account: the payee is relying on the financial strength of the bank to make payment, not the funds in your account, so it's considered a guaranteed payment with no risk the check will bounce. The bank will charge a small fee for this service.

Since a bank account is a form of legal contract, you must be over 18 to have one by yourself. Minors can open accounts by having an adult listed on the account as a joint owner, who will have full legal authority over the account. If you're under 18, you can access money in a joint account by using your debit card and through electronic banking. When you're old enough and want to have the account by yourself without the adult as joint owner, you need to close the account and open a new one.

Another type of bank account is a certificate of deposit (CD). CDs are used for long-term savings and commit your funds for a term of months or even years, during which you can't use the money without paying a financial penalty. In return, CDs pay a higher rate of interest than regular savings accounts. Annual interest rates paid for a 6-month certificate of deposit averaged about 7.5 percent per year in the 1970s, about 10.0 percent in the 1980s, and about 5.5 percent in the 1990s. In stark contrast, from 2009 to 2013 the interest rate for 6-month CDs averaged only 0.5 percent per year.[3] It's unlikely that a low-interest-rate environment will last forever, but even at 0.5 percent per year, an account with $5,000 in it will generate $25 per year in earnings—better than under a mattress, and much safer.

AUTOMATED TELLER MACHINES

Bank ATMs are electronic devices where you can bank without a teller just by using your debit card: withdraw cash, check account balances, make a deposit, transfer funds between accounts, pay routine bills, and sometimes even perform some non-bank transactions like buy postage stamps. ATMs can be found inside grocery and convenience stores, at public entertainment venues, in airports, bus, and train stations, as stand-alone centers in commercial areas, and of course at bank branches. There are over 400,000 ATMs in the United States alone, and your bank card will usually even work in an ATM in another country, dispensing the local currency instead of U.S. dollars. As mobile and electronic banking become more prevalent, ATMs may go the way of bank branches and become harder to find in the future. For now, however, they're an important part of the banking infrastructure.

Each bank owns a certain number of ATMs. Some ATMs are owned by companies that aren't banks at all, but almost every ATM is part of a network that allows you access to a large number of ATMs beyond those owned by your bank. What's important to consumers about these networks are the fees they may be charged to use the ATM. Most banks don't charge account holders any fees for using an ATM the bank owns, but non-bank ATMs often charge transaction fees. Any ATM not owned by your bank is an out-of-network ATM and could result in your paying two separate fees: a fee to the owner of the ATM machine and a fee to your own bank for processing an out-of-network transaction. Pay close attention to the rules that govern ATM usage with your bank account and choose your ATMs carefully.

PREPAID DEBIT CARDS

The debit card associated with your bank account is linked to that account, and all the purchases you make using that card immediately reduce the balance in your account. Banks and other financial service companies also issue *prepaid debit cards* that aren't linked to any bank account. Instead, consumers pay upfront to load money onto these cards using another form of payment, such as cash, a credit card, or an electronic transfer. These debit cards then have a value equal to whatever the purchaser paid for them minus any fees, and they can be used at any merchant accepting debit cards. With most prepaid debit cards you can only spend up to the amount loaded onto the card, while a debit card linked to a bank account allows you to spend as much money as the bank account holds. Banks, drug stores, and other retailers sell prepaid debit cards, most of which can be reloaded with additional funds after the initial balance has been spent.

Some consumers find these cards a useful alternative to a bank account, and their use has expanded greatly in recent years. Many people use these cards as gifts, since they work just like cash. However, almost all of these cards charge fees for their purchase, so it might cost $55 for a $50 card, and there can be additional fees as well for setup, transactions, inactivity, and reloading. While they look just like bank account debit cards, they don't always offer the same protections for a lost card or a transaction dispute. It can also be difficult to compare fees between different cards. Some cards even offer an "overdraft protection" feature, blurring the line between a debit and a credit card and potentially exposing a user to surprisingly high fees.

OTHER FINANCIAL INSTITUTIONS

Banks are at the center of our economy, but they aren't the only kind of financial institution you'll encounter. Other kinds of financial institutions specialize in offering different products and services that you may need throughout your life:

Insurance Companies. Insurance is a product you purchase to compensate you in the event of some calamity or loss. Insurance can protect your home, automobile, belongings, health, and life. These firms offer many financial products to consumers and hold substantial assets to cover claims. They're supervised by insurance regulators in each state.

Brokerage Firms. Stock market investments are typically made through a brokerage firm. A brokerage firm's business is to buy and sell securities such as stocks, bonds, mutual funds, government debt, and other investments for itself and its customers. They can also offer their customers bank-like products such as checking accounts and loans.

Credit Card Issuers. The average consumer has more than three credit cards in her wallet at any given time. Credit cards can be issued by banks, retail merchants, petroleum companies, and specialty credit card companies. Credit card issuers extend large amounts of credit to individuals and businesses.

Investment Banks. Large businesses and corporations have special needs for financial services. Investment banks help issue debt and equity, advise clients about acquisitions and divestitures, and engage in financial engineering. A firm today can be both a commercial bank and an investment bank at the same time, which wasn't always the case.

Private Equity Firm. These firms solicit investment funds from large, sophisticated investors such as wealthy families, pension funds, endowments, and insurance companies. They then use these funds to buy and operate a portfolio of different businesses. These companies and funds aren't traded in the public stock markets, hence the term *private*.

Hedge Funds. A hedge fund solicits investment funds in the same manner as a private equity firm but doesn't own and operate businesses. Instead, hedge funds make complex and speculative investments, engage in high-frequency trading, take positions that benefit when markets fall, and trade commodities and derivatives.

Commercial Lenders. Businesses seeking loans can borrow from banks or, if they're large enough, from capital markets or institutional investors. Specialized commercial lenders also make substantial loans to businesses. They operate like banks with respect to loans, but they don't have the branch networks or take deposits the way banks do.

Investment Managers. Many types of firms manage investments on behalf of owners or beneficiaries. Pension funds, investment firms, mutual funds, wealth advisors, trustees, and endowment managers all act as professional managers for investments. These managers can operate as subsidiaries of other financial institutions or as independent firms.

FEES AND SERVICES

Banks are businesses that charge fees for their services, but if the only way a bank earned its revenues was to charge you for checking and savings accounts, it wouldn't have a sustainable business model. Banks do two things with the money you deposit: they hold it for you when you need it (to pay a merchant via debit card or online transfer, disburse as cash from an ATM, or cover checks you've written), and they pool it with other funds to lend out at interest. Banks make a profit on the lending activity, but they wouldn't have the funds to sustain their business without your deposits. Once you start doing business with a bank you usually stay a customer for a long time, so the bank can rely on having your deposits around to help fund its lending business. Still, fees are an important source of banking revenue. As a consumer, it's important for you to understand them.

Many banks charge a *monthly account fee*, generally between $5 and $25, to help pay for the branch network and the technological infrastructure that provides account security and transaction processing. For many people with low incomes or who maintain low account balances, bank accounts are expensive. Banks often waive the monthly fees for special types of accounts, like student accounts; if you have multiple accounts at the bank (for example, a checking account combined with a savings account or a loan); or if you maintain a balance above a certain level. Banks sometimes limit the number of no-charge transactions each month (for example, no more than three ATM withdrawals per month without an extra fee). There may also be fees for stopping payment on a check you've written before it has been cashed, getting printed account statements, closing your account within a few months of opening it, making or receiving certain electronic transfers, using the online bill payment systems, and an inactivity fee for *not* using your account. And these are just a few examples.

One fee to really worry about is the *overdraft fee*—a charge around $30 that banks impose when there isn't enough money in your account to cover a check you've written. Young people don't usually have much extra money, and sometimes their account balances get close to zero. The risk of using checks comes from the delay between when you write a check and when it clears your account. It's easy to lose track of your spending and suddenly find that you have less money in your account than you need to cover the checks you've written. You're less likely to overdraw your account using a debit card, an ATM withdrawal, or an electronic payment, because those transactions are posted almost immediately, and payments won't get processed if you don't have enough money in your account. Debit cards linked to your bank account impose overdraft fees only when you accept an overdraft plan. Overdraft plans for prepaid debit cards add money to the debit card to cover spending once the card has a zero balance and charge an overdraft fee for the service. This is almost always a bad deal, so you should never accept these plans. Without the overdraft plan, when your debit card hits a zero balance the transaction is declined, but you won't pay a big overdraft fee.

Banks don't know whether a check will bounce until it goes through the banking system. The bank of the payee presents it to your bank for electronic payment. In turn, your bank looks at your account to see if you have enough money. If so, the bank deducts it from your account and all is well. If not, the bank returns your check to the payee unpaid and charges you an overdraft fee. The merchant who deposited your bad check into her account is charged a service fee of around $25 by her own bank for the so-called returned deposit. This merchant will expect you to pay that bank fee as well, plus you still owe the merchant for the amount of the check. All in all, the total fees for a bounced check may cost you over $50 for *each* bounced check. You can avoid these fees by linking your checking account to a savings account, credit card, or overdraft loan, and while there are fees associated with using this protection, they're much lower than the total cost of a returned check. Using online payments and debit cards (without overdraft protection) can almost eliminate the risk of these types of fees.

RECONCILIATION

The way to keep careful track of your money and avoid overdraft fees is to reconcile your bank account statement to your check register. A *check register* is a small lined booklet, usually attached to your checkbook, designed to record every transaction in your account so you can track your account balance in real time. Even if you don't write many checks, keeping an accurate register is the most important tool you have to monitor your account balance. A few times a week you should go online and compare your running balance in the check register with what the bank shows as your balance. Or, when you receive your monthly bank statement, you can compare the transactions recorded in your register with those reflected in your bank statement. The act of comparing your check register and your account statement and making any adjustments is called *reconciliation*.

Reconciliation is required because of mistakes and timing differences. It's possible your bank made a mistake: a deposit of $250 was recorded as $25; the bank charged you a fee that was supposed to be waived; the same item was processed twice. Possible, but unlikely. Banks have multiple systems in place to ensure accuracy in the account balances, so if you think the bank made a mistake, check yourself before contacting them. More likely *you* made a mistake: forgetting to write down debit card transactions; making an arithmetic error; not recording legitimate bank fees. It's also possible that an online vendor charged you a different amount than you thought, or you forgot to record a recurring payment in your register. Importantly, keeping an accurate register allows you to quickly identify on your bank statement any transactions you didn't make and report them to the bank as unauthorized.

Timing differences occur when a transaction is reflected in your bank account after you recorded it in your check register. For example, if you write a check on July 5 and it's not presented to your bank until July 15, for ten days your balance will appear higher than what's really available. Maybe you had an automated payment set up on a day that fell on a holiday, delaying its posting to your account. If you wait for the printed account statement to be mailed to your home instead of checking it online, you may find a debit card transaction from the end of your statement cycle that wasn't recorded until the following month's statement, another timing difference.

The reconciliation example in Table 4.1 shows that several adjustments must be made for the check register and bank statement to balance. The account owner kept good track of her routine transactions, all of her ATM cash withdrawals, and her checks. She accounted for the direct deposit of her paycheck. However, she forgot to record a deposit made toward the end of the month, and she also overlooked two small debit card transactions from a vending machine. The other needed adjustment she made was for check 1127, which she wrote on July 17, but it hadn't cleared her account by the end of the month. Even though the bank thinks she has that $100 available, because she tracked it in her check register, she knows she doesn't.

Table 4.1   Reconciliation Illustration

Bank Account Statement

Account Summary		
7/1/16	Beginning Balance	$522.25
3	Checks	$150.00
8	Withdrawals / Debits	$312.95
2	Deposits / Credits	$525.00
7/31/16	Bank Fees	$5.00
7/31/16	Ending balance	$579.30
Account Detail Checks		
7/12/16	1126	$35.00
7/20/16	1128	$90.00
7/26/16	1129	$25.00
Withdrawals / Debits		
7/4/16	ATM location 005675	$50.00
7/8/16	Debit purchase Stubhub, Inc.	$31.00
7/15/16	Debit purchase Amazon.com	$20.95
7/16/16	Debit purchase Joe's Pizza	$12.00
7/20/16	ATM location 005690	$100.00
7/25/16	Debit purchase snack vending	$1.50
7/31/16	Debit purchase Kroger, Inc.	$96.50
7/31/16	Debit purchase snack vending	$1.00
Deposits / Credits		
7/15/16	Employer direct deposit	$500.00
7/28/16	Check deposit branch 00114	$25.00
Bank Fees		
7/31/16	Monthly service charge	$5.00

(continued)

Table 4.1   Reconciliation Illustration *(continued)*

Personal Check Register

Date	Item	Amount	Balance
			$522.25
7/4/16	*w/d cash*	*−$50.00*	*$472.25*
7/8/16	*d/c concert tix*	*−$31.00*	*$441.25*
7/9/16	*1126 gas bill*	*−$35.00*	*$406.25*
7/15/16	*d/c Amazon*	*−$20.95*	*$385.30*
7/15/16	*paycheck*	*$500.00*	*$885.30*
7/16/16	*d/c pizza*	*−$12.00*	*$873.30*
7/17/16	*1127 bike repairs*	*−$100.00*	*$773.30*
7/18/16	*1128 MasterCard bill*	*−$90.00*	*$683.30*
7/20/16	*w/d cash*	*−$100.00*	*$583.30*
7/25/16	*1129 flowers*	*−$25.00*	*$558.30*
7/31/16	*d/c Kroger*	*−$96.50*	*$461.80*

Reconciling Adjustments:		**Bank Balance**	**Register Balance**
		$579.30	*$461.80*
	Forgot 2 vending		*−$2.50*
	Forgot bank fee		*−$5.00*
	Forgot deposit		*$25.00*
	1127 not cleared	*−$100.00*	
	Correct balance	*$479.30*	*$479.30*

Source: Author's analysis.

MOBILE PAYMENT SYSTEMS

Smartphones have become the primary tool not just for electronic communications but increasingly also for shopping and spending through *mobile payment systems*. Three of the better known services for smartphone users are Apple Pay, Samsung Pay, and Android Pay. These systems facilitate secure transactions with merchants online and in stores that have communication-enabled payment terminals, creating another way to purchase goods and services or even transfer money from one phone to another. These "wallet" systems are an emerging technology that will evolve rapidly, but what they have in common is a link to a credit or debit card account, as if the smartphones are replacing your physical wallet holding the plastic cards with all your account information. The charges incurred by using these mobile payment systems will end up on your credit card statement or be deducted from your debit card balance or linked bank account.

Another popular mobile app is PayPal, which started as an online payment system embedded into eBay, then evolved into a robust payment system for Internet and mobile transactions. It's now a widely accepted form of payment through smartphones or any Internet service. Like other mobile systems, PayPal can consolidate your credit card and bank account information, making that information a single source for using your spending accounts. With PayPal, you link credit cards or bank accounts that actually fund the purchase, use PayPal balances, or move money between PayPal and your linked accounts. PayPal's Venmo service is specifically designed for mobile devices and facilitates transactions directly between smartphones. Venmo keeps balances you can use for other Venmo transactions, or you can transfer money to and from your bank accounts and debit cards. Today, these mobile payment systems can replace the cards associated with bank and credit card accounts. Soon, they may replace the accounts themselves.

ELECTRONIC BANKING

All of banking relies on electronic computer systems to track balances and carry out transactions. You use these systems when paying with credit and debit cards, checking your account balance online, direct-depositing your paycheck, making online payments, transferring funds between accounts, using mobile payment applications, or accessing ATMs. Behind the scenes of our banking system are two giant *electronic banking* networks where transfers into and out of bank accounts are matched up. Each network is called an *Automated Clearing House*, or ACH. All checks in the United States are now converted into ACH payments; in the old days, paper checks actually were sent back and forth between banks. Online bill payment transactions originate in the ACH system and don't need to be converted. Fewer checks are being used today in favor of direct electronic payments or debit and credit cards (which are handled through another system), but there are still billions of checks processed every year, in addition to the other transactions handled by these networks.

For each bank, the ACH networks process and total all the direct electronic transfers, checks, ATM transactions, and other payments and net this against all the deposits and other receipts such as incoming electronic payments. The bank may receive a net payment or have to make one. Each bank then takes all that information and processes it against all the accounts at that bank. Each day, the thousands of U.S. banks must allocate these transactions across the millions of bank accounts they hold, and this is done automatically and securely by computers. It takes amazingly complex and sophisticated hardware and software to make this work right; if you think of any bank as a really big computer system with an occasional bricks-and-mortar office, you wouldn't be far off.

DEPOSIT INSURANCE

In 1933, during the Great Depression, Congress created the *Federal Deposit Insurance Corporation* (FDIC) to protect depositors in case the bank that held their money became insolvent. Today, each depositor is protected with insurance up to

$250,000 per bank, funded by premiums paid by the member banks, and most advertising will mention this fact. Almost every bank in the U.S. is covered by this insurance plan, so depositors need have no fear about recovering the value of their deposits, even with the total collapse of their bank. Credit unions have their own deposit insurance system, also giving protection up to $250,000 per depositor at each credit union.

The FDIC insurance applies only to bank deposits. As banks have offered more financial services besides bank deposits, it's possible to have an account at a bank that's not covered by insurance. Typically, these would be brokerage accounts holding stocks and bonds. Regulations require that banks make very clear in their marketing efforts that these accounts are *not* insured.

The *Federal Reserve Bank*, often called "the Fed," is the nation's central bank, composed of twelve regional banks throughout the United States and the controlling Board of Governors in Washington, D.C. Congress created the Fed in 1913 and gave it broad legal authority over the national banking system. The Fed operates one of the two payment processing systems along with other primary responsibilities:

Central Bank: The Fed is the central bank for the United States, processing bank transactions involving the federal government and transactions between banks themselves.

Money Supply: Through its Federal Open Market Committee, the Fed regulates the national money supply by establishing reserves banks must hold, setting interest rates for Fed loans, and purchasing government securities.

Lender of Last Resort: The Fed lends money to banks and other financial institutions that are having temporary liquidity problems or otherwise face an emergency, to avoid systemic breakdowns of the financial system.

Regulator: The Fed has direct responsibility for ensuring compliance with laws for a large sector of the banking industry, undertaking audits and inspections with a large staff of investigators.

Other government organizations besides the Fed, at both the national and state level, ensure that banking laws and regulations are followed. For example, government rules establish how much capital banks must hold in reserve against losses; require that banks establish systems to prevent fraud or unauthorized transactions; limit the concentration of risk in bank loan portfolios; and mandate nondiscrimination in lending.

Some banking experts think the complexity of modern banking requires increased regulation of banks and greater scrutiny by regulators. Other analysts feel that banks have been unfairly blamed for problems in the economy that weren't their doing, and more regulations will prevent banks from providing capital to support economic growth. Because of the influential role banking plays in the national economy, and the numerous legal requirements already imposed on banks, bank regulation will continue as an important and debated topic.

BANK SAFETY

One of the primary causes of the Great Depression was a "run" on banks, where the threat of a bank's insolvency caused depositors to rush to their banks and demand full return of their deposits. Banks could comply with these demands only for the first few depositors, then their cash was gone and the depositors were turned away empty-handed. This caused banks to call in their loans, demanding that borrowers repay their loans at once, which they were often unable to do. These effects combined to shake consumer confidence, shrink the economy, and topple the banking sector. The bank runs triggering the Great Depression weren't our country's first, but they were probably the worst. Plummeting confidence in the financial system can lead to so-called banking panics.

Banking panics can occur because we use a fractional reserve system. Banks keep a small *fraction* of their deposits as cash *reserves*, available to meet the cash needs of depositors. Banks lend the rest of the money to other customers who build businesses or buy homes. The popular Christmas movie *It's a Wonderful Life* illustrated this dynamic in a scene where George Bailey calmed a mob of depositors demanding their money back by explaining that their money wasn't at the bank but was, instead, invested in their neighbors' homes and businesses.

Today, as during the Great Depression, banks can't convert their loans to cash quickly in order to pay off depositors. What's different now is that all banks have deposit insurance, so depositors need not rush to their bank for cash if the bank is in trouble. While it's still possible to lose confidence in the financial system, deposit insurance virtually eliminates the risk of a bank run. Other financial panics can still occur, of course, but not from fear of losing bank deposits.

NOTES

1. The Vanguard Group, Inc., "How America Saves 2014" (Valley Forge, PA: June 2014).

2. National Credit Union Administration, "Industry at a Glance," June 30, 2015 (6,159 credit unions); Federal Deposit Insurance Corporation, "Statistics at a Glance," September 30, 2015 (6,270 commercial banks and savings institutions).

3. Board of Governors of the Federal Reserve System, Economic Research & Data, Statistical Releases and Historical Data, "Selected Interest Rates (Daily)—H.15," December 19, 2013; Author's analysis.

FIVE

Budgeting and Spending

A budget is a plan for all of your income and all of your spending. The goal of budgeting is to make sure your total spending is less than your total income, so you'll have extra money around for surprises. Not everything can be predicted in advance. Maybe you want to get your friend a gift and intended to spend $25, but you find something perfect for her that costs $35. Maybe you've had an accident and need to make a co-payment on your health insurance you hadn't anticipated. Or maybe you really want the new iPhone and don't want to wait until you've saved up for it. With a well-designed budget, spending for all these things may be possible.

Not only does a budget allow you to handle surprises, it also helps you avoid them. By knowing accurately in advance how much income you'll be generating and how much money you'll be spending, you can balance the two. When income and expenses are in balance, you won't be generating any debt. With a good budget you won't come to the end of the month and be unable to pay the rent or utility bills. A good budget will instill financial discipline and allow you to build a strong foundation as your income and spending needs change throughout your life.

HOW TO BUDGET

The first step in preparing a budget is to compile a detailed list of all your income and all your expenditures. A monthly cycle is probably the best period to analyze, but a good budget should plan a whole year going forward. Tracking expenses and income is a tool to get you started: it looks *backward* to see what you've been doing in the past. A budget, on the other hand, looks *forward* to predict what you'll earn and spend in the future. You can do this simply with some pencil and paper, or you can use various apps—for example, Spendee or Mint—to organize and categorize your income and spending. Keeping a budget doesn't have to be a lifetime commitment: experts disagree whether regular tracking (which is hard to maintain) or a short-term budgeting effort (which can become obsolete) is the better approach, but it's widely agreed that any thorough budgeting effort will pay you great rewards.

Start from scratch and estimate every component of spending in the coming year. Use your past spending as a guide. Similarly, what do you expect your income to be in the next year? Let's say you're a recent college graduate. While you were in college your income was limited to whatever amount your parents could afford to give you as support, plus any part-time and summer job earnings. Now you have a job that nets you, for example, $2,650 per month (after payroll deductions) for the next year—but your parental support and the part-time earnings will stop, so your job earnings are all you'll have available to spend.

On the spending side, particularly as you move from being dependent on your family for support to becoming financially independent, you'll face some big changes. Your food and housing were probably provided for you by your parents or by your college. Now, you'll have to pay for this yourself. Your health insurance was probably covered by your family or under a school plan; your new employer will probably offer a health insurance plan, but you'll have to pay some of the premium. Other spending categories will be new to you, and those will be hard to budget. It's tedious work to research what things cost, but that's what's required, whether it's your cell phone service or your gas bill. The good news is that once you do the "up-front" work for the first time to estimate what it costs to lead the lifestyle you can afford, then subsequent budgets will be much easier.

Many financial planning experts suggest rules of thumb for how much of your income to allocate to certain categories of spending. For example, one guidance suggests limiting your housing expenses to 30 percent of your income, and another suggests limiting your monthly commitments (housing and loan repayments) to no more than half of your income. There are many free guides available online or from libraries that give detailed assistance for creating a budget, if you need help. Here are several suggestions to keep in mind:

Don't over-consume housing: Housing and related costs are by far the single largest component of most people's budgets. Especially when you're young and less experienced with control of your own money, err on the side of slight discomfort in your living situation in order to keep the costs down. This can mean having more roommates than you like, living in a less desirable neighborhood, having a smaller apartment, or traveling farther to work. The good news is that as you get older, your housing quality will likely keep improving.

Little things add up: You can easily burn a few hundred dollars a month without realizing it, from daily Starbucks to take-out dinners, from health-club memberships to iTunes downloads. Drink free coffee at work if provided; cook at home; join the Y; enjoy the radio. Once you have your own income the urge to spend is great. *Resist that urge at every turn.* Be thrifty now, so you'll have the opportunity to be extravagant later.

Build a large cushion: You'll encounter many surprises in life that will impact your finances. It may be hard to predict in any given month what will come up: one month it could be a large traffic fine, another month you may need to buy something for your apartment, and the next month it could be time to replace your computer. Over the course of a year these surprises will even out, but you need a cushion in your budget to cover them.

EVERYDAY SPENDING

Write down everything you spend money on for a one-month period: every single cent. A month may seem like a long time, but since many expenses—cell phone bills, rent, and credit card statements to name a few—recur on a monthly basis, a shorter period risks missing some important routine expenditures. Tracking for more than a month can't hurt, but it's a laborious process and not necessary for you to get a good sense of where your money is going.

Let's consider a student who lives at home and depends on one or two parents to provide necessities like food, shelter, and education. Here are some other things that even a student living at home might spend money on: entertainment, such as movies, concerts, plays, and parties; food, such as snacks and meals while outside the house; gifts for friends; clothing or items for special events like Halloween or school dances; personal care items such as makeup, breath mints, or skin care products; money for gasoline or for public transportation fares; and accessories for a computer or phone such as apps, e-books, video, and music.

Now let's consider a college graduate who's working at her first full-time job and living in an apartment with a roommate. The things that a young person wants to spend money on while living at home will still be of interest ten years later, just in a more adult version: entertainment, gifts, and electronics are always in style. So none of that spending will likely go away. Added to that list of items, however, will be some new ways to spend money: paying back college debt; rent and utilities, including your cell phone and Internet connection; all of your groceries; insurance for your health and property; expenses related to a car if you own one; furnishings for your living space; all of your clothing; travel for vacations or to visit friends and family; and of course, putting money away as savings.

SAVINGS AND EMERGENCIES

Financial planners recommend that you include in your budget two important categories of spending: savings and emergencies. It may sound odd to describe "savings" as a category of "spending," but it's a good practice to set aside money for savings, just as you'd allocate money for other budget priorities. Sometimes this is called "pay yourself first," to emphasize its importance. Budget as much as you can for savings; it will be easier to control your spending if you don't even have the money around where you can be tempted to spend it. Many employers offer a savings plan through the payroll system, so money is deducted from your paycheck before you even see it.

An emergency fund isn't for the monthly surprises that inevitably occur, but is instead designed for a very serious occurrence, such as losing your job, becoming temporarily disabled, or supporting a family member in crisis. Many experts recommend what will seem like an impossible goal: having six months' worth of spending in an emergency fund. This is a goal you can work up to gradually, even if it takes several years to achieve. During any emergency situation you'll cut back your expenses as much as possible, but you absolutely must have an emergency fund.

SAMPLE BUDGET

The following table shows an example of a budget for the recent college graduate mentioned previously.

Table 5.1   Sample Budget

Income	
Monthly Salary	$3,200
Payroll deductions for taxes, insurance, 401(k)	$550
Available Income	$2,650
Spending	
Rent, gas, electricity, and property insurance	$650
Groceries, snacks, lunch, restaurants, take-out	$600
Loan payment on college debt	$350
Phone, cable, entertainment, transit pass	$200
Personal care (drugstore items, hair and makeup, medical costs)	$200
Durables including clothes, furnishings, gifts	$150
Cushion for repairs, replacements, surprises	$100
Emergency fund build-up	$100
Savings in addition to 401(k)	$100
Vacation and travel fund	$100
Charity	$50
Unbudgeted spending	$50
Total Spending	$2,650

Source: Author's analysis.

AUTOMOBILES

Let's move from routine spending to major expenditures. One major expenditure you may consider is a car. If you live in most cities you probably have no need to own an automobile and should rarely even need to rent one. Many cities have extensive networks of public transportation, offer densely populated neighborhoods where many destinations are within walking distance, and provide multiple options for short-term rides from taxis, Uber, Lyft, Zipcar, Maven, Car2Go, and traditional car rental companies. Major car rental companies usually don't rent to drivers under 21, charge extra fees under age 25, and require a credit card: take your business elsewhere if you can. Even if you think you'd like to have a car in the city for the occasional cross-town jaunt or weekend getaway, forget about it: cars are very expensive to own and operate anywhere, much more so in a city.

If you don't happen to live in a big city—and that would cover about half of all Americans—then the possibility of owning your own car has probably crossed your mind more than once. In some places a car is a necessity, and it may even be a requirement for your job. So first decide if you really need one. If there's any other reasonable option, use that instead. Think of car ownership as a last resort: there's much more to it than you ever thought possible.

Every car must be registered, typically by paying a modest annual fee to the state where you reside (license plates with your name or other custom lettering are extra). Some states and municipalities also impose an annual property or excise tax based on the car's value (you can't play games here by trying to claim the car is worth less than it really is; the motor vehicle departments have good data). You should find out in advance what that tax is—it can be hundreds of dollars per year.

You'll need to have a driver's license, of course, but also one more thing to legally operate a car on the public roadways: automobile liability insurance. In all but a few states every driver must have insurance in case of an accident. Driving a car without this insurance is a crime, and drivers need to carry proof of insurance in the car with them. Rules vary by state about what minimum coverage is required, but you can expect to pay no less than $500 per year and likely in the range of $1,000 annually for automobile insurance.

Even new cars don't last forever, and most cars over five years old no longer have a warranty, so regular maintenance and repair costs are another fact of life for car owners. Even with a warranty, you'll incur costs for routine maintenance such as oil changes, new wiper blades, replacement tires, and cracked windshields. The frequency and cost of repairs will vary dramatically by the age and condition of the car, but it's easy to average $500 or more every year on automobile maintenance.

You'll also pay for gasoline, tolls, and parking. Gasoline will be a large cost for most drivers, as it can run between $0.10 and $0.20 per mile depending on the gas mileage of your car and the gasoline price at the pump. Some highways, bridges, and tunnels charge users a toll for using them, so this can add to the cost of any trip. Once you arrive at a destination you'll have to pay to park your car—at a parking lot, parking meter, valet, or garage. If there isn't street parking or a parking space included with your residence, then you'll have to find parking near where you live. Avoid parking tickets, and if you get one, deal with it: ignoring tickets when issued will add a fine, and parking authorities will eventually hunt you down, then tow your car or immobilize it with a "boot" if you don't pay.

You might somehow be given a car, otherwise you'll need to buy one yourself. You'll face many questions: lease versus buy; new versus used; dealer versus Craig's List; cash versus financing. Consult a car buying service for information about quality, features, repair history, and range of prices for the model you're considering. *Consumer Reports* offers well-regarded and low cost car reports, for example. Avoid debt: save up enough money for the car you want before buying it. Leasing is the same as borrowing money, the interest charges are just hidden: don't do it.

A late-model used car (less than 5 years old) will be much less expensive than a new car, and will still give you plenty of good miles during its useful life (the average car on the road today is over 11 years old). Using the Internet to buy a car directly from someone you don't know will probably save you money, but it's risky. Car dealers are in business to make a profit, and a good car dealer will want to earn your loyalty and treat you right. Investigate online ratings of dealers or consult friends and relatives for their recommendations.

RENTING AN APARTMENT

At some point you'll transition from your parents' home, college dormitory, or temporary group living quarters to a place of your own. Many young people share apartments, since having one or more roommates can provide lower rent, immediate social support, and additional shared resources (maybe one roommate has a car). Having roommates can also reduce privacy and create occasional lifestyle friction, but it's good training for later in life when you may have a more permanent roommate situation.

Renting an apartment is a substantial financial commitment. Whoever signs the lease will be legally responsible for making all the payments, so even if there's an "understanding" among the roommates, the person or people who sign the papers are ultimately responsible. If not all roommates are on the lease, a short letter of agreement among roommates is a good idea, something most people can write themselves. Leases typically require a security deposit of one to two months' rent as protection against damages and unpaid rent, and the first month is due when you sign the lease. This means you'll need a bundle of saved money just to start your lease, up to three months' rent to cover these costs.

Make sure you understand whether the landlord provides any utilities as part of the rent: heating, cooling, electricity, and Internet are all services you'll want. If these utilities aren't provided, someone will have to open an account and will ultimately be responsible for all the charges. All roommates should understand that they're collectively responsible not just for the rent and any damage to the apartment, but for the other living expenses as well. Groceries are an area of potential conflict among roommates, so make sure you have a system for managing and sharing food costs, paper goods, and cleaning materials. Having laundry facilities in or near the apartment is also a great benefit.

Furnishing an apartment can be costly: beds, tables, desks, chairs, electronics, appliances, shelves, kitchen items, lights, window shades, and more. Maybe you can get used furniture from family or friends. Give this some thought before moving in, remember who owns what, and try to allocate expensive items across the different roommates. There *will* be a parting of the ways, perhaps sooner than anyone intends. Be sure to get the landlord's permission in writing if you alter the premises, and also a clear understanding whether you must return the unit to its original condition upon leaving (for example, if the landlord allows you to paint a bedroom lime green, does she expect you to repaint it white before you leave?).

Living together with a romantic partner raises many issues beyond the scope of personal finance, but many of the same roommate concerns will arise: who's legally responsible for the lease and utilities; who owns what of the furnishings, books, DVDs, and so on; what costs are shared and what are kept separate. When you decide to move in together, breaking up is, unfortunately, one possible outcome. Despite its decidedly unromantic character, keep this possibility in mind, so the inevitable emotional pain of breaking up won't cause financial pain, as well.

OWNING A HOME

Owning a home has long been part of the American Dream, providing a sense of permanence, belonging, security, and pride. Sometimes it's simply assumed this is a goal that everybody should share, but owning a home isn't necessarily the right objective for everybody. A home will probably be the most expensive thing you ever buy. A government study estimated the median value of U.S. homes during 2010 through 2012 (half are more, half are less) at around $175,000, but this varied dramatically by state and region. In California the median home was worth $360,000, and in Michigan it was less than $120,000, for example.[1] Prices have increased in most places since then, and because of the cost, most people must borrow money to afford a home. Lenders require some portion of the purchase price be paid in cash as a *down payment*. A good rule of thumb is that you should have 25 percent of the home's cost saved in advance, to pay for the down payment on the loan and other costs associated with buying a home.

Every home will also require maintenance and upkeep; unless the home is less than 10 years old, you can expect to spend about 1 percent of the purchase price, on average, every year in maintenance costs. You'll have to pay property taxes and also buy homeowner's insurance; these costs can range from $500 to $1,000 for the insurance and 0.5 to 2 percent of home valuation for taxes each year. Like an apartment, you'll need some home furnishings and will incur up-front costs such as moving and installing utilities. In some places condominiums are a popular form of ownership, where many of the routine expenses are rolled into a single monthly fee. (A condominium is a separate unit in a complex like an apartment building where the common property such as lobbies, driveways, and lawns is owned collectively.) Of course, if you borrow money to buy a home, you'll also have a monthly mortgage payment to make.

Some people think of their homes as an investment. A home can increase or decrease in value like a financial investment, but it appears to be missing an important feature of what investments provide: a regular return such as interest or dividends. By living in a home you own, however, you're avoiding the cost of renting, so the money you save on rent is a direct return on the money you spent buying your house. It's as if you're renting your home to yourself. But it's not a simple financial analysis to compare buying a home versus renting one.

RENTING VERSUS BUYING

The *transaction costs* associated with buying a house include broker's fees (paid by the seller), title insurance, loan fees, and transfer taxes. Even if they're rolled into the loan, you still pay them one way or another, and it can take several years of appreciation in your home's value just to recover these costs. In comparing renting versus buying, it's important that the options are close equivalents in neighborhood quality, house size, and amenities. You should make realistic assumptions, especially about the housing price appreciation you expect, because these will drive the outcome of this analysis. In rising markets too many people assume this trend will last forever. This country's experience during 2008–09, when housing prices collapsed and took years to start increasing again, should serve as a cautionary tale.

The illustration in Table 5.2 uses a five-year time horizon, in which you start with $40,000 in available savings (for a down payment if buying a home, or left to earn interest if renting one); pay 1 percent of the purchase price for closing costs that are rolled into the loan amount; and incur no other selling costs besides paying a broker. It also ignores the effect of taxes, which are usually minimal anyway, or the time-value of money. (Many people mistakenly think that the income-tax mortgage interest deduction should compel home ownership; in fact, all it does is reduce your effective interest rate a little.) The other assumptions are made clear in the illustration. In this case, it turns out that the cost of ownership over the five-year period exceeds the cost of renting by about $1,115 per year. If the owner stayed in the house a few years longer, or if housing prices increased more rapidly, this would make ownership a more attractive option.

COLLEGE

If you're considering entering college, are currently enrolled, or have finished in the last few years, it can't have escaped your attention that college is a huge expense. Perhaps you're paying for it yourself, working your way through and taking some loans. Perhaps you've heard your parents express their anxiety about how to pay for it. Or perhaps you're fortunate to have a combination of savings and grants that will cover most of the costs. Whatever your situation, having an awareness of your

Table 5.2   Rent Versus Buy Analysis

Starting Savings	$40,000	
Renting Option		**Annual Costs**
Monthly Rent Year 1	$1,000	$12,000
Annual Increase	3% simple	
Monthly Rent Year 2	$1,030	$12,360
Monthly Rent Year 3	$1,060	$12,720
Monthly Rent Year 4	$1,090	$13,080
Monthly Rent Year 5	$1,120	$13,440
Utilities	$200/month	$2,400
Maintenance	Included	
Taxes	Included	
Renter's Insurance		$500
Five-Year Costs	$78,100	
Interest Rate on Savings	2% annually	
Savings at end of 5 years	$44,163	
Earnings on Savings	$4,163	
Five-Year Cost of Renting	$73,937	$14,787
Ownership Option		**Annual Costs**
Purchase Price	$200,000	
Annual Appreciation	2% simple	
Down Payment	20% = $40,000	
Closing Costs	$2,000 added to loan	
Mortgage Loan	$162,000	
30-Year Mortgage Rate	6% annually	
Monthly Payment	$971	$11,652
Utilities	$200/month	$2,400
Maintenance		$2,000
Taxes		$2,500
Homeowner's Insurance		$1,000
Five-Year Costs	$97,760	
Selling Price	$220,000	
Seller's Brokerage Fee	5%	
Sale Proceeds	$209,000	
Mortgage Balance	$150,750	
Net Proceeds	$58,250	
Profit on Savings	$18,250	
Five-Year Cost of Ownership	$79,510	$15,902

Source: Author's analysis.

college expenses and how to manage them is important, because they're likely to be a central feature of your financial life for many years.

There are different types of colleges: for-profit and nonprofit; two-year and four-year; private and public. For-profit colleges have received criticism in recent years, although there's nothing inherently wrong with this type of school. For-profit schools tend to focus on practical training or career specialties, like computer programming, graphic arts, cooking, and health care. They offer nontraditional formats like online classes and attract many part-time students. The number of for-profit schools has grown in recent years, leading to allegations—certainly overbroad—that they exploit the financial-aid system to leave students deeply in debt without improving their career prospects.

Public community colleges offer good educational value, flexible schedules, and practical courses of study designed for quick entry into the job market. The community college systems also include technical schools, business colleges, career centers, and apprentice programs with local industry. Community colleges typically offer two-year degrees and can serve as an entry-point for some students into four-year degree programs at other colleges. Public universities typically grant four-year degrees and have resources to offer a wide range of study options, from nursing to engineering, liberal arts to business. Private colleges and universities provide a similar range of academic options as the public institutions, supported by endowments instead of tax dollars (an *endowment* is a fund from accumulated gifts that generates income to be used for scholarships and operations).

The cost of college is substantial. The most expensive item is tuition, but students must also pay for room, board, books, health insurance, activities, and certain other fees. Every school publishes a list price for tuition and fees, but only a very small number of students pay the list price. Most students receive some amount of grant, scholarship, or aid—money that doesn't need to be paid back and that serves to reduce the *net price* of college. Most students (and their families) are eligible for subsidized loans, and while these loans have to be paid back—and therefore don't lower the cost of college—they can allow a student to attend an otherwise unaffordable college.

The total annual cost (tuition, room, board, and fees) of a four-year private college or university in the United States today is around $45,000 with a range roughly between $30,000 and $65,000. Fortunately, the average level of grants is around $20,000 so the net price averages $25,000 per year. For four-year public schools the average total cost is $20,000 with grant aid of $6,000 bringing the net price to around $14,000. For two-year public schools the net price after grants is about $7,000 per year, which can be reduced even further for students living at home.[2] For a four-year degree the total investment is between $50,000 and $100,000, which explains why the average student with loans graduates college owing about $35,000 in debt.[3] There are many *net price calculators* online to help students understand the true cost of college, but study them carefully: loan aid isn't the same as grant aid, and net price calculators don't treat different types of aid consistently.

Should the likelihood of having $35,000 or more in student debt discourage you from considering a four-year college? Not at all: college is one of the best investments you can make in yourself. Numerous studies show the financial value of a college education: college graduates earn about twice as much money each year as those who don't attend college, and over a lifetime the net benefit of a college education is *in excess of a half-million dollars*.[4] For most people, the high cost of a college education will eventually be worth the financial investment. More importantly, a college education helps create a responsible, curious, and informed citizen, which is critical to the successful functioning of our society.

Just because college has a tremendous financial payoff, however, doesn't make it the right choice for everybody. Not every person will benefit from a college education, nor is financial success guaranteed just because you receive a degree. Matching your skills and interests to the type of education you seek after high school is important: many young people would be far better off at community college studying for a particular job than at a four-year school acquiring general knowledge. There are many ways to train for jobs or acquire skills that lead to ready employment besides attending four-year colleges.

Whether you choose to study welding at a community college or philosophy at a four-year private university, planning for college costs is important. Every state offers tax-subsidized college savings programs called 529 Plans. Numerous organizations offer scholarships to worthy students. The federal and state governments offer scholarships, direct aid, and subsidized loan programs; some of these loans can be forgiven after college for certain types of jobs or based on income. College financing options are complex, numerous, and constantly changing, so it's advisable to consult resources at libraries, college counselors' offices, and online. No matter your circumstances, you can afford college if you work hard to make a financial plan.

CHILDREN

As you mature you'll consider whether to become a parent. There are many reasons to have children, and only in modern times have these reasons *not* been fundamentally economic: a little more than a century ago, a primary motivation to have children was to produce additional workers for the family farm or business, and to take care of aging parents when those parents became too frail to work. Today, most child labor is illegal, and numerous government programs assist the old and infirm.

If young couples thought about the costs of raising children, they might never reproduce. As parents, you'll have to pay living costs not just for yourselves, but for additional little creatures as well: food, clothing, housing, transportation, child care, education, personal care, recreation, and health care. The government estimates that it costs on average about $250,000 to raise one child to the age of 18 in the United States, ranging from $150,000 to $450,000 depending on where you live and a family's affluence.[5] And this doesn't even include college. Yikes!

Child rearing if it happens will likely be some years off for you, so you don't have to plan yet for the financial impact of having children. What you do need to keep in mind as a young adult, however, is that you'll be facing very large expenses down the road, a road you're rapidly traveling. To meet these burdens, you'll need to budget carefully, spend cautiously, save aggressively, and invest prudently.

VALUE

You might engage in hundreds of small, routine transactions every month, and by doing so you develop a good idea what prices for these things should be: which stores have better grocery prices, which gas station offers the lowest price, and where you can get a reasonably priced haircut. When you buy something less often, it's harder to judge whether you'll get a good deal. The more money you spend, the more effort you should take to compare prices and features before making a decision. A good rule of thumb is to have three different options whenever you're considering making a sizable purchase.

There are two components to *value*: price and quality. Price isn't always so simple. There's the purchase price, of course, and it's easy today to compare multiple offers using online sellers. But there are also sales taxes, delivery charges, setup fees, and disposal charges that might be added. Then consider the lifetime cost of ownership: sometimes the product requires something consumable (ink for a printer, CO_2 for a SodaStream), so you must factor that into any purchase analysis. Finally, everything breaks, so the cost of repairs and how readily they can be made should also be included in your decision making.

The likelihood that something you buy won't function as expected or will otherwise be unsatisfactory is an element of quality. You can't always determine quality in advance of using a product or service, but you can consult online ratings, seek the recommendation of a trusted friend, or do research in a consumer magazine. Being aware of qualitative differences in a product or service may be enough to tip the balance when prices are close. A low-cost product that's known to fail early in its life may well be less attractive than one that costs more but is known for its durability: you get to decide whether you want to pay more now, or later.

CONSUMERS BEWARE

Watch out for termination fees or "evergreen" renewal clauses in any agreement for purchasing services like cellular phone plans, health club memberships, computer software, or utilities. These are *contracts*, and an *evergreen* clause renews the contract for another term unless you explicitly opt out. Leaving your service provider early might trigger large termination fees. Service agreements can be many pages in length, written in language that's hard to understand, and include terms that two reasonable people would never agree to. But consumers don't have the opportunity to negotiate with large service providers—it's take it or leave it. You must find the language in these contracts that governs termination and renewals, and follow it carefully for example, by giving notice of termination far enough in advance to avoid being charged a painful termination fee.

Many retailers offer an *extended warranty* when they sell you a product. Experts recommend that you *never purchase* one of these warranties. Most products come with warranties from the manufacturer, and many retailers offer generous terms for returning the products they sell, whether it's online or from a local store. Walmart, for example, allows returns on most goods up to 90 days. Consumer products, especially in the case of electronics, usually fail right out of the box or soon thereafter, if they fail at all. So the retailer return policy, or the standard warranty from the manufacturer, is all you'll need in the vast majority of cases. Extended warranties usually run at the same time as the manufacturer's standard warranty, so you get less extra coverage than it appears. Extended warranties are one of the most profitable add-ons for retailers, which means they're a bad deal for consumers.

Finally, you should avoid so-called "rent to own" purchases. In this type of a transaction, the consumer makes a monthly rental payment to the retailer for one or two years, after which the consumer owns the property—furniture, a television, or an appliance, for example. These are actually expensive loans, with high fees and hidden interest rates. If you don't complete all the payments, you must return the property to the retailer and will lose all the payments you've made. A better approach is to save your money until you can afford to buy what you want and avoid this type of hidden borrowing.

NOTES

1. U.S. Census Bureau, "Home Value and Home Ownership Rates: Recession and Post-Recession Comparisons from 2007–2009 to 2010–2012," Table 1 (data from 2010–2012), November 2013.

2. The College Board, "Trends in College Pricing 2015," Table 7, October 2015.

3. Jeffrey Sparshott, *The Wall Street Journal,* "Congratulations, Class of 2015. You're the Most Indebted Ever (For Now)," May 8, 2015.

4. See Pew Research Center, "The Rising Cost of *Not* Going to College," February 11, 2014.

5. U.S. Department of Agriculture, "Expenditures on Children by Families, 2013," August 2014.

SIX

Credit and Debt

For thousands of years, human progress was slow. Advances in arts, sciences, literacy, technology, and the human condition came in spurts, but most people, for most of history, lived at a subsistence level, barely able to survive. This changed dramatically with the advent of democratic capitalism and the industrial revolution. Over the last two centuries, billions of human beings have improved their material living standards at the greatest rate in the history of mankind through application of market-based systems that order our economies. Fundamental to the operation of these markets is lending and borrowing money.

At the root of a market system is *capital*—wealth that has built up beyond the subsistence needs of those who accumulated it. It normally takes any one person a long time to accumulate enough wealth to have anything left over after providing for basic needs. Some people—through good luck, skill, ambition, or position—are able to generate wealth more rapidly. The extra wealth that people have available for use beyond their daily needs is called capital, and capital fuels growth in a free-market economy.

In a modern free-market economy we often use financial institutions to connect users of capital with sources of capital. Someone seeking capital may invest in a business, purchase an expensive asset like a house or a car, or cover short-term spending on daily needs. Someone offering capital can provide it to make an investment in owning a business, which is permanent, or to make a loan, which is temporary. In this chapter, we focus on providing capital through the most common types of loans.

LOANS

A *loan* is a transfer of money from a lender to a borrower under specified terms for the repayment of that money. A loan is always expected to be paid back: if you don't have to pay it back, it's a gift, not a loan. There are informal loans, such as a sister lending her brother $10 to go to the movies, and there are formal loans, for example, between a bank and a consumer that require mounds of documents to define the terms. Some loans need to be repaid quickly, such as within one month, and other loans can be paid back over many years or decades. Loans can be repaid in pieces or paid back all at once. The great flexibility of loans makes them a versatile tool for matching people who need money with those who have money to lend.

Interest is the cost for the use of borrowed money; think of it as rent. The lender requires interest for three reasons. First, the loan might not be repaid, so the lender must be compensated for this risk of loss (also called "credit risk"). Second, the owners of capital (those providing the loan) need a return on their money, otherwise they have no incentive to lend. Finally, the lender has to pay operating costs to run its lending business. Sometimes borrowers also pay fees to the lender to analyze the loan and prepare the documents; we call these *transaction costs*.

TIME VALUE OF MONEY

Because money can earn a return, people naturally prefer to have money today rather than money tomorrow, all else being equal. This is called the *time value of money*. Consider a choice between receiving $100 today or $100 in five years. In five years, $100 will almost certainly buy you less of everything than $100 today because of inflation. Moreover, you can also earn interest on that money (or some other return) and have more than $100 in five years. Another example is the Mega Millions lottery jackpot, where the stated prize is much larger than the "cash option." A $15 million grand prize (before taxes) might translate to $9 million received today because the grand prize is paid out over 30 years. Money received today is worth more than money received tomorrow.

Time value is based on understanding that interest charges on borrowed money require you to pay back more money the longer you hold onto it. Let's say you borrow $100 today at 10 percent annual interest; time value means you'll have to pay back $110 a year from now, $121 in two years, or $133 in three years. Time value also explains *indifference*: in a world with 10 percent interest rates, you should be indifferent—have no preference one way or the other—between $100 today and $110 a year from now.

COLLATERAL AND REPAYMENT

If there's a big risk a borrower won't repay a lender, the required risk charge might make the interest rate so high the loan would be unaffordable. One way to reduce the risk of nonpayment, and lower the interest charge, is to have some *collateral* backing up the loan. Collateral is something of value that will be forfeited if the loan isn't repaid.

For example, if you borrow money to buy a car, the car itself will be collateral to secure repayment of the loan. Lenders would much prefer you repay the loan instead of repossessing the vehicle, but if something goes wrong and you can't repay it, the lender will reclaim the car, sell it, and use the procceds to pay down the loan. Because the vehicle has substantial value and can be sold quickly for cash, the risk of the loan is reduced, and the lender can offer car loans at affordable interest rates.

Not all loans have collateral, so the borrower's ability to repay the loan out of her income or assets is an important factor in a lender's willingness to make a loan. A lender devotes energy and resources to assess the ability of a borrower to repay the loan, a process called *underwriting*. Underwriting can be as simple as confirming that the borrower has a job, or it can take weeks of research and analysis of documentation furnished by the borrower.

MORTGAGES

A *mortgage* describes a loan made to purchase real estate, typically a person's home. Technically, the term "mortgage" refers to using your home as collateral to secure a loan, but in common usage it usually refers to the loan itself. In the United States, there's about $10 *trillion* worth of home mortgage debt outstanding today, covering 50 million homes (out of 75 million owned homes in the U.S.) and another 40 million rental units.[1] That's a lot of debt. Mortgages are the number one type of borrowing for American consumers.

One important feature of a mortgage is whether the interest rate is fixed or variable. Typically, variable rate loans start with lower interest rates, but can rise several years out after being reset. Another feature is whether you'll pay back the loan a little each month, or all at once at the end of the term. The length of the loan is also important: some loans can be as short as 5 years, but the 30-year mortgage loan has become the standard in the United States. Some mortgage lenders charge fees for their expenses in documenting a mortgage loan, so this can be another difference between loans.

A *home equity loan* is simply a mortgage loan made after you've owned a house for a while. Instead of using a loan to buy a house in the first place, you use a home equity loan to borrow more money on top of the initial mortgage loan. You can do this when you've accumulated enough of a difference between the home's value and the amount of the original loan—called *equity*—so the bank can lend you additional money secured by the home. Some people unwisely use the proceeds from home equity loans for frivolous purchases such as boats or vacations, but the proceeds can also be used to make improvements to the house that increase its value.

Local governments maintain official records of real estate ownership, called *title*. Since real estate secures a mortgage loan, we use title registries to record a mortgage and to release the property when a loan is paid off. As a result, lawyers and title insurance companies get involved with every mortgage, and their services are costly. Real estate brokers, building inspectors, and other professionals may also be required in a real estate transaction. Like all secured loans, if the borrower doesn't pay the money back, the lender will *foreclose* on the property and use sale proceeds to pay off the loan. Despite these costs and risks, home ownership would be impossible for most people without mortgage loans.

INTEREST RATES

Every kind of loan has a charge for the use of the money, called *interest,* which is typically expressed as a percent per year. The amount of money someone borrows is called the *principal,* and interest is figured by multiplying the interest rate times the principal amount.

Example: Interest rate of 12 percent per year, with a principal loan amount of $1,000, for a term of one year. The total interest charge will be $120 per year. At the end of one year, the borrower will owe $1,120.

This example illustrates simple interest. Unfortunately, that type of interest calculation is only used among friends. Among financial institutions things are a bit more complicated, starting first with *compound interest.* To compound interest means to pay interest on the interest. That's a terrific thing when you're a lender (for example, if you have a savings account, the interest you earn will be compounded). As a borrower, it increases how much total interest you pay and complicates your calculations. Let's use the same example as above with interest compounded monthly.

Example: Interest rate of 12 percent per year, with a principal loan amount of $1,000, for a term of one year. With monthly compounding, the monthly interest rate will be 1 percent (12 percent divided by 12 months per year). Table 6.1 shows the first month's interest charge will be $10, and the balance at the end of month one will be $1,010. The second month's interest charge will be $10.10 (1 percent times $1,010 balance), and the ending monthly balance will be $1,020.10. And so on. At the end of the year the borrower will owe $1,126.84 using compounded monthly interest instead of $1,120.00 using simple annual interest. So the *effective interest rate* is about 12.68 percent, not 12.00 percent.

Table 6.1   Compound Interest

Monthly Compounding	Beginning Balance	Monthly Interest	Ending Balance
Month 1	$1,000.00	$10.00	$1,010.00
Month 2	$1,010.00	$10.10	$1,020.10
Month 3	$1,020.10	$10.20	$1,030.30
Month 4	$1,030.30	$10.30	$1,040.60
Month 5	$1,040.60	$10.41	$1,051.01
Month 6	$1,051.01	$10.51	$1,061.52
Month 7	$1,061.52	$10.62	$1,072.14
Month 8	$1,072.14	$10.72	$1,082.86
Month 9	$1,082.86	$10.83	$1,093.69
Month 10	$1,093.69	$10.94	$1,104.63
Month 11	$1,104.63	$11.05	$1,115.68
Month 12	$1,115.68	$11.16	$1,126.84
Total Interest		$126.84	

Source: Author's analysis.

Now let's consider interest compounded daily, taking the 12 percent stated annual interest rate and dividing it by 365 days to get a daily interest rate of about .0329 percent. If you compound that daily interest rate every day for an entire year, you'll owe $1,127.47 at the end of the year, giving you an effective interest rate of 12.75 percent, not the 12.00 percent that was indicated.

Most financial institutions use daily interest for their calculations on their accounts and loans. Mortgages, because they're designed to receive fixed payments once a month, typically use monthly interest calculations. Borrowers may see interest rates expressed as an Annual Percentage Rate (APR), which accounts for various fees and costs so consumers can compare loans more easily. The APR will almost always be higher than the stated rate because of these adjustments for fees and other costs.

AMORTIZATION

In the examples above we assumed the loan amount (principal) would be paid back at the end of the year. This is called a *lump-sum* or *balloon payment*. We also assumed that the interest would be accumulated during the year to be paid at the end, with no interest payments made during the year. The financial term for accumulating the interest is called *accruing*. Both of these conditions, however, can change depending on the type of loan. Most loans require interest payments during the term of the loan, and many loans also require that some repayment of principal be made before the end of the term. When there's partial or complete repayment of the principal during the term of a loan, this is called *amortizing*.

Home mortgage loans are the most common type of amortizing loan. Some mortgage loans allow for partial repayment of principal over the term of the loan, leaving a significant balloon payment at the end. To make a balloon payment or when interest rates drop, homeowners usually *refinance* and use proceeds from a new loan to pay off the balance on the old loan. Most mortgage loans, however, are completely amortizing and pay off the full principal amount during the length of the loan.

Example: Interest rate of 4 percent per year, principal loan amount of $100,000, term of 30 years. Using monthly interest, the cost for the first month is $333.33, which is 4 percent divided by 12 months times $100,000. To amortize the principal, we divide $100,000 into 360 equal pieces (30 years times 12 months), so the borrower would pay back $277.78 of principal every month and have a zero balance at the end of 30 years. So the first month's payment would be $611.11 (interest of $333.33 plus principal of $277.78).

During the second month the loan balance would be only $99,722.22, because we paid back $277.78 the month before. Therefore, the interest charge for the second month would be less than previously, a total of $332.41. The monthly principal payment would remain $277.78, bringing the total monthly payment for interest and principal to $610.19, $0.92 less than the previous month. This pattern would continue every month as shown in Table 6.2: fixed principal, decreasing interest charges, total declining payments.

Table 6.2   Mortgage Payments

	Beginning Balance	Principal Payment	Interest Payment	Total Payment	Ending Balance
Declining Payment Mortgage Loan					
Month 1	$100,000.00	$277.78	$333.33	$611.11	$99,722.22
Month 2	$99,722.22	$277.78	$332.41	$610.19	$99,444.44
Month 3	$99,444.44	$277.78	$331.48	$609.26	$99,166.66
Etc.					
Fixed Payment Mortgage Loan					
Month 1	$100,000.00	$144.09	$333.33	$477.42	$99,855.91
Month 2	$99,855.91	$144.57	$332.85	$477.42	$99,711.34
Month 3	$99,711.34	$145.05	$332.37	$477.42	$99,566.29
Etc.					

Source: Author's analysis.

Although a fixed principal repayment schedule is completely amortizing, you can see the loan payment changes every month. This places an administrative burden on lenders to recalculate a new payment every month and on borrowers to adjust their budgets. Many people like having a fixed payment every month, so with just about any calculator or spreadsheet you can figure this out. All you do is enter the amount of the loan, number of months for the payback, and the monthly rate of interest. The calculator or computer will produce the fixed monthly payment that reduces the loan balance to zero at the end of the last period. (In Microsoft Excel, it's the Formulas / Financial / PMT function.)

Using the example in Table 6.2, the fixed monthly payment for 30 years is $477.42, about $134 less than the initial payments under the declining payment method. After making the $477.42 payment every month for 30 years, you'll have entirely paid back the $100,000 and paid a 4 percent annual interest rate on the outstanding balance, as it changed every month. Table 6.3 shows the total payments over 30 years will be $171,869.51, and the total interest payments ($71,869.51) will be almost as much as the amount of the principal loan repayment ($100,000). A shorter term of 10 or 20 years reduces the total interest payments, but it also raises the monthly payment. The early payments are mostly interest—for example, the first payment on the 30-year loan has $333.33 in interest and only $144.09 in principal repayment. Toward the end of the term this ratio is reversed, with most of the payment going to principal, and very little applied to interest. This is a natural feature of a fixed payment amortizing mortgage loan.

CREDIT CARDS

A *credit card* is a plastic card embedded with identifying information on a magnetic stripe and computer chip. The card represents an account used by the owner

Table 6.3   How Total Interest Varies with Term of Loan

Term	10 Years	20 Years	30 Years
$100,000 Loan 4 Percent Interest			
Monthly Payment	$1,012.45	$605.98	$477.42
Total Payments	$121,494.17	$145,435.28	$171,869.51
Total Interest	$21,494.17	$45,435.28	$71,869.51

Source: Author's analysis.

to purchase goods and services from vendors who are in the credit card network, which is a transaction processing system. Every month, the issuer of the credit card sends the account holder a statement showing the purchases made on the card. At this point the account holder has a choice: pay the balance in full (by auto bill-pay, electronic transfer, or using a check), or pay only a portion of it. If you don't pay the full balance, the amount you owe becomes a loan with interest. There are many types of credit card issuers, including banks and other large financial institutions, and also retailers such as Macy's and Target.

The largest credit card networks in the United States are Visa, MasterCard, Discover, and American Express. They're separate networks, and many vendors accept only one or two of them. The vendor agrees to pay the network a fee for the use of the network and for processing the transactions (this is called an *interchange fee* and is about 3 percent of the transaction amount). Through the network, the issuer makes an immediate payment to the vendor for the value of the credit card transactions it processes. This speedy collection of the money is one of the reasons vendors are willing to pay the interchange fee to the networks. Another reason vendors accept credit cards is they're a preferred form of payment by many consumers, so not accepting credit cards can hurt the business.

Since the issuer immediately pays the vendor but gives you about a month to pay your account, you've received a short-term loan (credit) from the credit card company. There are over 1 billion credit cards outstanding in the United States, with nearly $1 trillion in debt on them at any given time. However, only about two-thirds of credit card holders use their cards as *credit* cards by carrying balances for more than the length of the billing cycle. The other one-third of credit card holders use their cards as *transaction* cards by paying their balances in full every month. These users are essentially getting an interest-free loan from the credit card company.[2]

If you're among the two-thirds of users who *don't* pay the balance in full every month, a credit card is a bad deal. Credit card issuers charge high rates of interest, generally between 12 percent and 24 percent annually on outstanding balances, which start the minute you make a purchase—no free credit for any length of time. If you miss a payment or are late, the card company will charge you high fees that are added to your balance and on which additional interest must be paid. It's very seductive to buy something with a credit card and pay for it down the road, but this has created financial nightmares for millions of well-meaning consumers who overused these cards and suddenly found themselves buried in debt. Heed this advice: **never carry a balance on a credit card** unless it's an emergency.

Shopping around carefully for the right credit card is worth the effort. There's no reason for a young person to have a card that charges an annual fee ($50 to $100 per year)—these cards have advanced features like airline points and zero foreign transaction fees, something worthwhile only for higher-spending users. Some cards give you rebates, for example 1 percent of purchases (giving you some of the interchange fee the network charges the merchants). Find a card with low late fees and interest rates in case you accidentally miss a payment or suffer an emergency where you must carry a balance. Also look for a long "grace period," the time between the statement closing and the due date of your payment, and consider automating your monthly payments through your bank account.

AUTOMOBILE AND PERSONAL LOANS

An automobile loan is money lent by an affiliate of a car dealer, an automobile financing company, or a commercial bank used to purchase a vehicle. Because it's a secured loan, if you don't keep up with the monthly payments and can't work out a deal with the lender, you'll lose the car. In many cases, the borrower will still be liable to pay any remaining balance after the car has been repossessed and sold. You can seek a *non-recourse* loan where the lender will have no right to come after you if the loan is unpaid—the lender must look only to the collateral (the car) in the event you don't make all the loan payments. Dealer affiliates are more likely to offer non-recourse loans, but they're costlier.

Most automobile loans require a down payment of 10 to 20 percent and are structured as fully amortizing with fixed monthly payments. In some cases, you can get a car loan with a balloon payment that has low monthly payments, but at the end of the term there's a big payment due. An *automobile lease* is actually a loan in disguise. Lenders calculate their lease rates by estimating the selling price of the car at the end of your lease, called the *residual value*. The difference between the selling price of the car (minus any required down payment) and the residual value is the amount that must be financed. The leasing company applies its internal interest rate (which by law must be disclosed to you) to calculate the monthly payments. Lease payments are usually less than loan payments because the leasing company owns the residual value at the end of the term, lowering the amount financed. With a purchase financed by a loan you must borrow more, but you own the car when you're done making payments.

Personal loans can be made for any purpose, for example to consolidate credit card debt or make home improvements, and they aren't usually collateralized. Many banks, consumer finance companies, and online lenders offer these loans with varying terms, interest rates, and payment options. Borrowers must show proof of income and will pay higher interest rates because the loans have no collateral. These loans can be set up as a *line of credit*, where you have an account that you draw on as you need the money, paying interest only on what you borrow. Or these loans can be set up so you get all the money up front and pay the loan back on a fixed schedule.

CREDIT REPORTS

One of the tools a lender will use during the underwriting process is a credit report. A *credit report* is a compilation and analysis of historical financial transactions that reflect the financial character of a potential borrower. There are three major credit reporting agencies in the United States: Experian, TransUnion, and Equifax. They provide services to lenders by issuing credit reports on potential borrowers—you—that help lenders make decisions about how much and on what terms to offer credit.

A credit report contains four types of information. It provides *identifying information* about the potential borrower, such as Social Security number, name or former name, address, and birth date. The report also has a section showing the *history of credit* offered to you in the past, whether a mortgage, credit card account, automobile loan, or a merchant's line of credit. Included here are payment and balance history, late payments, and maximum credit limits. Another section shows all the *inquiries* for your credit report made in the last two years; these might come from opening credit card accounts or applying for a mortgage. Finally, the last section of a credit report shows *public records* such as bankruptcies, lawsuits, wage garnishments, foreclosures, and liens. It also shows any collection agency activity to collect unpaid debts.

One of the most important elements of every credit report is the *credit score*. About 60 years ago a company called Fair Isaac Corporation (FICO) developed a data-driven model to assess credit-worthiness (started by two techies with the last names of "Fair" and "Isaac"). They created the concept of a numerical "credit score" and have been refining it ever since. All three of the credit report companies use some version of the FICO scoring system, which produces scores from 300 to 850 (higher is better), and lenders rely on this score extensively. The two most heavily-weighted factors in the FICO score are the payment history and amount of debt owed. These factors consider the extent of delinquencies, negative legal items, on-time payments, number of accounts with debt, total balances, and loan payoffs, among other things. The FICO score also considers how long you've had credit, the type of credit you've used, and the frequency of requests for new credit. Most scores are between 600 and 750, with 700 and up generally considered good. FICO isn't the only scoring system, but it's the leader.

Many employers and insurance companies also check your credit report to learn about your financial character. Because of the importance of credit reports, the government regulates their use to help improve the accuracy of the information and ensure that consumers are treated fairly. Under law, consumers are entitled to receive one free copy of their credit reports each year through a joint venture established by the three national credit reporting agencies (to order, visit www.annualcreditreport.com or call 1-877-322-8228). There are numerous "imposter" sites that claim to offer free credit reports, but there's only one official site run by the three agencies. You're also entitled to a copy of your credit report if you're denied an application for credit, insurance, or employment. It's a good idea to periodically review your credit report for errors: both the credit reporting company and the entities providing credit information are required to correct inaccurate or incomplete information. If you discover errors in your credit report, contact the credit reporting company and the information provider in writing.

PAYDAY LENDING

Payday lending is a form of credit that seems like cashing a paycheck in advance, but in fact these transactions are loans. *Payday loans* rely on the future payment of wages from a borrower's regular job, and don't require any collateral. A borrower provides employment documentation showing the amount of her weekly paycheck, typically a pay stub (this is the documentation that comes with paychecks showing gross wages, taxes, and other deductions). The lender gives the borrower immediate cash, often in the form of prepaid bank cards, based on how much the borrower will receive on her next payday, minus the lender's fees. When the paycheck arrives, the borrower is expected to repay the loan in full by signing over her paycheck, although often the loans are extended for additional periods.

The payday lender's fees are high for a short-term loan, making this an expensive way for people to obtain credit. Single women, minorities, those without college degrees, and lower-income families use payday lenders at a much higher rate than other groups. This has prompted strong criticism and increased regulation of these lenders. Some studies have shown that borrowers use these loans responsibly, without incurring high default rates. Other studies find that these loans are predatory and exploit desperate borrowers. There's vigorous debate about how useful these loans are, but there's no doubt they're expensive and should be avoided except as a last resort.

DEBT COLLECTION

If everything goes well, a loan can be a beneficial transaction for both borrower and lender. The borrower can purchase something she desires that wouldn't have been possible without the loan, and the lender can make a profitable transaction by pairing its capital with someone who needs it. Not everything always goes well, however. People lose their jobs, incur sudden expenses such as hospital bills, or prices skyrocket putting pressure on family budgets. Sometimes people get deeply in debt simply by not paying attention to their borrowing and spending. Lenders will work with borrowers who run into temporary difficulty and modify the payment schedule—they want to have you back as a return customer, after all—but they're businesses and ultimately will run out of patience with a borrower who can't repay a loan. Once a lender decides the borrower can't repay even a modified loan, the debt is turned over to another department in the lender's company or to a third-party debt *collection agency*. This is called sending a debt for *collection*.

The debt collection process is stressful for consumers, many of whom already have other complications in their lives that may have triggered the financial problems. Debt collectors and collection agencies can be persistent, disruptive, and aggressive. As a result of harsh collection practices, the federal government has passed several laws to help protect consumers. Under current law, for example, debt collectors can't use abusive or threatening language, must limit the time and place they contact you, must give you detailed and accurate information about the debt, and must stop contacting you if you request this in writing. This won't prevent the collection effort from being reported to the credit agencies or stop any legal action, so it's best to work out a debt with a lender before it's sent to a collection agency.

RESPONSIBLE USE

It would be unaffordable for most people to buy a home until they were very old, if it weren't for the existence of a well-functioning mortgage lending market. It would be impossible for many drivers to own their own cars without the ability to take out an automobile loan. Many promising teenagers would be unable to attend college without the availability of student loans. And modern consumer spending would be inconceivable without the presence of the merchant-based credit card system. Clearly, there are many positive attributes of using credit and debt.

On the other hand, the widespread and relatively easy availability of credit today allows some consumers to become indebted beyond their abilities to repay. Many people don't factor in the possibility of some problem surfacing in their financial lives, and have no cushion should things go wrong. Financial distress often results from excess indebtedness, and this places a huge burden on personal relationships and individual well-being. Avoiding debt entirely is probably the best strategy of all, but that may be impractical for most people. If you must incur debt, the safest way to do so is cautiously, sparingly, briefly, and with a well-conceived and realistic plan to pay it off.

NOTES

1. Board of Governors of the Federal Reserve System, Economic Research & Data, Statistical Releases and Historical Data, "Mortgage Debt Outstanding," One- to four-family residences, September 2015, U.S. Census Bureau, "2013 Housing Profile: United States," American Housing Survey Factsheets, owner-occupied units, May 2015.

2. Tamara E. Holmes and Yasmin Ghahremani, "Credit Card Debt Statistics," http://www.creditcards.com/credit-card-news/credit-card-debt-statistics-1276.php, accessed November 28, 2015.

SEVEN

Bankruptcy

One of the many good reasons to acquire financial literacy—the purpose of reading this book—is to help achieve your goals in life, many of which require careful attention to your money. A huge roadblock to achieving your life goals will be running into financial distress. Unresolved money problems can ruin every dream you have. Even with a good financial plan, some things may be out of your control and place a crushing burden on your financial condition—a serious illness or terrible accident that leaves you unable to work and facing large medical bills, for example. Whatever the reason causing financial distress, it's important to recognize your problem if it happens, and deal with it forthrightly. One of the tools for dealing with financial problems is the bankruptcy system.

WHY BANKRUPTCY?

The challenge of unpaid debts has been around for much of human history. The Bible teaches to forgive debts every seven years, but that didn't catch on everywhere in the ancient world. The early Greeks, for example, didn't allow debt forgiveness and enslaved the whole families of those with unpaid obligations. Things weren't much better in early England, where many U.S. legal and financial customs originate: you could be imprisoned or even executed for not paying your debts. Ultimately, punishment for unpaid debts gave way to rehabilitation, and by the end of the Great Depression the United States had created our modern bankruptcy system.

Bankruptcy is simply a legal process by which debts are eliminated or greatly reduced, so the honest debtor can make a fresh start. People in financial distress usually have much more debt than assets and insufficient income to change that very quickly. Through bankruptcy your debts are reduced or *discharged* (eliminated forever) in a way that leaves you with enough income and assets to maintain a reasonable living standard.

When a debt is cancelled through bankruptcy somebody loses money—the lender. You could say the Greeks had it right, that taking a tough stand on borrowed money keeps people honorable. Morality aside, bankruptcy is a practical response to a common financial problem. Dealing with financial distress in an orderly, low-cost way will collect as much money as possible to pay off debts and return the debtor to productivity. Creditors, who are often experienced businesses, can quantify the risks of bankruptcy and manage the cost of bad loans. The victims of financial distress are usually unsophisticated, low-income individuals who got in over their heads financially. So bankruptcy is an efficient process to reset an unbalanced situation.

TYPES OF BANKRUPTCY

The bankruptcy process is almost entirely governed by federal law and administered through the federal court system. It's in the U.S. Constitution: "The Congress shall have power . . . [to establish] uniform laws on the subject of Bankruptcies throughout the United States." People often refer to bankruptcy as "Chapter 11" because the bankruptcy laws are found in Title 11 of the federal code, and the section dealing with business bankruptcies in Chapter 11 of Title 11. Got that? For consumers, Chapter 7 governs a *liquidation,* where the debtor's assets are sold and the debts discharged quickly, and Chapter 13 controls a *debt adjustment,* where the debtor creates a payment plan and debts are paid off over several years.

Bankruptcies are for individuals, not families. Chapter 7 is the simplest form of bankruptcy, limited to people earning below the median income (middle of the range) in the state where they live. The median income in 2015 for a single person was a bit more than $40,000 in South Carolina, Georgia, Montana, and Tennessee; near $50,000 in California, New York, Minnesota, and Wyoming; around $60,000 in Connecticut, Maryland, New Jersey, and Alaska; and about $45,000 in most of the other states.[1] If your income exceeds the state median there are more complicated income tests that might allow you to use Chapter 7, but it won't be assured. You're also required to take an approved credit counseling course before filing for bankruptcy, and you can use Chapter 7 only once every eight years. If you're not eligible for Chapter 7 then you must use Chapter 13, or you won't be able to use bankruptcy at all.

A Chapter 13 bankruptcy has eligibility limitations based on the total debt amount, not income. You can use a Chapter 13 bankruptcy if your *unsecured* debts don't exceed $400,000 and your *secured* debts are less than $1.2 million (these limits are adjusted periodically). Most people considering bankruptcy should fall within these limits. You'll have to take a credit counseling course, and the limit on repeating a bankruptcy after going through Chapter 13 is only six years. In Chapter 13 the end result is a repayment plan that lasts three to five years, during which the debtor makes installments to repay a *portion* of the debts. How much the debtor has to pay off is determined by a complicated analysis of the debtor's income, the kind of debts, and the total amount owed. In Chapter 7 there's no repayment plan, and assets are simply sold to repay as much of the debt as possible.

If you qualify, a Chapter 7 liquidation is simpler, faster (all done in under six months), usually less costly, and allows you to keep all of your income once the bankruptcy process begins. However, there may be some advantages to Chapter 13: a broader class of debts can be discharged, you get to keep most of your assets, and your credit report will be affected for a shorter period of time following bankruptcy. Chapter 13 can be preferred particularly when the debtor owns a home and wants to keep it, and it may also be better if there are cosigners on some debts. In practice, many debtors don't really have a choice between the two forms of personal bankruptcy. The complexity of even a basic bankruptcy requires that a debtor hire an experienced bankruptcy attorney to assist with the process, in almost every case.

EXEMPT PROPERTY

You don't usually lose all of your assets through bankruptcy. Certain assets are *exempt* from the process, meaning they're protected from having to be sold in a liquidation, or they don't count in developing your repayment plan in a debt adjustment. If an asset is exempt, you'll get to keep it all the way through bankruptcy. Which assets are exempt depends on where you live, however, since each state has its own law on the specific assets, and how much of each asset, that can be exempted from bankruptcy. The federal bankruptcy law also has exemptions, and you get to choose whether to use those or the state exemptions, except in a few places where you *must* use the state exemptions. Exemptions in a debt adjustment bankruptcy (Chapter 13) work a little differently than in a liquidation bankruptcy (Chapter 7), but they're the same exemptions in the same amounts.

Home equity—the value of your home minus the loans outstanding—is called the *homestead exemption*. Some of your home equity can be retained through bankruptcy; the federal limit is about $23,000 (all the federal limits adjust every three years). You can keep $3,700 of value in your car, $2,300 in business tools and books, $1,600 in jewelry, all your life insurance, and over $12,000 in general household goods like clothing, furniture, and electronics.[2] There's even something called a "wildcard exemption" that can protect any asset you choose, up to $13,000. Importantly, all retirement accounts below $1.3 million are also exempt (although it's hard to imagine someone earning below the median income with such a large retirement account). State exemptions are usually different. For example, the homestead exemptions exceed $250,000 in Massachusetts, Minnesota, Montana, Nevada, and Rhode Island, and the states of Florida, Iowa, Kansas, Oklahoma, South Dakota, and Texas offer *unlimited* homestead exemptions.[3]

If you own a home, keeping it through a bankruptcy won't be easy. Often there's little home equity to protect under the homestead exemption, and residential home mortgages won't be reduced or discharged through bankruptcy. If you have equity in the home below the exemption, and you can make the mortgage payments, you'll probably be able to keep your house (under Chapter 13 you'll have to bring the mortgage loan entirely current during the plan period). Any equity above the exemption will have to be used to pay creditors. If the debtor can't make the mortgage payments or otherwise work out a deal, the lender will probably foreclose. In some states the borrower may be liable for any *deficiency* between the mortgage debt and the home's value, another push toward bankruptcy. A debtor should consider whether it's better to just walk away from the home, hard as that may be, given that bankruptcy is all about a fresh start.

DISCHARGE OF DEBTS

The bankruptcy process gives debtors *protection* from their creditors, at least for a while. The first thing that happens after filing for bankruptcy is that the debtor receives an *automatic stay*: all debt collection efforts must cease at once, and you can stop paying on your debts. A creditor listed on the bankruptcy filing will receive notice from the court and can't proceed with further activities against you while the case is ongoing, with just a few exceptions. This means no more calls from collection agencies, no more new lawsuits against you, the automatic stay can even stop a utility disconnect or home foreclosure (for a little while, at least). A creditor that intentionally violates the stay can be fined. The stay won't always keep someone from being evicted, but it gives the debtor some breathing room.

The benefit at the end of the bankruptcy process is a *discharge* of your debts. A discharge means that the debt, or a portion of it, will be considered null and void, and will never need to be paid. It's final, complete, and irreversible except in cases of fraud. In a liquidation case, all of the debts (with a few exceptions) will be discharged at the end of the process: none will remain. In a debt adjustment case, the portion that's reduced through the process will be discharged at the end of the three- to five-year period *if* the debtor successfully completes the payment plan. Whatever debt isn't required to be paid under the plan is discharged completely and forever. Because discharge is such a powerful benefit from bankruptcy, the law limits its use to once every 6 or 8 years, depending on which form of bankruptcy the debtor uses.

Here's an idea for a clever college student: borrow all the money you need for college, graduate, get a good job, then immediately declare bankruptcy and wipe out all your college loans. Sorry, the bankruptcy system is on to that. There was a major overhaul of the bankruptcy laws in 2005 to respond to complaints of abuse from the creditor community, so today certain types of debts can't be discharged. A lien or security interest in property pledged to pay a loan isn't extinguished in bankruptcy, which is why debts secured by collateral always get paid first. The creditor gets the money or the collateral, even in a bankruptcy. It's the unsecured creditors, those without collateral behind a debt, who take the biggest losses in a bankruptcy. But not every debt can be voided.

There are 19 categories of debts that by law can't be discharged through bankruptcy.[4] At the top of the list will be student loans, taxes, and government fines— do you see a pattern? (These are all usually owed to the government.) You can't discharge alimony or child support, nor can you get rid of debts arising from accidents you caused while intoxicated. Any debts resulting from the debtor's fraud, theft, or embezzlement, or a judgment in a lawsuit where you injured someone intentionally, won't be discharged. If you forget to list a debt on your bankruptcy filing, oops, that won't be discharged. A debt adjustment case offers slightly broader discharges than a liquidation, but in either case, some debts may have to be fully repaid in order to go away.

BANKRUPTCY PROCESS

A system of 90 federal court districts across the United States administers the bankruptcy process, each with its own clerks, judges, and staff (there's at least one federal court district in each state, and some states have several). The *bankruptcy trustee* is at the center of this process, typically a private-sector lawyer or accountant appointed by and working on behalf of the government, who takes charge of each bankruptcy case. The trustee sells the debtor's assets, distributes the proceeds to creditors, and generally oversees the case. The judge resolves any disputes, interprets legal issues, and puts the final stamp of approval on the resolution of the case. It's almost impossible for a debtor to complete and file the court papers properly without hiring an attorney. The trustee, even if she's a lawyer, works for the court system, not for any of the parties in a bankruptcy case.

Ironically, you can't be totally broke and go bankrupt: you'll need at least $1,000 to start a bankruptcy case and maybe even more. That's because you'll need to pay your lawyer's fees, court costs to file the bankruptcy papers, and costs for the mandatory pre-filing credit counseling. You start by taking a complete inventory of your financial life: all assets, debts, income, and expenses. It's important to be completely honest at the start because anything omitted might be considered a fraud on the court and cause the case to be dismissed. It will be a hassle to compile this information, which includes contact information for every creditor, but since the automatic stay only applies to creditors who get notice of the bankruptcy, it's important to be thorough.

After putting together all the financial information, there's not much for the Chapter 7 debtor to do. There's usually one brief meeting you have to attend where the trustee will ask you questions. Most bankruptcy cases are no-asset liquidations, where there's nothing for the trustee to sell because all the assets are within the exemptions. These cases get moved along very quickly. In a Chapter 13 case the debtor must come up with a payment plan that satisfies the creditors, subject to the rules governing how much of a debtor's income can be applied toward debts. There can be a good deal of negotiations here before the repayment plan gets confirmed by the judge. Once the repayment plan is confirmed, the debtor moves on to a new financial life, making routine payments to the trustee under the plan, who distributes that money to creditors. Although the discharge of debts doesn't technically occur until the end of the three- to five-year period, the stay on collection and enforcement actions remains in place the whole time.

Under either type of personal bankruptcy, the debtor doesn't determine who gets paid, the trustee does. The debtor will either lose all her assets in a liquidation (above the exemptions) or make a single payment to the trustee under a payment plan, and in both cases the trustee deals with paying off the debts. For creditors there's a pecking order of who gets paid first: priority claims (taxes and legal fees, for example), then secured claims (anything with a lien on it, up to the value of the property), then all the rest (unsecured claims) get paid *pro rata*. This order can be helpful to the debtor: a non-dischargeable tax debt, for example, gets paid first out of available assets, and that's good for the debtor after bankruptcy. Unfortunately, the debtor has no control over this.

AVOIDING BANKRUPTCY

Although bankruptcy can improve a debtor's financial condition and give a debtor a fresh start, it should be considered a last resort. Bankruptcy is emotionally painful, involves much work, is costly, and often attaches a stigma. It has a negative impact on your credit score and will raise the cost of obtaining future credit. You'll lose your assets or your future income. And you won't be able to do it again for at least six years, if you get into worse financial trouble later. Still, the alternative to a bankruptcy is continuing to live with unmanageable debts and the emotional trauma of financial distress. If the situation seems hopeless, is there any other route?

To generalize, financial distress results from one of two conditions: an ongoing and regular mismatch between income and spending, or an unusual event that hugely impacts your life. If you have an ongoing problem with money—living on the edge, from paycheck to paycheck—you have a double problem to resolve. First, you must change your habits: cut up those credit cards, cancel the cable service, no vacations for a while, no eating out; maybe get a second job, ask for a raise, look for a higher-paying job, see if you qualify for government benefits. All painful. Then, you have to deal with the problem, the overhang of debt those bad habits created. If it's just some bad luck that created the spiral—a large medical bill or being in-between jobs for a while—you only have the debt to deal with.

One approach is to negotiate with your creditors. If you have many creditors, large debts, and nothing left after your living expenses, this won't work. But if you have some extra money after paying for your basic needs, a creditor may prefer to work out a payment plan for a portion of the debt, rather than getting nothing in a bankruptcy. If there are many creditors this will be difficult, and you may need to use a professional debt consolidation agency. Hospitals and other medical providers often negotiate their bills down and establish payment plans for large debts. Debtors have less leverage with secured loans (car loans and home mortgages), but in most cases a creditor would rather have you paying on the loan than put you into bankruptcy, even if it takes a "haircut" on the balance.

Sometimes doing nothing is the best solution. If you don't have many assets, or all your assets are below the exemption amount, there's no point in a creditor coming after you. It may be annoying to hear from debt collectors, but federal and state laws limit how intrusive they can be. To collect on a debt a creditor has to sue you in court, obtain a judgment, find an asset you own, and go through a legal process to seize it. If you have a regular job, letting them sue you isn't the best idea, since your wages can be *garnished* to pay the judgment, where the employer receives a court order to take money out of your paycheck. But if you're a student with no income and a large debt, the creditor may decide you're not worth going after and just let it go. After a while a debt becomes unenforceable, and it dies a natural death—in most states it takes 3 to 6 years, but in some states debts can be collected for as long as 10 years.[5]

CREDIT COUNSELING

Within six months of filing for bankruptcy protection a debtor must take an approved credit counseling course. Each bankruptcy district maintains a list of approved agencies that offer this service, it doesn't take long to complete, and the cost is low. This course helps find options besides bankruptcy, but you're not obligated to follow any of the advice you receive. Without proof of completing credit counseling, the bankruptcy court must dismiss your case. Following your bankruptcy filing you must take an *additional* course on debtor education; without finishing that course the court won't discharge your debts, and that would be a big problem for you. There's another approved-provider list for this service, often the same firms that are the credit counselors, all of which must be nonprofit organizations and offer reduced fees or waivers where necessary.

Numerous credit counseling, debtor education, and debt management services will also help consumers with their money or to keep them from needing bankruptcy. The impulse to seek help from a professional expert is a good one; however, there are risks involved from choosing an agency that's more interested in making money than helping you fix your problems. Some firms even work on behalf of creditors. So here are a few tips in choosing an appropriate agency:

- Look for an accredited, nonprofit agency. Accreditation and membership organizations include the National Foundation for Credit Counseling, the U.S. Department of Housing and Urban Development, the Association of Independent Consumer Credit Counseling Agencies, and the Better Business Bureau. Just being on the bankruptcy court's approved list isn't enough.
- Look for a firm that provides free information, a clear description of fees in writing, and has a process for reducing or waiving fees if necessary. A good agency will have free educational downloads and course videos you might find helpful, before you sign up for anything.
- If you have any doubts about the legitimacy of the firm you're using, check with your local consumer protection agency (every state has one) or the attorney general's office, which maintains information about complaints and fraud.

With some agencies you may be asked to enter into a debt management plan (DMP). This is where the debtor makes a single payment to the agency, which distributes the money to creditors, similar to how the bankruptcy process works but doing so by agreement, without a court. The agency negotiates with your creditors to accept partial payment, and you pay the agency a setup charge and monthly fees to administer your payments. Credit counselors try to eliminate late fees and interest charges, allowing you to stretch out your payments and keep the debt from growing, whereas under a DMP you might get some of the debt eliminated. A DMP can be a legitimate option, but be on guard: there have been numerous complaints to regulators about DMPs that overpromised results and overcharged fees.

BUSINESS BANKRUPTCIES

The bankruptcy system covers business bankruptcies under Chapter 11, where a business will reorganize its affairs, typically reducing its debts and emerging from bankruptcy to continue its business. Special sections in the code deal with cities (Chapter 9 governed Detroit's 2013 bankruptcy, the largest municipal bankruptcy ever), farmers and fishermen (Chapter 12), and international bankruptcies (Chapter 15). Individuals operating a business can use Chapter 11, although that's rare, and businesses can use Chapter 7 to liquidate, just as an individual can.

A business reorganization under Chapter 11 starts with a bankruptcy court filing that lists the business's assets and liabilities, each creditor and the amount owed, business contracts, a detailed income and expense statement, and additional financial information. Chapter 11 reorganizations can apply to a corporation, partnership, or LLC; a sole proprietorship will use the personal bankruptcy system. Usually debtor businesses initiate the bankruptcy, but a small group of creditors can force a company into an *involuntary bankruptcy*. The bankruptcy filing triggers immediate relief: all debt collection activities against the business must stop, and the business can stop payments to creditors while the bankruptcy is pending. There are a few exceptions where a creditor, with permission of the court, can proceed against a company's assets once the bankruptcy case has started.

A company in Chapter 11 bankruptcy becomes a "debtor-in-possession" (DIP), with current management controlling the assets and operating the business under supervision of the bankruptcy trustee. It takes fraud or other extraordinary circumstances for a court to appoint a trustee to take direct charge of the company. While there's often anxiety and uncertainty among employees, customers, and suppliers of a company going through a Chapter 11 reorganization, almost everything operates normally during the bankruptcy while management develops its plan. The reorganization plan creates a new financial structure for the company, sometimes disposing of assets and making other changes to how the company will operate after the bankruptcy is over. After all, there was usually something wrong with the business operation itself in order to cause the bankruptcy.

Complex bankruptcies can take years for a reorganization plan to be approved, although most companies emerge from a reorganization in six to twelve months. During that time the company will need funds for its operations, called "DIP financing," since neither lenders nor vendors can be forced to keep doing business with a company in bankruptcy. Lenders who make DIP loans are at the top of the list when it comes time to get paid back, and they receive attractive interest rates. Vendors of a DIP are called *trade creditors* because the debts they're owed result from routine business transactions—selling goods and services. Trade credit also serves as financing for DIPs.

Unfortunately, trade creditors are usually *unsecured* and have no rights to specific assets of the bankrupt company. Banks and commercial lenders, on the other hand, are usually *secured* parties with liens on the company's assets, and they get paid first. Secured lenders usually get paid most or all of their money, and unsecured creditors get paid little or none of their debts. Many vendors choose to continue to do business with a DIP despite the fact that the old debts may never be repaid. There's nothing a typical supplier can do about the money it was owed, but going forward, having a customer is better than not.

If you work for a company that reorganizes under Chapter 11, you'll probably keep your job and get paid all your back wages and benefits. If you work for a business that supplies a company in Chapter 11, you'll probably keep doing business with them. But if you're an owner of a company in Chapter 11, you'll probably end up with nothing after the reorganization. Secured creditors get paid first, and only if they're paid in full do unsecured creditors get anything. In rare cases unsecured creditors get paid in full, otherwise they share pro rata what's left. If all the creditors are paid in full, then, and only then, do business owners receive any payments. That's why equity interests (ownership) are the riskiest, and offer the highest potential returns: you can lose it all in a meltdown. Creditors often become the new owners of a company emerging from bankruptcy, exchanging unpaid debts for equity in the reorganized company.

If a company can't operate during Chapter 11, doesn't develop an acceptable reorganization plan, or is unable to secure DIP financing, the bankruptcy will be converted into a Chapter 7 liquidation. If managers know that there's no hope to reorganize the business, then they'll start the process under Chapter 7. This is like a liquidation under individual bankruptcy, except there are no exempt assets, no concern about the debtor's living expenses, and no discharge of debts. The company ceases operations, and the trustee takes over with the sole objective of maximizing the proceeds from asset sales to distribute to the creditors. A liquidation doesn't always end the owners' problems, for example, if they personally guaranteed a debt of the company, but from the company's point of view, the Chapter 7 process closes the doors forever.

AFTER BANKRUPTCY

Returning to personal bankruptcy, there will be a point when it's all over—after the Chapter 7 discharge is approved, or after the Chapter 13 debt repayment plan has been completed. At that point the debtor returns to a "normal" financial life. What does this look like? No more collection agencies, garnished wages, or repo men for starters. You should be cautious with debt, which is probably what got you in trouble in the first place. Obtaining credit will be a little harder and more expensive, at least for the 8–10 years your credit report will show the bankruptcy, but it won't be impossible. Obtaining prepaid credit cards, retailer credit, or (if you kept a home mortgage through the bankruptcy) successfully paying down your mortgage will help rebuild your credit score. If you're employed when you seek bankruptcy protection, it's against the law for your employer to fire you because of it. There's a good chance your employer will find out, so honesty with your employer may be beneficial in the long run.

If you're looking for a new job, however, your bankruptcy can hurt you. While government employers aren't allowed to consider your bankruptcy in a hiring decision, private employers face no such restriction. Some employers may deem certain job functions, such as those dealing with money and banking, as too sensitive to entrust to someone with a history of money problems. Employers can require a credit check as part of the job application process and use negative credit information to reject you, so don't lie about your bankruptcy. The best approach is to be ready to explain how you got yourself out of trouble and why it won't happen again. Developing new habits of thrift and debt avoidance, rebuilding your financial track record, and being honest about the money problems you overcame will give you that fresh start in life the bankruptcy process offers.

NOTES

1. U.S. Department of Justice, U.S. Trustee Program, Means Testing, "Median Family Income Based on State/Territory and Family Size," cases filed on or after November 1, 2015.

2. Kathleen Michon, "Federal Bankruptcy Exemptions," http://www.thebankruptcysite .org/exemptions/ federal.html, accessed November 28, 2015.

3. "50 State Homestead Exemptions & Other Bankruptcy Exemptions," http://www .legalconsumer.com/ bankruptcy/laws, accessed November 28, 2015.

4. 11 U.S. Code 523 (2015).

5. Ken LaMance, "Statute of Limitations for Breach of Contract Actions," http://www .legalmatch.com/law-library/article/statute-of-limitations-for-breach-of-contract-actions .html, updated August 2, 2012.

EIGHT

Investments

Once you've saved some money, you need to protect it and make it grow. An *investment* is anything of value you intend to hold for a later time that will produce some financial benefit: you expect a *return* on your investment. A return can take two forms: an increase in the investment's value, and the distribution of money to the investment's owner, such as an interest payment. Simply keeping money in a safe place for future use with no expectation of a return, say coins in a piggy bank, isn't an investment; that's safekeeping. Neither is buying a television: its value will decline over time, and you'll be using it right after you buy it. Depositing money in a bank savings account, on the other hand, *is* an investment: you're holding it for future use and will earn a small return. In the world of investments, we usually talk about *financial assets*, which are claims on valuable property that arise from agreements between two or more parties. Most financial assets are readily valued and can be easily converted into cash.

It's important to distinguish the type of account in which you may own an investment from the investment itself. You need an account at a financial institution to own most financial assets, such as a bank account, brokerage account, or retirement account. The account is a contract between you and the financial institution. The firm executes transactions you authorize, holds your assets for safekeeping, and provides you regular information about your investments, for example through monthly statements or available online. These accounts can hold almost any type of asset: a savings account, certificate of deposit, individual stock, stock index mutual fund, Treasury bill, money market account, corporate bond, or gold coins. Sometimes the financial institution holding the asset is also responsible for creating and managing the asset itself—that's usually the case with banks. Accounts at brokerage firms, retirement accounts, or at other institutions will often hold investments sponsored by other companies (e.g., your Fidelity retirement plan holding a JPMorgan Chase CD). Think of an investment account as the bag holding all the assets inside of it. The bag is necessary, of course, but it's what's inside that really counts.

COMPOUNDING

Don't despair at the possibility of earning in the range of 0.5 percent per year on your investments for the rest of time. The interest rate on a six-month bank CD has averaged about 6 percent per year over the last 50 years (but since it lasts for half a year, you'd earn 3 percent on your money during that period).[1] The U.S. stock market returned about 10 percent annually during the previous century, and long-run estimates going forward are in the range of 7 percent annually.[2] Interest rates and investment returns will change over time, and you won't be locked into low rates forever, even if the current rates and returns seem unappealing.

Taking a long-term view on interest rates and investment returns is important because of the power of *compounding*, which is earning a return on previous earnings as well as a return on your initial money. The cumulative effect of compounding over many years can be very large. To illustrate this, it's helpful to use a simple type of investment as an example: a bank savings account.

When you borrow, lenders charge interest for you to use their money. Here, as an investor, you're the lender, and the bank needs to give you a return on your money in order for you to part with it. As a customer of a bank you may not feel like you're making them a loan, but you are. The money you're lending is the *principal*, and when the return is agreed upon up front, we call this the *interest rate*. The interest rate describes how much money the borrower will pay the lender annually, expressed in percentage points. Multiplying the interest rate by the principal gives you the interest amount earned in the first year. When you add the interest amount to the principal, you have a larger investment to earn interest in the second year.

Bank accounts pay interest; the returns from other investments can be described as *profits, earnings, capital gains, dividends, and appreciation*. These terms are just different ways to describe distributions of cash from the asset or increases in value of the investment. These other forms of return are indicated as annual percentage rates, as well, and they can also be compounded. However savings are invested, the return can be expressed as an annual percentage rate of return, just like an interest rate, and by using an annual percentage rate of return we can see the effect of compounding.

Example: A savings account with $1,000 principal paying an annual interest rate of 2 percent, with no money added to the account. If every year the bank sent you a check for the interest you earned, you'd receive $20 each year. At the end of 20 years, you'd have received $400 in total interest payments, and you could also collect the initial principal for a total of $1,400. If, on the other hand, you left the earnings in the bank account each year, the earnings would also generate interest (compound), and at the end of 20 years you'd have a total of $1,486. That's $86 more than if you collected the earnings every year. This greater return occurs because

Table 8.1   Impact of Compounding Returns on $1,000 Initial Investment

Total Return: Value of Investment with Simple Interest, Not Compounded

	2%	4%	6%	8%
10 years	$1,200	$1,400	$1,600	$1,800
20 years	$1,400	$1,800	$2,200	$2,600
30 years	$1,600	$2,200	$2,800	$3,400
40 years	$1,800	$2,600	$3,400	$4,200
50 years	$2,000	$3,000	$4,000	$5,000

Total Return: Value of Investment with Compounded Interest

	2%	4%	6%	8%
10 years	$1,219	$1,480	$1,791	$2,159
20 years	$1,486	$2,191	$3,207	$4,661
30 years	$1,811	$3,243	$5,743	$10,063
40 years	$2,208	$4,801	$10,286	$21,725
50 years	$2,536	$6,318	$18,420	$46,902

Source: Author's analysis.

the $400 in "simple" interest payments was kept in the account earning interest instead of being paid out.

You don't realize the gains from compounding unless you keep your money invested. At higher rates of return the effect of compounding is much greater. For example, with the same $1,000 invested for 20 years at an 8 percent annual return (something like what the stock market should generate over long periods of time), the compounded value is $2,061 more than without compounding. Table 8.1 illustrates the powerful effects of compounding returns: your initial $1,000 if left alone for 50 years at an 8 percent annual return would be worth almost $47,000.

The *Rule of 72* is a handy way to estimate the length of time it takes a compounding investment to double in value. You divide 72 by the fixed interest rate, and the result is roughly the number of years it takes for the investment to double. For example, at 4 percent interest an investment will double in about 18 years (72 divided by 4 is 18), and at 8 percent return (about what the stock market should do long term) it will take about 9 years to double (72 divided by 8 is 9). The Rule of 72 is surprisingly reliable, predicting doubling time within one-half year for interest rates above 3 percent.

UNDERSTANDING RISK

You've probably heard about someone making a "killing" from some sort of an investment. Indeed, some investments can produce spectacular profits, but what you don't hear as much about is the opposite—some investments lead to spectacular losses instead. Certain types of investments aren't likely to produce big returns.

A savings account, for example, is a safe investment but won't pay you much interest. Perhaps you see a relationship: safe investments have lower returns than risky investments. But what does it mean to be a risky investment?

Scholars and professional investors have developed many ways to measure risk. One measure of risk is the *volatility* of an investment, which measures how likely investment returns are to jump around and vary from high to low. Another way to measure risk is to think strictly about the downside: how likely are you to lose some or all of your investment principal? There's nothing wrong with the common understanding of risk when we think about investments—that you might lose your money, but there are also technical ways to define and measure that likelihood. There's a basic relationship between risk and return: the higher the risk, the higher the return, and the lower the risk, the lower the return. Importantly, these returns are what you can *expect* over a long period of time: the risk comes from the possibility of losing money at certain times during that period, and you also might *never* achieve the return you expect.

When we consider a loan, for example lending your money to a bank in the form of a savings account, we run the risk that the bank will go out of business and not be able to pay us back. That's called *credit risk*, and for a federally insured bank, that risk is zero (up to $250,000 covered by deposit insurance). Credit risk also arises in speculative investments, for example buying stock in a start-up pharmaceutical company, where you might lose your entire principal and never get any money back. Another form of risk comes not from losing value, but from difficulty in getting your money back. For instance, if you purchased vacant land for an investment project, it could take months or years to sell that land and get cash in return. This is called *liquidity risk*. There are also macroeconomic factors in the economy that can change, such as overall interest rates or investor psychology, influencing how investments as a whole will behave. This is called *market risk*. Regardless of the source of risk, they all result in volatility of returns and the possibility of loss.

Every person has a unique feeling about investment risk, which is called *risk tolerance*. Some people like taking chances and will be comfortable with a high level of risk in their investments. They need to be prepared for the possibility that exhilarating highs will be accompanied by unsettling lows in how their investments perform. Other people are risk-averse and will be uncomfortable taking many chances with their money. They'll prefer conservative investments and sleep very well at night, particularly during times of global turmoil that tend to cause most investment values to drop rapidly. They also need to be prepared for relatively modest returns. There's no free lunch here: the possibility of high returns means the possibility of high losses, and avoiding the risk of loss means avoiding the possibility of large gains.

THE STOCK MARKET

You can't follow a newsfeed, go to a website, receive a tweet, listen to the radio, or read a newspaper for very long without coming across a reference to the stock market. Sometimes the "stock market" is used as a guide for how the overall economy is doing (it's a *leading economic indicator*, predicting how the economy will perform in the future), and there are many different stock markets, not just one. There are also many ways to measure what happens in a stock market, which is a collection of different investments, not a single asset. Before we can understand a stock market, however, we need to understand what "stocks" are, and why there's a "market" for them.

You need money to start a corporation, and the organizers raise that money from their own savings, friends, family, and outside investors. In exchange for giving a corporation money, the corporation gives its investors *shares* of *stock*. These shares represent ownership interests in the corporation: all the shares together reflect complete ownership of the company, while a fraction of the shares reflects a portion of ownership of the whole company. Example: A corporation with $100,000 in capital from 100 investors who each contributed $1,000. Each investor would own 1 percent of the corporation, and be entitled to 1 percent of the profits and 1 percent of the proceeds from the sale of the company. These ownership interests are sometimes called *capital stock*, or simply "stocks." Alternatively, this same corporation could be formed by one person alone with a $100,000 investment, in which case she would own 100 percent of the capital stock and be entitled to all of the company's profits or sale proceeds.

A corporation can issue its shares in different *classes*, for example, *common stock* is the basic form of ownership, while *preferred stock* has superior rights to receive the company's profits. Corporations that raise their funds through networks of friends, family, and associates are called *privately held* corporations, meaning their shares aren't traded with the general public. Promoters utilize the *stock market* if they need to raise a lot of money to start or increase the size of a corporation. These markets facilitate the sale of stocks to the general public by requiring government registration, information disclosure, and adherence to strict procedures about how and to whom stocks may be sold.

When a company raises money using the stock market for the first time it's called an *initial public offering* (IPO). When a company subsequently raises money it's called a *secondary stock offering*. In both cases the money raised goes directly to the corporation to use for its business purposes. Once a company's stock is *listed* on a stock market, owners can sell their shares to other investors, and new investors can buy shares from existing investors, all through the stock market. Most people carry out stock market transactions—trading—using the services of an intermediary firm, called a *broker*, whose job is to facilitate the buying and selling of stocks, among other things.

There are many different stock markets throughout the world. Each market is organized as a *stock exchange* where buyers and sellers communicate prices, agree on transactions, and transfer funds. In the United States, the leading stock exchanges are the New York Stock Exchange (NYSE) and the National Association of Securities Dealers Automated Quotation system (NASDAQ). The leading foreign exchanges include those in London, Tokyo, and Hong Kong. Each exchange has its own rules about the types of corporations it will list. For every buyer there must be a seller, they must agree on the same price, and money must change hands. Electronic exchanges have proliferated in recent years, greatly increasing the number of transactions that take place. For example, the NYSE routinely trades more than one billion shares worth over $40 billion every business day.[3]

Many factors can influence the price of a company's stock. First and foremost is the company itself: is it profitable, is it growing, does it have a good management team, is its industry attractive, are its customers loyal? Highly trained professionals called *analysts* study public companies to assess their prospects, issuing reports and recommendations about whether to buy, hold, or sell a given company's stock. Market sentiment is another important factor influencing stock prices: is the economy growing, is the government running a deficit, is unemployment rising, are there inflation worries, is the banking system at risk? Finally, emotions and psychology can affect investor sentiment and influence the price of stocks, especially in the short term. *People* make investment decisions, and people can behave erratically, overreact, and even panic, all of which will be reflected in the prices of stocks.

MUTUAL FUNDS

You don't have to be rich to invest in the stock market, but you can't just walk into the office of the NYSE and buy some shares. You need an account at a *brokerage firm*, and there are many "discount brokers" whose account minimums and transaction fees are low. You can set up an account over the phone or by completing an online form with your personal and financial information, then transferring funds to the account at whatever the minimum level is for that broker (usually $500 to $1,000). Through a brokerage account you can buy almost every type of investment available. Many people experience excitement when buying and selling stocks and enjoy the process of researching and analyzing different companies. But beware: buying individual stocks is almost always a bad idea.

Scholars and analysts have studied stock markets for a long time and have discovered you can minimize your risk by *diversifying* the stocks you purchase. Instead of buying one or two stocks in companies you favor, you should buy ten or twenty stocks in companies that have different businesses and are likely to have variability in how each company performs under different economic conditions. Some companies do well in downturns, others do well in boom times, some businesses are volatile, others are generally stable: mixing different types of companies will diversify your *portfolio*, which is another name for the investments you own. Buying twenty stocks that are all retailers (Walmart, L Brands, Gap, Macy's, Kohl's, etc.) *won't* give you a diversified portfolio, but it will be better than holding just one retail stock.

Even if you buy twenty stocks that give you a well-diversified portfolio, you need to pay regular attention to what's happening at each company. Conditions can change in a hurry, and if you're holding twenty stocks in your portfolio, one or two of them might be headed for trouble at any moment. Managing twenty stocks can also be costly because of the transaction costs of buying and selling each one, and holding twenty small positions isn't efficient. Some analysts have demonstrated that a "buy and hold" strategy where you make investments for the long term, and hold them for many years, is superior to actively trading in and out of investments, incurring higher fees and exposing yourself to risks of market timing. But even if you're highly disciplined and stick to a buy and hold strategy, managing your own portfolio that's large enough to be diversified is a lot of bother.

The financial services industry has developed a solution to the problem of managing a diversified portfolio: the *mutual fund*. A mutual fund is a pool of stocks managed professionally by a firm that offers fractional interests in the fund to investors. An investor can buy shares in a mutual fund, allowing the management company to make investment decisions about the individual stocks owned by the fund. Most mutual funds can be purchased without any brokerage fee, but there are still costs. The fund itself must buy and sell the stocks in the fund, the professional investment managers must be paid for their services, and the firm that sells the mutual fund shares and manages the customer accounts also has expenses. These total costs are typically lower than holding a portfolio comprising actively traded individual stocks. In recent years, *exchange-traded funds* (ETFs) have become popular. These are simply the equivalent of mutual fund shares sold on stock exchanges instead of being sold directly by the mutual fund company, offering investors real-time pricing and greater transactional flexibility.

A portfolio or mutual fund is *actively managed* when it engages in routine trading based on timing, individual analysis of investments, or industry trends. There's a longstanding debate in the investment world about whether actively managed stock market investments produce better results than a passive investment strategy (described below). Some funds and managers have produced extraordinary results for a long period of time; many other actively managed funds have done poorly for a long period of time. The famed Peter Lynch produced average returns in his actively managed Magellan Fund of *nearly 30 percent per year* for a 23-year stretch ending in 1990, when he retired.[4] But were these amazing results skill or good fortune? The hard part is finding the Peter Lynch–type results *before* they happen. Instead, the passive investment strategy many investment experts recommend is the regular purchase of mutual funds or ETFs based on stock market indexes.

MARKET INDEX FUNDS

A *stock market index* is a measure of a collection of stocks, usually representing a large number of different companies, which reflects the broader stock market. For example, the S&P 500 is an index of 500 of the largest companies traded on U.S. stock exchanges, compiled by the Standard & Poor's company (S&P), a leading investment information firm. The actual numerical value of the index is less important than how that number changes over time: was the index up, down, or unchanged from an earlier period? An index shows the trend in the stock market. There are around 5,000 publicly traded stocks in the United States; the S&P 500 represents the largest 10 percent by number and covers around 80 percent of the total value on the U.S. exchanges.[5] As a result, this index is widely seen as a barometer for how the whole stock market is performing.

Another well-known index is the Dow Jones Industrial Average, an index of 30 of the leading companies traded on U.S. exchanges, sometimes referred to simply as "the Dow." The index, named after its early founders, contains few industrial companies today, reflecting the evolution of our economy away from manufacturing toward technology and service companies. The current operators of this index choose their 30 stocks very carefully, to represent the whole economy through the largest companies in multiple business sectors: Procter & Gamble (consumer products), Disney (entertainment), Pfizer (pharmaceuticals), McDonald's (food), Boeing (aerospace), IBM (computers), and JPMorgan Chase (banking) are members of this club. Although the Dow is less representative of the market as a whole due to its relatively small number of companies, it remains highly influential because of its historical importance and widespread use by news outlets.

Maintaining these indexes is hard work. prices must be collected from multiple exchanges in real time, companies must be added and subtracted as they go out of business, get acquired, or otherwise evolve, and various adjustments must be made to reflect the finer points of publicly traded shares (dividends, stock splits, etc.). Many investment firms and high-speed traders rely on stock indexes for their work, so they pay the operators of these indexes to get this information in real time; the rest of us hear about the indexes after the fact, such as "the S&P 500 closed up 22½ points today." Such reports aren't very helpful unless you know where the index started and can do fractions in your head, but some of the better-educated journalists do a better job for their audience by reporting the percentage change in these indexes.

Investment managers have created mutual funds that mirror these indexes, called stock market *index funds*. Since the S&P 500, for example, contains about 80 percent of all the stock market value in the United States, a mutual fund that contains the same stocks as the S&P 500 index will be representative of the entire stock market. You can also buy funds based on the Wilshire 5000 index that contain nearly all of the publicly-traded stocks in the United States, or indexes that track particular sectors of the economy. When you buy a share in an index fund, you're buying a piece of the stock market that's balanced the same way as the index itself.

Index funds are *passive:* investment managers aren't making subjective decisions about which stocks are good or bad based on intensive research and sophisticated analysis, but instead are simply following a mechanical process of keeping the stocks in the mutual fund balanced just like the index itself. This keeps administrative costs low, and many advisors think investing in broad-based index funds provides the best return at the lowest risk over the long term. There are about as many stock mutual funds available as there are individual stocks, but only a few market indexes that constitute the "whole market," so a buy-and-hold index-fund approach appeals to investors who wish to do other things with their time than study different stock market investments.

Making a fixed investment at the same time every month, or *continuous automatic investing,* is a disciplined way to build a portfolio. You could, for example, set up your bank account to buy $100 of a market index fund every month, without further action on your part. This fixed-dollar automatic approach creates *dollar-cost averaging,* where you buy fewer shares during market highs and more shares during market lows, taking advantage of market dips and avoiding the risks of trying to time the market. This also creates the discipline needed to save regularly, without reacting to emotions during the inevitable stock market swings. This program also implements a buy-and-hold strategy, since you won't be evaluating whether to exit a bad individual investment. You'll only sell a market index fund when you need to use the money.

BONDS

When a company needs capital it issues *securities,* which are contractual obligations between the company and the investor. Equity securities are shares of stock representing ownership, and holders of stock get paid from the profits of the company in the form of *dividends,* which are periodic payments of a portion of the profits. When a company wants to borrow money as debt, it can issue a security called a *bond,* and make periodic interest payments to the bondholders. Bonds are sometimes called *fixed-income* securities because their interest payments don't change. After bonds have been issued by a company they can be traded on the stock exchanges, even though they aren't stocks at all. Exchanges trade all forms of securities, not just stocks, but the "stock exchange" name has stuck. Like most investments, you buy a bond through a brokerage account.

Someone who buys shares of stock is an owner; someone who buys a company's bonds is a lender. A bond pays a fixed rate of interest, whereas a stock *may* pay a dividend, and if it does, that dividend can be changed at any time—or even suspended. Interest payments on bonds are rarely suspended. A bond has a fixed date on which it will be repaid (its *maturity* date), unlike a stock, which has perpetual life (a stock can be sold to another person and sometimes sold back to the issuing company). A bondholder has a superior claim on the assets of the company in a liquidation: if a company goes out of business, the stock owners are the last people to get paid, after the bondholders. Stock prices also tend to fluctuate much more than bond prices. As a result of these differences, bonds are considered safer than stocks.

While only businesses issue stock, governments and government agencies can also issue bonds. For example, U.S. government-backed agencies package thousands of home mortgages together into a pool and sell them to investors as bonds. Cities, states, and the U.S. government itself all issue bonds, and except for the tax treatment of the interest payments, they share essentially the same structure as bonds issued by businesses. When governments don't have enough revenue coming in from taxes, issuing bonds is a way to raise money to fund their activities.

Buying bonds issued by the federal government is considered the safest investment a person can make. The safer a bond is, the lower the rate of interest it will pay, so bonds of a start-up company will pay a higher rate of interest than bonds issued by a longstanding, mature company. Typically, the longer the length of time before a bond matures, the higher its interest rate.

Like all investments, of course, bonds carry risk. Although bonds are safer than stocks, they can sometimes *default* and not be repaid in full. This is less true of government bonds, but even bonds issued by governments don't always get repaid in full: holders of Detroit's bonds lost billions in the 2013 bankruptcy, and investors in other local government debt have suffered the same fate. Bonds also carry *interest rate risk*. The rate of interest a bond will pay is determined by the level of interest rates at the time the bond is issued. If interest rates rise after that, the value of the bond will fall. If interest rates fall after the bond is issued, the value of the bond will rise. Somebody selling a bond before it matures may suffer a loss or enjoy a gain, even though the interest payments on the bond will remain the same throughout its entire life.

TREASURY SECURITIES AND MONEY MARKET FUNDS

Sometimes people want investments to be very *liquid* (easily and quickly converted to cash) but don't want investment risk. The U.S. government issues securities called *Treasury notes* (T-Notes) and *Treasury bills* (T-Bills). T-Notes have maturities from 2 to 10 years and pay interest every six months. There's such a large market for them that they can be sold at any time and converted to cash, but their values can change as interest rates fluctuate—the shorter the maturity, the less price change in the T-Note when interest rates move. T-Bills have maturities between four weeks and one year and are sold at a discount to their maturity payoff (called *face value*), so all the interest is collected when the T-Bill matures. The return on discounted securities is called the *yield*, which is equivalent to an interest rate. For example, you'd pay $999.27 for a 6-month T-Bill priced to yield 0.145 percent per year, and collect $1,000 when it matures. The U.S. Treasury Department also sells 30-year bonds, but these bear substantial interest rate risk from their long maturities. The securities issued by the U.S. government are considered the safest investments in the world, so their interest rates are relatively low. You can buy these securities directly from the government or at most banks and brokerage firms with little or no transaction cost.

Money market funds are another type of short-term, liquid, safe investment. The term "money market" refers to large-dollar transactions between banks and big businesses, sometimes of just a few days' duration, where companies borrow money. Because these obligations are the debts of the largest companies in the world, these short-term investments are considered safe. Banks, mutual fund companies, and brokerage firms package these securities into money market funds to sell to investors as shares where the value is always $1 per share. There are even money market funds that hold only U.S. Treasury securities, for an even safer (and lower yielding) investment. Some money market funds offer check-writing to make accessing your money easy. In a low-interest rate environment, however, the interest rates on money market funds are close to zero.

DERIVATIVES

Financial and investment firms routinely hire mathematicians, physicists, and computer scientists with PhDs to develop complex strategies and profit by trading securities. It's fair to question the social value of these efforts; proponents would argue that trading helps make markets efficient and improves the functioning of the economy. Some of these strategies involve the buying and selling of securities called *derivatives*. A young person starting to save and make stock market investments has no business getting anywhere near derivatives; but you should have some idea what these investments are all about, if for no other reason than to avoid them.

A *derivative* is a financial contract that changes in value based on another financial asset or indicator—its value is derived from something else. For example, you can have a derivative on an interest rate, on a stock or bond, on a stock index, on a precious metal like gold or silver, or on a currency. In reality, a derivative investor is taking a bet that the underlying asset or indicator will rise or fall. Why not, then, just buy the underlying asset or indicator? Derivatives are usually highly *leveraged*, using borrowed money or the terms of the contract itself to increase the return on the investment. An underlying asset may move 2 percent, but the derivative on that same asset could move 20 percent. Many derivatives take just one side of a risk: if the underlying asset goes up, the derivative increases in value; but if the underlying asset falls, the derivative loses nothing.

A *call option* gives the buyer the right to purchase a company's stock at a certain price for a period of time (usually a few months). If the stock rises during that time period, the owner of the call option can purchase the stock at the stated option price (called the *strike price*) and immediately resell it at the higher price, thereby making money (in practice, you'd just sell the option, which would rise in price). You purchase a call option from a financial investor or speculator willing to take the risk of the transaction at a price determined by complex mathematics. If you choose not to exercise the call option (because the stock price didn't rise), you lose the money you paid for the option—but nothing more. A *put option* gives the buyer the right to *sell* the stock at the strike price if the stock price falls, in effect betting against the stock and allowing you to make money when the value declines. There's also an options market for stock indexes.

The call and put options are two relatively simple derivatives. Specialized exchanges trade many types of derivatives, the most prominent being the Chicago Mercantile Exchange, and major commercial and investment banks around the world trade custom derivatives privately. Derivatives are very sophisticated investments, their complexity sometimes outpacing the ability of their creators to understand and manage their risks. Several global financial crises have been triggered in whole or in part because of derivatives gone bad, and government regulators around the world have struggled to keep up with these ever-changing products of financial engineering. Unless you're a professional investor with decades of experience in the financial sector, stay far away from derivatives.

COMMODITIES AND CURRENCIES

In 1983, Paramount Pictures released *Trading Places*, a movie starring Eddie Murphy and Dan Aykroyd. It tells the story of an old-line commodity trading firm whose two owners play a cruel practical joke on a younger member of the firm, leading to tragicomic results. Although decades old, the story it tells about commodity trading is essentially unchanged today. The film's characters explain that customers want to buy commodities such as coffee, orange juice, and gold, and trading firms help them do that. But why? Suppose you're a buyer for Starbucks: by purchasing commodity contracts on coffee beans, you can guarantee the cost of coffee in the future and keep expenses stable. That means Starbucks won't have to raise prices to its customers, at least for a while.

Trading commodities isn't for the casual investor: commodity contracts are derivatives. Commodities trade through commercial exchanges or as private contracts between large financial institutions. Examples include oil and energy, agricultural products, and precious metals. In a common transaction the buyer purchases the commodity at a fixed price for future delivery, say in 6 months; these are *futures* contracts. If the price of the commodity goes up, the buyer is protected since the futures contract has already set the price of the commodity. If the price of the commodity falls, the buyer loses the cost of the contract but no more, and can buy the commodity at the lower market price. Some commodity investors are *hedging*: fixing the future cost of a commodity because the investor uses this material in its business. Other commodity investors are *speculating*: taking pure financial risk as a trader. Like other derivatives, commodity trading is highly leveraged, so a small amount of money controls a much larger position.

There are also large and well-developed trading markets for futures contracts on the major worldwide currencies, through electronic exchanges or directly with other financial institutions. Because so many financial transactions take place as part of global trade, currency trading allows market participants to control the risk they face from a change in a currency's value. For example, suppose General Electric (GE) just sold $2 billion worth of power turbines for a dam in India, but it will be paid in Indian rupees converted as of the delivery date. If the rupee falls in value even 2 percent between the time of delivery and the time of actual payment, GE will lose $40 million on this transaction. By using currency futures, GE can protect itself from the change in currency value and lock in its profit from the turbine sale. Investments in commodities and currency futures are derivatives, and are suitable for financial professionals only.

OTHER INVESTMENTS

Some people collect porcelain figures, model railroads, baseball cards, or watches; others enjoy collecting stamps, coins, art, rare automobiles, and jewelry. Are these investments? *Collectibles* share one thing in common with financial investments, which is the possibility of rising and falling in value. But collectibles don't generate income while you own the object. Instead, these objects give the owner pleasure, whereas financial investments typically lack the emotional connection. While there are many active buyers and sellers of collectibles, these markets are typically illiquid with great variability in pricing. It's better to think of collectibles as a hobby interest and not an investment activity; if you build a collection of value, so much the better.

Real estate can be an attractive investment, offering the potential to generate regular income and appreciate in value. Lenders readily make loans against real estate, making it easier to buy. You can invest in office buildings, warehouses, hotels, shopping centers, raw land, farms, and apartment buildings. If you had sufficient capital you could directly purchase real estate, but many real estate developers create limited partnerships or LLCs and sell shares in them to investors. You can also purchase stocks of companies in the business of real estate development or management. Real estate investments are better suited for experienced investors or people who take an active interest in managing the investment property, although owning a mutual fund with real estate companies in it would be a prudent way to invest in real estate.

A *hedge fund* refers to an investment pool that essentially has no limits on what it does. It can trade stocks and bonds or commodities. It can borrow money and speculate on currencies. It can take positions that rise in value when the markets fall (called going "short"). There are also investment pools called *private equity* funds, which gather capital, sometimes leverage the pool with borrowed money, then buy operating companies. They hold these companies for 3 to 10 years, improve their performance, then sell them and return the profits to the investors. Neither hedge funds nor private equity funds are appropriate for most investors.

A *variable annuity* is an investment best thought of as a mutual fund wrapped up inside an insurance policy. These products can offer protection against investment loss and favorable tax treatment, but they're expensive and complicated. Variable annuities are appropriate for sophisticated investors in certain cases, but should be avoided by most young people.

LOSSES

A lot of psychology is involved in making investment decisions. Like most decision making, investment decisions tend to be better when they're the product of careful deliberation of objectively considered facts, not the impulsive reaction to news of the moment. This is especially true of recognizing that an investment decision isn't working out, and taking steps to exit. This will be less of an issue if you regularly purchase stock index mutual funds and follow a buy-and-hold strategy:

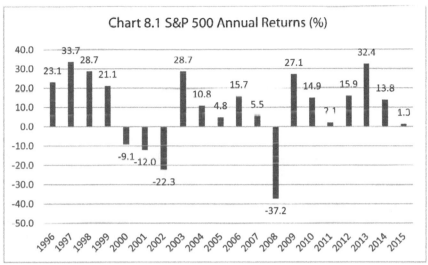

Chart 8.1 S&P 500 Annual Returns (%)

Source: Moneychimp.com, Author's analysis.

you won't have to weed out any "bad apples" in your portfolio. Even using this strategy, however, you must confront the inevitability of losses.

Investments rise *and* decline in value: that's their nature. Looking at Chart 8.1, you'd feel pretty good if you owned an S&P 500 index fund in 1997 or 2013, when returns exceeded 30 percent. But how would you feel in periods like 2000–2002, losing substantial money three years in a row, or after the collapse in 2008? If you carefully research an investment, determine it's a good fit for your goals and risk tolerance, and include it as part of a mix in your overall financial plan, chances are it will be a good investment even during troubled times. That doesn't mean your investment won't lose value for a period of time. Just have confidence in your investments for the long haul. Financial crises, bad economies, recessions, and market panics all come and go. But good investments will eventually rebound, and patient investors will be rewarded.

SAFETY OF FINANCIAL MARKETS

The Great Depression started with the collapse of the stock market in October 1929. Although many factors led to and prolonged that decade-long financial crisis, dramatic wealth losses from the market's collapse stunned investors and shook people's faith in our economy. The federal government created the Securities and Exchange Commission (SEC) in 1934 to enforce what became a series of federal laws to improve disclosures about investments, reduce market manipulation, and regulate the people and firms that promote stock market investments. These federal laws supplemented state laws that had been ineffective in curbing rampant speculation and price manipulation by unscrupulous operators. The SEC today remains a powerful regulator of financial markets, investment firms, brokers, and investment advisors so the general public can rely on the integrity of the stock market. An analogous organization, the Commodity Futures Trading Commission, performs regulatory oversight over the exchanges and firms trading futures in commodities, currencies, and other derivatives.

Two organizations protect investors from losses caused by the financial firms handling stock market investments. The Securities Investor Protection Corporation (SIPC) is a federally created nonprofit corporation that insures investor accounts in the same way the FDIC insures bank deposits. Importantly, the SIPC doesn't protect against market-fluctuation losses or fraud; it covers losses up to $500,000 per account from the insolvency of brokerage firms. The Financial Industry Regulatory Authority (FINRA) is a private corporation authorized by Congress to regulate its member organizations of securities brokers and dealers. FINRA disciplines and fines individual brokers and firms that violate its regulations, and is the first place an aggrieved investor will go after suffering financial losses because of malfeasance by an investment firm or individual advisor (such as excessive trading or commingling of funds). Most brokers require their customers to use FINRA to settle disputes, making this an important function of the organization. The SEC has oversight authority over FINRA, although it operates independently.

NOTES

1. Board of Governors of the Federal Reserve System, Economic Research & Data, Statistical Releases and Historical Data, "Selected Interest Rates (Daily)—H.15," December 19, 2013; Author's analysis.

2. Aswath Damodaran, "Annual Returns on Stock, T. Bonds, and T. Bills: 1928 - Current," data for S&P 500 geometric average 1928–2014, New York University, January 5, 2015; Rick Ferri, "30-Year Market Forecast for Investment Planning, 2014 Edition," U.S. large-cap stocks with 2% inflation, Forbes, January 9, 2014.

3. New York Stock Exchange, Transactions, Statistics and Data Library, "Daily NYSE Group Volume in NYSE Listed, 2015," January 1, 2015—October 30, 2015.

4. Eleanor Laise, "Can Anyone Steer This Ship," *Wall Street Journal,* April 23, 2011.

5. Dan Strumpf, "U.S. Public Companies Rise Again," *Wall Street Journal,* February 5, 2014; S&P Dow Jones Indices, "S&P 500 Fact Sheet," McGraw-Hill Financial, as of October 20, 2015.

NINE

Avoiding Financial Scams

Someone is always trying to separate you from your money. In most cases that's appropriate: you're given the choice to buy or sell something in a voluntary transaction. In exchange for your money, you receive a product or a service that you value more than the money (or else you wouldn't have bought it). The buyer and the seller are both happy. Unfortunately, some people don't play by the rules; they lie, cheat, or steal. When someone does this intentionally and systematically to take your money or other objects of value, that's a financial scam.

Financial scams can be hard to see. Some require gaining your confidence; others may be a form of extortion; often there's an element of deceit; there may even be outright theft. Criminals are constantly evolving their techniques to steal from you, and as technology advances, the fraud landscape will continuously change. There are no sure-fire ways to make sure you're never ripped off. However, being aware of some of the common forms of these scams may help you avoid them, and following some "best practices" in your financial life can further reduce the risk of losing money to fraud.

PYRAMID SCHEMES

A *pyramid scheme* is a fraud where investors are promised large returns, often from a clever investment nobody thought of before, but there's no legitimate investment taking place. Instead, new investors keep piling in money based on the reported success of previous investors, and this new money (the bottom of the pyramid) is used to provide large returns to early investors (the top of the pyramid, who are persuaded to keep investing their fictitious profits). These frauds are discovered after suspicion arises about the unusually large returns, someone investigates, and the scheme falls apart—hopefully before the operator disappears with any funds remaining.

In the early 1900s, Charles Ponzi worked for a bank and observed the owner paying twice the interest rate on deposits as the competition, resulting in huge inflows of deposits. The bank's loans couldn't earn enough to pay the promised interest, so ultimately the bank's owner absconded to another country with the bank's remaining money. Learning from this, Ponzi promised investors they could double their money in three months by exploiting the international postage stamp system. Like many pyramid schemes it sounded somewhat credible, but it was just too good to be true. In Ponzi's case he couldn't make much money on the postage stamp transactions, so he relied on dazzling promotions of his scheme to bring in huge amounts of money, some of which was paid out in big returns to early investors (most of whom reinvested). After suspicions arose Ponzi hired a publicity agent, but the agent discovered the fraud, leading to Ponzi's downfall and imprisonment. It was such a famous scam that forever after we've called these frauds *Ponzi schemes*.

Bernard Madoff ran a successful, legitimate back-office investment trading firm in New York for about thirty years. He also ran a separate business managing money for charities and wealthy investors which, it turned out, was fraudulent. Unlike Ponzi he didn't promote crazy-high returns but instead promised consistent returns just a little better than "the market." That was his selling point: year in and year out, in up markets and down, he would deliver good performance. Too good. Investors always got their money when requested, and Madoff used his past success and sterling reputation to gain new clients. Despite investigations over the years, the fraud went undetected until the financial meltdown in 2008, when new investments dried up and Madoff couldn't sustain the charade. The largest known fraud in history, there were at least $17 billion in losses with many investors (including major charities) completely wiped out.[1]

Pyramid schemes don't always target the rich: many of Ponzi's investors were poor. Two red flags should arouse suspicion: *unusually high returns* and *overly consistent results*. Other characteristics of pyramid schemes are difficulty in receiving payments, investment strategies that are secret or too complex to be explained, lack of transparency with financial information, anything that's "risk-free," and using unlicensed agents to sell the investments. In sum, if something sounds too good to be true, it is.

OTHER INVESTMENT FRAUDS

Promoters *tout* a publicly-traded stock to increase awareness of a small or thinly traded company. This is done through social media, newsletters, bulletin boards, websites, and blogs devoted to investments. Sometimes this touting is fraudulent, making false claims about exciting developments in the business that could make the stock double or triple overnight. An organized campaign to tout a stock's amazing but make-believe future can build interest in the stock and entice many people to buy in a short period of time. This drives the price up, at which point the promoters bail out and the stock price collapses, leading to losses for most investors. This method of fraud is called *pump and dump*.

Another sign of fraudulent investments is a link to an off shore business, a foreign investment opportunity especially in a developing or rapidly growing economy, or a "prime bank" overseas that only special investors have access to. It's possible for foreign investments to be legitimate, but they won't be promoted with urgency, by unlicensed brokers, or with promises of large returns. Legitimate foreign investments are sold through well-known companies, offer voluminous disclosures, don't make extravagant promises, and have well-established relationships in the United States.

Any newsletter, bulletin board, website, social media posting, or investment seminar that offers you a hot tip is suspect. Investment professionals do research to find undervalued companies and offer good investment advice ahead of the pack, but legitimate advisors won't create a sense of urgency, demand fees up front, require immediate payment, start a short countdown, or promise huge returns. The fanciful investments change with the times: green energy, oil and gas, social media, and China investments have all been the objects of popular investment frauds in the last decade. It's not always easy to sniff out a fraud; you have to be on your guard to avoid becoming a victim of investment fraud.

IDENTITY THEFT

Identity theft occurs when a criminal uses your personal data, such as your Social Security number, bank account, or credit card number, to commit fraud and profit at your expense. Identity theft (also called *identity fraud*) describes frauds that rely on using your personal information to steal your assets or incur liabilities in your name. The victim usually doesn't know about the fraud until well after it happens, and therefore isn't able to stop it beforehand. Identity frauds recently have used health insurance or tax collectors as the basis for the fraud. False communications using personal information threaten fines, demand repayment of phony debts, or insist on buying health insurance. Frightened victims then make payments to these scammers, often using prepaid debit cards.

A common form of identity fraud is stealing credit card account numbers from receipts, phone calls, compromised payment terminals, or hacked databases and making charges on the accounts. Fortunately, even though it's a hassle to cancel your credit card and get a new one, federal law limits cardholder liability to a maximum of $50, and it's zero if you report the fraud promptly after you discover it. More worrisome is a criminal accessing your bank account through your debit card PIN, account number, or online password, since that risks your entire account balance. Look for signs of tampering, especially at non-bank ATM terminals, which could indicate the installation of "skimmers" that steal your debit card information. In practice, banks usually absorb the cost of fraud but only after a great deal of pain and suffering on the part of the account holder.

The most important piece of information allowing identity fraud is your Social Security number (SSN). Your SSN is used in every form of credit application, and someone who has it can take out loans in your name. It's also used in your tax returns, and filing a fraudulent tax form to obtain a refund is a common form of identity theft. Schools, employers, hospitals, and health insurers use your SSN as a personal identifier, so routine communications may include it. Experts recommend you never carry your Social Security card with you, that you be very cautious before disclosing the number, and that you protect financial records and other documents that have your SSN printed on it.

After identity fraud has occurred, a victim has three separate issues to resolve. First, identity fraud and the financial losses that result are crimes under both federal and state law, so the people who carry out these acts are criminals and subject to prosecution. Law enforcement officials may want a victim's help in bringing the criminals to justice. Second, a victim must eliminate any debts and recover stolen assets; it can take a lot of work to unwind the illegitimate transactions. You're never liable for a debt you didn't incur, even if a creditor thinks it was you who borrowed the money, but creditors can take a lot of convincing. Finally, a victim must restore her credit rating from the three major agencies. The U.S. Department of Justice maintains a section on its website with step-by-step instructions for victims of identity fraud, which you can use if you ever have the need.

Avoiding identity theft requires vigilance and practices that keep your personal information safe. Here are a few ways to reduce the chance you'll become a victim:

- **Personal Information**. Never give out your personal information, including Social Security number, birth dates, or names of family members (which are used to authenticate identity), unless it's during a communication that you initiated with a party you're certain is legitimate. Don't respond to unsolicited requests for personal information in the mail, over the phone, or online. Never give out a password under any circumstances.

- **PIN Numbers**. Protect your PIN numbers by never writing them on a debit card or on paper in your wallet, and don't allow someone to observe you enter numbers at a machine. Keep all personal identifying information in a safe place at home. Low tech is best here: any computer file you have is hackable, so use pen and paper.

- **Snail Mail**. It's possible for someone to redirect your U.S. mail to another address, so if you stop receiving mail contact the post office at once. Don't let your mail sit around without being picked up, as personal information is at risk in mailed documents. If you'll be away for more than a few days, have the post office hold your mail.

- **Statements**. Review banking, credit card, insurance, investment, and other financial statements carefully and frequently, online or as soon as they arrive. Also check your transaction receipts. These reviews will be your first line of defense to spot any fraudulent transactions. If you don't remember a transaction, even for a small amount, make the call. Pay attention to your billing cycles; if anything is late, contact the appropriate company.

- **Garbage**. Get an inexpensive shredder and use it on any financial or personal papers before discarding them. Tearing up papers isn't enough. Cancel and cut up old credit or debit cards. Collect your transaction receipts and shred them after they're no longer needed. Assume that someone will go through your garbage looking for your financial information.
- **Credit Reports**. Get a free copy of your credit report each year and review it carefully. Inquire into any unusual information, such as credit applications, collection efforts, and unpaid balances. If you think you've been a victim of identity fraud, activate the "fraud alert" feature with one of the credit reporting agencies, automatically sending it to the other agencies to reduce the risk of further damage.

SAFE COMPUTERS

If someone else has access to your smartphone, tablet, laptop, or computer, your personal life and financial information can be exposed. Following best practices about information security on these devices can protect your financial well-being. The first step is to protect your data with a backup system for all your devices: just do it. Equipment sometimes fails, and malicious software can penetrate even the best defenses and destroy or corrupt your data. Another "just do-it" practice is to install a good security program to prevent computer viruses, spyware, and malware from gaining access to your devices. These programs can steal your valuable information as a first step in committing a bigger theft: login IDs, passwords, financial account information, anything on your device is at risk. There are numerous security programs commercially available that also provide continuous updates.

Wireless Internet networks are extremely convenient but notoriously risky. The wireless signal between your computer and the hotspot modem is a radio wave that can be intercepted with simple equipment by people up to no good. When you're connected by a network cable to other computers or the Internet, the connection doesn't use radio waves and can't be intercepted as easily. You should be wary when using wireless networks and seek networks that are password-protected. Even then, avoid transmitting financial information except on a wired network such as a fixed workstation at an office. Be careful as you move from hotspot to hotspot to log into the right network: avoid anything that looks suspicious or has a similar name to the Wi-Fi connection you're seeking. Virtual private networks (VPNs) provide an additional layer of security for e-mail and Internet through encryption of your communications.

Cell phones are also a source of risk, since they're essentially portable computers. Smartphones are susceptible to losing any information contained in e-mails, so experts suggest locking your phone and being wary of apps from an open-source environment (the iPhone has strict controls over its applications; Android apps, on the other hand, carry greater risk). Back up the content on your phone, since if you lose the phone, it's stolen, or is otherwise electronically compromised, your valuable information can lead to financial loss. Consider security apps for your smartphone. If you use your smartphone for mobile payments, you'll use your fingerprints for security, which offer greater potential security, but the technology is in its infancy.

Every device, website, online magazine, and account can require a password for access. Experts suggest you use complicated passwords, change them on a regular basis, and never write them down. That's great advice, but entirely impractical. A properly secure password will be at least twelve characters in length, mix alpha in upper and lower case, numeric, and symbols in a combination that has no word meaning, such as yT9q%hm71M$b. That will be a hard password for a criminal to decipher, but even harder for a user to remember.

A more practical, if less secure approach, is to choose a handful of passwords you can easily remember in a combination of words and numbers that won't be obvious to other people. Birthdates, street addresses, and phone numbers are all public information, but how many people know your locker number, height in inches, or your best time for running a mile? Coupled with a word that has meaning to you and nobody else (your favorite author, TV program, or foreign country) you can create an alpha-numeric combination that you can remember and others can't easily figure out. Changing passwords annually is a good practice. For sensitive communications like access to bank or financial accounts, consider a more complicated password that you write down in a safe place in case you forget. Software programs can store and manage your different passwords securely, but those programs aren't foolproof, and the jury is still out on their effectiveness.

Social media is the central communications framework for young people today, providing entertainment, companionship, and useful ideas. Social media also serves as a bulletin board for personal information that can be used to hurt you, including financially. Don't share personal information outside your trusted network, including birthdays, travel plans, your address, names of family members, and anything that uniquely identifies you. Thieves are clever and can use social media to commit frauds against you.

INTERNET SCAMS

Internet communications through websites, social media, and e-mail serve as tools to increase productivity, enhance friendships, solve problems, and make our lives more meaningful. Criminals use these same methods to obtain identifying data, such as passwords and banking information, or even direct payments of money, through unsolicited communications, called *phishing*. Sometimes these messages promise benefits by requesting personal data or something in return. These communications can also introduce malware, spyware, or viruses that destroy your data or steal it without you realizing it. One common form of spyware is called a keystroke logger, which captures every keystroke you make and sends it back to the criminal without you knowing it. Even the best password isn't secure if the criminal can watch you type it.

Here are tips to recognize phishing, avoid Internet scams, and keep malicious software from causing financial fraud:

- Never open an attachment to, or click on a link in, a message from a person you don't know; or if it comes from a name you recognize but doesn't have any message of explanation; or if it contains a brief, innocuous message such as "thought you might like this" or "document for you"; or if there's anything the least bit suspicious about it. If unsure, send the message back and ask the sender if she really sent it; better yet make a phone call.

- Nobody you know lost all their money in a foreign country and needs your emergency financial assistance. This will never, ever happen.

- Nobody from a foreign country wants to buy anything from you, requiring that you contact them with your financial information so they can arrange to do business with you.

- There's no shipment from Federal Express, DHL, UPS, the U.S. Post Office, or any other legitimate carrier, that was unable to be delivered and caused them to contact you with a link to claim your package. Shipping companies leave physical tags at your residence when they can't deliver, they don't send you an e-mail. If you read the messages carefully, you'll usually find something suspicious (wrong domain names, faulty logos, etc.).

- If you get a confirmation for any travel plans you didn't make—hotel, plane, train, bus—this is bogus and an effort to get you to click on something you'll regret.

- You didn't win the lottery, especially a foreign lottery. Never, ever will this happen. You'll never get a legitimate e-mail announcing your good luck. If you're a lottery winner, it's because you bought a ticket and are holding it in your hand.

- Nor are you the beneficiary of an estate, will you be receiving an inheritance from a wealthy person, or have you won a financial prize from a philanthropist that you didn't apply for. These things are all possible, they just won't be communicated through e-mail, Facebook, or Twitter. You'll get a certified letter from a lawyer—and then you should still be skeptical.

- Amazon, Walgreens, Walmart, and other retailers didn't send you a coupon to claim a cash award, give you money for completing a survey, or send you a gift card that needs activation. There are legitimate promotions from retailers out there, but what can give these and other fraudulent efforts away is the extraneous text at the bottom of the messages (to get through spam filters), the sender's not-quite-official domain name, and the large amount being promised.

- There's no money for you to claim in Nigeria, Zambia, the rest of Africa, or anywhere else in the world. As a rule of thumb, if any communication promises you some large payment, whether from a customs service, broker, foreign representative, or otherwise, but you have to send them something first—cash, money order, wire transfer, credit card number, or personal information—it's a scam.

- Nobody legitimate from any company will ever ask you to disclose your password, either in an electronic form, over the phone, or in response to a message. If you forgot your password, you'll reset it yourself through a series of electronic messages and links that you control.

BITCOINS

A new form of currency called *bitcoins* has been introduced to the world economy. Typically, money is issued by a government under the authority of law, but bitcoins aren't issued by any government. Bitcoins are a digital currency created by complex computer algorithms that, in theory, will limit their total circulation, creating scarcity and thus value. Owners of bitcoins possess an access key that gives them rights to the bitcoin's value. The access key is how you use a bitcoin in a transaction and realize its value, so if that's lost, so is the value of the bitcoin.

Bitcoins are accepted as currency for transactions by a limited number of merchants, and therefore can be considered a form of money. One important difference between bitcoins and traditional forms of money is that the value of bitcoins can vary dramatically. Normal currencies can change value as well, but much more slowly. Because of this volatility, many analysts deem bitcoins to be more like a commodity: a material that's bought and sold as a speculative investment.

Bitcoins themselves aren't usually fraudulent, although they can be used to perpetrate scams and have been associated with illegal drugs, weapons, and criminal activity because of their inability to trace. Even if used legitimately they're a risky investment, not simply a high-tech form of payment. Many bitcoin holders must convert them to other currencies for purchases because of the small number of vendors accepting them. Financial institutions have become interested in the technology behind bitcoins, which uses "blockchains" for record-keeping and might be adaptable to commercial transactions. As a currency, however, the credibility of bitcoins is still evolving. Most people should avoid bitcoins and other digital currencies until their stability and acceptance increase.

GET RICH IN REAL ESTATE

Numerous charismatic, articulate, and persuasive promoters have produced slick videos promising to turn you into a millionaire overnight, teach you how to make thousands of dollars working at home, or show you the path to easy money. Some of these videos promote real estate investment as the key to wealth and promise to share the secrets to success. You don't even need good credit or cash for down payments, they tell you. These videos show fancy cars, extravagant mansions, and beautiful people, featuring testimonials from regular folks who got rich by following the real estate investment secrets that you, too, can learn. It's all a lie. A number of these con artists have been fined by the government, sued by victims, and even gone to jail. But not all of them.

You'll be asked to pay for these secrets, in the form of seminar fees and purchase of DVDs, audio tapes, and books that describe how to get rich in real estate. Sometimes these purchases deceptively lead to recurring fees every month on your credit card or bank account, for ongoing "advice" from the promoters. The advice in these seminars and media isn't necessarily fraudulent on its face—which is why so many people are taken in   it's just never going to make you money. The typical get-rich-in-real-estate program is to find a property, convince the seller to sell it to you with no money down and to finance it for you (the seller issues you the loan), sell the property for a large profit, then repeat. A variant has you purchasing distressed properties out of bankruptcy or foreclosure for virtually nothing, with little money down and using the seller's financing or other creative borrowing. Works in theory, not so much in practice.

Real estate isn't the only realm of the infomercial-starring, seminar-hawking, book-peddling scam artists. They've created and hyped products and services that promise miraculous cures, immediate weight loss, free money, government giveaways, enhanced memory, greater brain power, and easy cash-generating businesses. Like with many scams, there's a little bit of truth behind each of these claims, but ultimately very little of value. The promoters make money selling victims "advice" in DVDs, books, or seminars, sometimes starting with a free seminar that leads to an expensive seminar where you learn the "real secrets" of the business opportunity. Or it can be in making bogus claims for health benefits of the books or products being sold. Any program that offers something for free, claims no risk, will reveal a secret system, promises to transform your life, or requires little effort for success, is invariably a scam.

MULTI-LEVEL MARKETING

Be cautious about any business opportunity using *multi-level marketing* (MLM), sometimes also called *network marketing*. Well-known companies such as Shaklee, Amway, Avon, Thirty-One Gifts, Mary Kay, Tupperware, and Primerica all use forms of MLM. This is a direct-selling distribution system where salespeople earn fees both for their own sales (for example, receiving a commission or markup) and for the sales of people they recruit into the sales force, creating a "downline" organization that can produce multiple levels of income. MLM often relies on the individual connections of the sales force to recruit or sell products to friends, family, and acquaintances, turning personal relationships into commercial ones. The potential exploitation of these relationships for financial gain has opened MLM to criticism. MLM agreements can also require the salesforce to actually purchase inventory from the company, increasing the financial risk to the salesforce if the goods can't be resold.

Numerous reputable businesses use MLM, providing legitimate goods and services. Unfortunately, some MLM firms make questionable claims about their products, lending an aura of inauthenticity to the entire enterprise. The MLM system can seem more like an investment scheme camouflaged as the marketing and selling of products and services, because people are driven to move up in the sales pyramid (by recruiting more downline sellers called *distributors*) rather than market the products and services to actual customers. Some MLM promoters misrepresent the business prospects or exaggerate the likelihood of large incomes, and emphasize becoming rich from the efforts of future recruits who create the pyramid levels. When a substantial portion of sales are made to other distributors in the network, it's a sign the business is unsustainable. Another red flag is having to purchase goods and own the inventory, as opposed to simply receiving a commission when a sale is made.

MLM firms have been subject to negative articles in the business press and have faced repeated scrutiny and legal action from government authorities. Despite the bad reputation MLM has developed, and perhaps because of social media, some newer businesses nonetheless choose to rely on MLM because the personal connections required for network marketing can build a large user community supporting the business. Using MLM is also a low-cost way for a startup to build excitement and sales quickly. MLMs offer flexible jobs that can provide supplemental income, but success ultimately depends on the efforts, talent, and determination of the worker. MLMs that sell products or services of questionable value, rely on salespeople to purchase inventory, or require aggressive recruitment of new distributors, should be treated with great caution.

DAY TRADING

Day trading is the short-term buying and selling of publicly traded securities, usually with sophisticated computer software. It's called *day trading* because it relies on fast execution of trades exploiting small price movements, with few positions held overnight, as distinguished from long-term "buy and hold" investing with only occasional trades. Since all you need is computer software and the Internet, day trading can take place from anywhere, including your home. From the suggestions made in advertisements, you'd think that day trading is an easy way to make a large income, perfect for the student or young adult. Some promoters emphasize how quickly you can get rich from day trading and that there's little risk. This is all a fantasy.

A typical financial scam involves fraud and theft, rather than excessive hype and unrealistic expectations, which is where day trading fits in. It's easy to set up a brokerage account to actively trade investments: it doesn't take much money, the brokerage firms aren't selective about their customers, and many firms provide the analytical and trading software for free. These firms may also lend you money, using the assets in your account as collateral, allowing you to make even more investments. This is called increasing your *leverage*. Some investments are naturally leveraged, allowing you to control assets worth much more than their indicated value. It's possible, in theory, to start with a small sum of money and turn it into a large sum of money quickly through stock market trading.

Unfortunately, making money on a sustained basis by day trading is extremely hard to do. On the other side of trades is usually a professional investor with years of experience and an understanding of market psychology: do you expect to get the better of her? Although trading costs per transaction are low, they can add up over time and take away from any potential profit; only the brokerage firm will be happy. The software shows you fancy charts looking backwards that seem impressive, but they explain the past and don't predict the future. Markets trend quickly up and down, requiring constant vigilance, and prices can react to news unpredictably. Markets reflect the decisions of human beings who are prone to frailties, emotions, and errors of judgment. You can lose all your money through day trading, and if you borrow through your trading account, you'll be on the hook for that money, too.

GAMBLING

Gambling is any game or contest where there's a financial payoff due to chance or randomness. That doesn't mean there's no skill in some of these games: card playing, casino dice games, horse racing, fantasy football, and sports betting all rely on expert knowledge of the game. Bingo, lotteries, and slot machines, on the other hand, are entirely random games of chance where knowledge adds nothing to your chance of success. Sports fantasy leagues have become increasingly popular and offer large payouts, using performance of individual athletes from professional teams assembled into "fantasy" teams created by the participant. Fantasy leagues have come under scrutiny by state and federal authorities for operating as unregulated gambling systems. Whether these leagues are legal or not, since you pay to play, and you win money when your fantasy team is successful, it's still gambling.

Gambling has been around in the United States since the early settlements, ebbing and flowing in social acceptance with various moral, political, and economic trends, but always under the watchful eye of government. At a few points in U.S. history most gambling was outlawed, perhaps reflecting the American ethic of hard work, perseverance, and honest conduct as the keys to success in life, but that just drove gambling underground. The need for tax revenue and the public's appetite for gaming gradually led to widespread, legalized gambling throughout the United States. Most states allow gaming by charities, run lotteries, and permit betting on horse and dog races, while many states also allow commercial and riverboat casinos. Native American tribes, using their quasi-sovereignty and favorable legal rulings in the 1970s and 1980s, have created extensive gaming operations on tribal lands throughout the country.

If you gamble regularly you'll win once in a while, but over time you'll surely lose. The states' lotteries, tribal casinos, sports fantasy leagues, church bingo parlors, and other gaming operators all make money by creating a *house advantage*. For every $100 wagered, for example, the house will keep $5 and pay out $95. Since it may take only a $1 wager for the bet, the winner will see her $1 turned into $95 and feel great, but the other 99 people will be out $1 each. If you play this game 100 times, you'll probably win $95 once and lose a dollar 99 times, paying $100 overall to win $95. Each game, even one requiring skill, has a different house advantage, but it comes right off the top, so long-term gamblers will always lose money. The house advantage is about 20 percent in horse racing, 10 percent in sports betting, 5 percent in blackjack and roulette, 15 percent for slot machines, and over 40 percent for state lotteries (because their profits go to fund government programs).[2]

Why do people gamble if, over the long term, they're sure to lose money? There's the joy of playing the games themselves with their rules and strategies, and watching sports, racing, or card games can be more exciting if you've made a bet on the outcome. Many people enjoy the thrill of a huge payoff, however rarely, more than they mind the pain of a small loss, even frequently. Even when there's skill involved, the payoffs reflect the expertise of the other players, so betting on a favorite gives you a low payoff: the house *always* makes its money. Unfortunately, gambling can become addictive and destroy your finances, and it's often associated with the seedier elements of life. Disciplined, limited, and infrequent gambling might bring pleasure to some folks. For most people, however, it's a bad bet.

OTHER SCAMS

Every time a financial fraud is exposed and people learn to avoid it, a new one arises. Technology improves our lives but also makes losing money from scams even easier. Elderly people, in particular, are susceptible to financial fraud: their mental faculties may have faded, they may be easily confused, they're often trusting, and many live on their savings and investments. You can help older family members and friends by reviewing important financial decisions to make sure they involve legitimate transactions.

Criminals sometimes target a religious or social community, called an *affinity group*, by pretending to be a member and then persuading leaders of the group to tout an investment scheme. People are naturally trusting, especially when a leader has endorsed the project of another member. These scams rely on the trust and relationships among group members, and once the fraud is discovered, a natural embarrassment and closing of ranks can inhibit law enforcement from exposing the scam and punishing the criminals. Affinity group frauds have included Ponzi schemes, penny stocks, bogus brokerage accounts, bank account schemes, and misappropriation of funds.

Prepaid debit and gift cards have been involved in many financial frauds because they're hard to trace. One scheme asked victims to make tax payments on a lottery prize they had supposedly won using prepaid money cards. Another scheme involves people claiming to be bail bondsmen, bill collectors, lenders, or government officials demanding payment through these cards. Debit cards aren't themselves fraudulent; they're just the payment method used to perpetrate the underlying scam. Some of the card companies are modifying their technology to reduce the risk of fraud, but because of their anonymity, the cards will remain popular with criminals. The requirement to use a prepaid debit or gift card for payment should be a red flag about the possibility of fraud.

Another scam involves placing a lien on your property. A *lien* is a legal claim recorded against a property's ownership records to notify prospective buyers about the claim. Liens are a common and legitimate way to protect the interests of lenders and are typically filed against land and vehicles to secure mortgages and car loans. A lien on your property makes it hard or impossible to sell until the debt is paid and the lien discharged. Scam artists file liens against homes or threaten to do so based on bogus debts. Although it's a crime to file a fraudulent lien, property owners must go through expensive legal process to clear the title to their property.

If you hire a photographer to take pictures at your wedding and don't like the photos, that's not fraud, that's a commercial dispute. But if the photographer disappears with your deposit, that's fraudulent. People you hire to perform services for you are called *contractors*, whether they're fixing your car, putting a hard drive in your computer, or painting your apartment. It's impossible to completely protect yourself from contractors who fail to perform or who do a bad job. However, you can reduce the chance of getting ripped off by following these suggestions:

- Avoid anyone who's pressuring you, using aggressive sales methods, or promoting a "today-only" discount.
- Avoid doing business with contractors going door-to-door.
- Make sure contractors have legitimate identification.
- Ask for references and check them out.
- Beware of a deal that sounds too good. Ideally, you should have several estimates for any big project, so it should be apparent what the "market price" is.
- Get agreements in writing, including a warranty for the job.
- Watch out for cash-only discounts greater than 5 percent. There's no recourse if you pay with cash, and contractors asking for cash may be illegally avoiding taxes.
- Don't pay until the project is complete, and then use a credit card if possible. If progress payments are made, always hold back some payment until after completion.

CONSUMER PROTECTION

There are two major federal agencies that protect the financial lives of consumers. The Federal Trade Commission (FTC) through its Bureau of Consumer Protection investigates allegations of deceptive or fraudulent practices, educates consumers about their rights under the many federal consumer-protection laws, and informs businesses about their obligations to consumers under these same rules. Businesses that cross the line can be sued by the FTC. The FTC enforces consumer protections for credit cards, debt collection, identity theft, data security, lending practices, credit reports, telemarketing, and product warranties. If you have a problem in any of these areas, the FTC may be a great resource for assistance.

Congress created the Consumer Financial Protection Bureau (CFPB) in 2010 to help consumers avoid problems from debt. The CFPB has issued rules governing mortgages, credit cards, student loans, automobile loans, payday lenders, and consumer leases. The CFPB also educates consumers to make better decisions about financial products and services. If you have a problem with a payday lender, an unresolved mortgage dispute, or trouble removing wrong information from a credit report, the CFPB can help. The CFPB maintains a database so you can check and see if a firm you're dealing with has a history of consumer complaints.

Most states have passed laws that prohibit deceptive trade practices, such as untrue or misleading advertisements, mischaracterizing the quality or condition of a product (treating a used product as new, for example), selling counterfeit brands, or even using high-pressure sales tactics. Some states have separate agencies to enforce these laws, but most states rely on their attorney general's office. Serious misconduct might result in prosecution, fines, and even jail time, and in some cases an aggrieved consumer can win treble damages and recover attorney's fees. These cases are hard to win, however, and in low-dollar disputes, many unhappy customers take their complaints directly to the seller, seek the aid of the Better Business Bureau, or use the power of social media to embarrass the seller into fixing the problem.

NOTES

1. Jordan Maglich, "Madoff Ponzi Scheme, Five Years Later," *Forbes*, December 9, 2013.

2. Robert Hanum, "Casino Mathematics," *UNLV Center for Gaming Research*, June 5, 2012.

TEN

Insurance

Perhaps you own a cell phone, computer, some clothing and furniture. If you're older, maybe you have a savings account or 401(k) retirement fund, a car or some jewelry. If any of these things were lost, stolen, or destroyed you'd be unhappy, to say the least. As you continue in your financial life, you'll accumulate more things of value. How can you protect yourself from distress in the event of a calamity?

Insurance is the trading or spreading of risk through an agreement: the insurer promises to make a payment to the insured party in the event something goes wrong. In ancient times, merchants used insurance to protect their goods on voyages if a ship was lost at sea. Today, insurance constitutes a significant part of the financial services industry. Modern commerce wouldn't be possible without it, and insurance allows individuals to protect their personal property. The number of risks that can be insured continues to grow: protection against lawsuits, against loss of income from disability, against catastrophic health care expenses, against loss of life. Insurance contracts have developed to serve a ceaselessly evolving economy where new risks arise around every corner, such as identity theft or computer data loss.

HOW INSURANCE WORKS

Insurance transfers the risk of loss. In exchange for paying a *premium* to an insurance company, you'll be paid if you suffer a loss. You're trading a small, certain loss (the premium) to avoid a much larger loss. When a large number of people pay insurance premiums, and only a few of them incur a loss, the insurance company generates enough money to pay all the claims, operate its business, and make a profit for its owners. This is called *pooling risk*. The people who pay the premiums sleep better at night knowing they're protected, and the unfortunate few who have a loss can at least recover money from the insurance company.

There's a lag time between when a premium is paid to an insurer and when a *claim* is paid to an insured party. This length varies depending on the type of insurance. In health insurance, for example, there's little time between the payment of premiums and the payment of claims. The insurance benefit here is more from the pooling of risks: in any large group, only a few people will have major claims from serious health conditions, but every year the total premiums and claims come close to balancing. In life insurance, risk pooling also applies, but there's a long period of time between collecting premiums and paying claims. The insurance company's skill at investing the collected premiums long-term to pay claims well into the future is an important part of its operations.

Every state regulates its insurance companies, which must establish operations separately in each state. The regulations make sure these companies have the financial ability to pay the claims of their customers, who have paid premiums to these companies for exactly this purpose. State laws may limit the types of investments these firms can make to reduce the risk of loss from speculative investments. State insurance boards also make sure consumers can understand the insurance they're being sold, that sales information isn't deceptive, and the people involved in selling and administering insurance products behave ethically. Many states also regulate the prices of some insurance.

Insurance creates a legal contract between an insurance company and its customers; in the industry these contracts are called "products." These contracts set out the specific risks covered by the insurance, any exclusions, and other conditions. State regulators make sure the contract terms are clear, reasonable, and consistent with any state laws that might apply. These terms are important because disputes can arise about whether a claim is covered.

Insurance companies sell their products directly through their own employees called *agents*, or by using independent *brokers* who represent many insurance companies at once. Consumers can rely on a broker to do the shopping for them and compare products from different insurance companies. Using an insurer's agents, consumers may have greater confidence in the company's products. In either case, insurance can be very complicated, requiring years of training to fully understand. Agents and brokers usually specialize in insurance for businesses, called "commercial," or insurance for individuals and families, called "personal," so they can build their knowledge about specific products for each type of customer.

PROPERTY INSURANCE

Insurance can protect many types of property, from family homes to business inventory, from coin collections to railroad cargo. An important distinction in property insurance is between *real property* and *personal property*. Real property refers to land and buildings, while personal property refers to just about everything else, such as household furniture, clothing, and electronics. Land has always been special; local governments publicly record its ownership and sale, something not done for other types of property. In our legal system a building becomes part of the land (it's pretty hard to move a structure after it's built), so both land and buildings are considered real property. However, land and buildings are valued separately, and typically the value of the land can't be insured against loss: if the house burns down, for example, the land will still have its value.

Homeowner's insurance is a widely available product used to insure the value of homes against damage or loss. These policies protect the home *and* its contents. If your parents own the home you live in and have a mortgage, they'll have this insurance since it's required by lenders. Homeowner's insurance is still a good idea even if the mortgage is paid off. Common risks these policies cover include damage from fire and storms, theft of contents, and structural failure such as a roof collapsing. People who live in flood zones must be careful because most homeowner's policies don't cover flood damage. A separate program administered and subsidized by the federal government insures flood damage in the United States.

Here's some good news for young people who live at home or at college: if somebody steals your bicycle or computer (even from a dorm room), homeowner's insurance on your parents' house will cover it. But then there's a little bad news for everybody: most policies have a *deductible*, which can be $250 or $500 that you absorb before the policy pays you the balance of a claim. Another feature of property insurance is whether the policy pays *replacement cost* or *actual cash value*. If you have a claim for a three-year-old laptop and the policy covers personal property at actual cash value, you may receive nothing on your claim after absorbing the deductible. If the policy pays at replacement cost, your claim will be paid at the current price of a new laptop. These policies have higher premiums, naturally.

Homeowner's insurance also provides *liability coverage* as well, to protect against legal claims for common risks facing homeowners. For example, if someone visits your home, slips on the stairs, and injures herself, you might be sued for the costs associated with that injury. Whether or not you as the homeowner did anything wrong, the insurance company will pay for the legal costs of defending that lawsuit and any monetary damages that may result. These policies often provide liability coverage for the children who live at the insured premises, even though young people are rarely the subject of lawsuits.

Commercial property insurance follows the same principles as personal insurance. Businesses that own their offices, warehouses, and factories will want to insure those properties against casualty losses from natural disasters, theft, and other risks. Many firms own valuable business property, from communications and computer networks to sophisticated machinery and analytical devices. These, too, are insured under commercial property insurance policies. Unlike personal insurance, however, liability insurance is typically not bundled with the property insurance, because business liability risks are much more complicated than those facing a homeowner and her family.

TITLE INSURANCE

Homeowner's insurance covers the value of buildings but not the value of the land on which those buildings sit. You don't really need to protect the land itself unless you're in a special situation: farmers use crop insurance to protect the things they grow, landscaping is usually covered under a homeowner's policy, and if a tree fell in your back yard and damaged the lawn, you'd have coverage for the costs of removing the debris and grading the yard. The land itself can't really be destroyed. There's one way you can definitely lose the value of your land, however: if you don't actually own it.

We say you have *title* to land when you own it. We demonstrate title with a legal document called a *deed*, which is registered with a local government agency called a *registrar* of deeds. If you want to know who owns a certain piece of land, you go to the courthouse (or government office building or online) and find out. You can trace the ownership of land back hundreds of years. When you sell your land you transfer title by signing over the deed to the new owner, who then registers the deed. The land description and the deed documents must be very precise so disputes about ownership can be avoided.

When disputes about land ownership can't be avoided, however, the value of the property is at risk. Perhaps the boundary of the land was based on an object that no longer exists, like a stone wall; or there were multiple parties who owned the land and a signature is missing on a previous deed; or a portion of the land was sold earlier but not properly recorded. Resolving these disputes can take years, involve costly lawyers and *surveyors* (people who identify property boundaries), and prevent a disputed property from being sold. Owners of real property use *title insurance* to protect against these risks. The title insurance company researches a property before a sale occurs and issues a policy protecting a new owner against any challenges to her ownership. These policies are mandatory if you buy your property using borrowed money, and it's wise to get title insurance even if there's no mortgage.

RENTER'S INSURANCE

Owning land or a house might be some years in the future for you. Renting your own house or apartment, on the other hand, is something you may be doing already. Since you don't own the dwelling you rent, you don't need to insure its value against a casualty loss, such as fire or storm damage. But what about all your possessions inside, such as furniture, electronics, clothing, and housewares? These are your property, and you bear the risk of loss should anything happen to them. Again, if you're a student and still maintain your permanent residence with your parents, a homeowner's policy on your family home will cover your property in a dorm room or student apartment. If not, your personal property is at risk.

Insurance companies offer *renter's insurance* to protect personal property from many different hazards at a dwelling you rent, such as theft or fire. These products also provide liability coverage and protection for your property while traveling.

Like all property insurance policies, there will be coverage limitations and exclusions, for example, highly valuable objects such as jewelry or musical instruments may need to be *scheduled* (listed separately with a premium surcharge) in order to be covered. These policies have maximum limits (for example, $50,000 in total coverage), deductibles against claims (for example, $250), and higher premiums to cover replacement cost instead of actual cash value. Many landlords require renter's insurance before you can move in. Even if they aren't required, these policies are usually affordable, so once you're living on your own it's a good idea to buy one.

CARS AND OTHER VEHICLES

The automobile has become central to our culture: for many people cars aren't just a mode of transportation—they create personal identity and signify individual freedom. There are more registered cars on the roads in the United States than adults—over 250 million. *Automobile insurance* covers the risks associated with owning and operating a motor vehicle. State laws require anyone owning or operating a car to have insurance covering that vehicle or risk criminal penalty. Even if you don't own or use a car right now, there's a good chance car ownership awaits you in the future, which means automobile insurance awaits you, as well.

One component of automobile insurance covers the value of the car; this is a form of personal property insurance. You might have a lot of value to protect, since the average cost of a new car in the United States is over $30,000, and a typical used car costs half of that amount. If your car is stolen, or you back up against a light pole and wreck the trunk, or your engine catches fire and the car is a total loss, the property component of your policy will compensate the owner for the repairs (or value, if it's a total loss).

A second component of an automobile insurance policy is its liability coverage. Liability arises when the operator of a car is responsible for damage to *another* person or vehicle. Imagine, for example, that a driver is texting while driving, loses her focus on the road, and hits another car, causing an accident where all the occupants are injured and both cars damaged. Regardless of whether the texting driver receives a citation from the police, accidents like this can result in a lawsuit, and the careless driver will be financially responsible for all the costs of the accident: damages to the other car and injuries to the occupants of both cars, even if they're friends of the driver. Insurance companies try to resolve these matters without a lawsuit, but liability coverage requires the insurance company, rather than the driver at fault, to pay for any damages and legal fees.

Every automobile insurance policy has a deductible amount before the insurance pays anything, and sets *coverage limits* that cap the maximum amount payable for a claim. A policy that covers replacement cost up to $50,000 will be costlier than a policy that pays for actual cash value (used car price) to a maximum of $20,000. If your car is worth $25,000 and you have a $20,000 limit, the insurance company won't pay you the full value of your car if it's stolen. A policy with a maximum of $250,000 in liability coverage will cost less than one with a limit of $1 million, but provide less coverage in the event of a claim. *Minimum coverage* laws exist to make sure drivers have insurance with enough liability coverage to pay for accidents. States impose this requirement to make sure there are no uninsured drivers on the road. It's against the law to drive without insurance, and you can be punished if you do so.

Children and young adults are covered through the policies their parents have for family-owned vehicles. These policies list each authorized driver, and premium costs for families with young drivers are high, because young drivers get into more accidents than experienced drivers. Driving history (past accidents and moving violations) will also affect the cost. Once you establish your own home (college residences don't count) or get married, you're no longer eligible to be listed on a family policy and must get your own insurance. Likewise, if you don't live in a home with a parent or guardian who has an automobile insurance policy, you'll have to get one on your own.

If you're ever in an automobile accident, first see if anyone needs medical attention. Call for an ambulance if necessary, and be careful about providing first aid if you're not trained. You'll want to exchange insurance and contact information with the other driver, and take pictures of all the cars and the scene of the accident. If there are any witnesses you should get their contact information, as well. When there are no injuries or little property damage, it's not necessary to call the police. It's unwise to make any comments about who caused the accident to another driver or occupants. You may be flustered or distraught at the time of an accident, so if police do arrive just give them the facts. They can cite you for what you say, even if they weren't there to see the accident. Report the accident to your insurance company as soon as you can.

Other moving vehicles—such as motorcycles, boats, snowmobiles, ATVs, and jet skis—can be insured. In some cases this insurance is required: minimum coverage laws in most states apply to motorcycles, for example. These types of vehicles are valuable, so there's certainly a risk of loss to an owner. They also create the same liability risks as cars; reading news reports about injuries to people on jet skis should be enough to discourage most people from riding one. If you have the money to purchase these types of toys, make sure you budget enough to pay for the insurance that goes along with them.

HEALTH INSURANCE

Health insurance pays the costs of medical care and is perhaps the most common form of insurance in the United States. A little more than half of all Americans have private health insurance from commercial insurers such as United Healthcare, Aetna, BlueCross, or Humana (Chapter 12 explains public health insurance through Medicare and Medicaid). The vast majority of these private insurance policies are obtained through employers, who negotiate with an insurance company to offer a *group policy* to their employees. The average employer pays about

70 percent of the premium, so it's a good deal for employees to purchase this insurance: the average premium cost for a family under an employer group plan is about $17,500 per year.[1] There's also no income tax payable by the employee on the premium paid by her employer, so this acts as a tax subsidy of private health insurance. In 2016, the Affordable Care Act (ACA) started imposing substantial fines on large employers (more than 50 employees) who don't offer high-quality and affordable health insurance to their workers, which should increase the number of employers providing these plans.

Those who don't obtain health insurance from their employers can obtain health insurance in the *individual market*. Historically, these policies actually cost a little less than employer group policies, but because the entire cost was paid by the individual, they were considered unaffordable—the entire $17,500 for a family plan, for example, would be paid by the individual buying the policy. The ACA has changed everything in the individual market for health insurance, leading to standardized policies purchased through state exchanges, providing federal subsidies through tax credits to lower the cost of insurance, and imposing new rules on insurers making it easier for sick people to get insurance. The ACA is still a work in progress, and its overall economic impact continues to be hotly debated.

The *premium* is the cost of the insurance paid to the insurance company for the policy itself. You pay a premium each month whether you use any health care services or not. A second component of health insurance is called the *deductible*, which is money you pay directly to your health care provider (for example, a doctor or a hospital) before the insurance policy makes any payments. If you have a deductible of $500, you'll pay the first $500 each year for all the health care costs you incur. After you've paid the first $500, the insurance company will make additional payments on your behalf, but you'll also have to pay a portion of each bill from a health care provider, called a *co-payment*. For example, if you've met your deductible for the year and have a 20 percent co-payment, you'll pay $60 for a $300 x-ray and your insurance will cover the $240 balance. Your deductible and co-payments are subject to an annual maximum out-of-pocket amount, after which your insurance will pay 100 percent of the costs.

Individuals can establish a *health savings account* (HSA) to pay for medical care such as insurance premiums and out-of-pocket expenses. You deposit money into an HSA as you would a savings account, then withdraw the money for health care expenses as you need it. These accounts offer tax advantages but also impose restrictions on the money you've deposited, so you must be careful to estimate your annual expenses accurately.

Besides processing claims and making payments for your medical services, health insurance provides an important price-setting function by negotiating with providers about the costs of their services. If you examine any bill from a health care provider, it will show two costs: the "list price" for the service (for someone without insurance), and the "actual price" the insurance company has negotiated— on your behalf—to pay for that service. The list prices are largely unrealistic and arbitrary, since the vast majority of all payments received by providers are set by insurance companies (including the Medicare and Medicaid systems). Still, the price-setting feature of the agreements between insurers and providers is of value to consumers. This is why most insurance plans only permit you to use health care providers that have accepted their pricing schedules.

Health insurance varies markedly from other forms of insurance because it operates both as a prepaid health care plan in addition to true insurance. Insurance covers the risk of a *large, unlikely* loss. Health care expenses are typically frequent and not that large (a flu shot, doctor's visit, or mammogram), meeting neither condition of a true insurance contract. We've become accustomed in the United States to relying on health insurance to pay for routine, low-cost health care services in addition to insuring catastrophic events, such as cancer treatment or organ transplants. This is our system, however, so get used to it.

Young adults and students usually receive their health insurance from their families. If one or both of your parents are employed, they'll probably obtain family health insurance through their work. If you're in a family that receives Medicaid, you'll have coverage through the state-run program. If you're in college, you'll have the choice of a student insurance plan from your school or to remain on your family plan. If you're 26 or under, you'll have the option of maintaining coverage under your family insurance plan. Living in another state than your family usually means higher deductibles and co-payments for coverage "out-of-network," but that's better than having no insurance at all.

Some people don't have health insurance, although for the majority of these people that's only temporary. People who lose their jobs have the right to remain on their employer's group plan after their employment ends, often referred to as COBRA rights (the acronym for the 1985 law that established this). Under COBRA, former employees must pay the entire premium (including the 70 percent of the premium that the average employer pays), sometimes making health insurance unaffordable. Young people often feel they don't need health insurance: they're healthy and spend little on health care. This is a mistake, since young people need health insurance for catastrophic illnesses or accidents that can happen to anyone, young people included. *High-deductible policies* can give young people this protection affordably, even if they don't have a job or their employer doesn't offer health insurance.

DISABILITY INSURANCE

Young people don't expect to die, and by and large they don't: every year, only about 7 people in 10,000 between 15 and 25 years old die (that's 0.07 percent).[2] Neither do young people expect to become disabled by a physical or mental condition so severe that they require assistance to function. Such disability might be loss of sight or hearing, inability to walk, or a cognitive impairment limiting understanding. A young person in that 15 to 25 age group has more than a 5 percent chance of suffering a severe disability, which means you're 8 times more likely to have a severe disability than to die.[3] If you're severely disabled, how will you work, earn money, or take care of yourself?

People with some disabilities can function very well. Most blind and deaf people live productive and fulfilling lives with little assistance. Other disabilities require a substantial level of costly assistance, a burden for someone without family and friends to provide support. Social service agencies at the local and state levels provide direct assistance to families with disabled children and to severely disabled adults, but these resources are limited at best. Fortunately, there are insurance products available to help with the costs of caring for the disabled.

There are three main forms of disability insurance in the United States: the federal Social Security system, state-level workers' compensation systems, and private disability insurance. The Social Security system (see Chapter 12) runs two programs providing financial benefits to people with disabilities. Each state runs insurance programs (usually through private insurance companies) to provide replacement income to workers injured on the job, called workers' compensation (also covered in Chapter 12). Finally, either individually or through an employer, people can obtain disability insurance from a commercial insurer such as UNUM or Prudential.

Disability insurance is expensive, and many people avoid buying it. It's costly because of the prevalence of disability in the United States: by age 60 about 1 person in 5 will claim a severe disability, making it difficult to earn a living.[4] With people working into their 70s and living into their 80s, succumbing to a disability when you're 50 or 60 can have severe financial consequences. When you're a young person, the odds will be in your favor for some years to come. Nevertheless, if your employer offers a disability policy as a benefit, consider taking it up. Should you be among the unfortunate few to become disabled, the government programs will help, but having your own disability insurance policy will further protect your income as you get older.

LIFE INSURANCE

As noted above, a young person's risk of dying is very low. Even when you reach your early 40s, your risk of dying each year is less than 0.2 percent.[5] Yet life insurance is one of the most widely sold forms of insurance in the United States. People have many reasons to buy life insurance. For example, in the early part of the twentieth century many people bought life insurance policies for their children because if the children died there'd be nobody to take care of the parents in old age. The insurance benefit paid out on a child's death would compensate for that financial loss. Some wealthy people use life insurance to reduce estate taxes when they die. The primary reason to buy life insurance today, however, is to replace the income of a person who dies, for the benefit of the people who depend on that income.

Life insurance works just like other forms of insurance. The owner of a policy makes a relatively small premium payment each year, and if the insured person dies, the insurance company makes a large payment (the policy amount) to the *beneficiaries* named in the policy. The policy owner, insured, and beneficiaries can all be different people. A typical example might be a husband (as owner) insuring the life of his wife (the insured) for the benefit of the couple's children (the beneficiaries). Life insurance policies often require that the insured person have a medical exam; the younger you are and the better your health, the lower the cost of the policy. The insurance company is pooling risks and investing the premiums for claims years down the road; older, sicker people have a higher risk of death so the premiums must be higher to compensate.

There are two basic forms of life insurance. *Term insurance* is a policy where the *face amount* is paid if the insured dies during the term of the policy, which can last just one year but usually runs between 10 and 20 years. Annual term policies increase in cost each year, whereas a *level-premium* term policy has a fixed premium for the entire term. At the end of the term the insurance expires, and the insured must seek another policy if she wants more insurance. As an example, a 30-year-old, non-smoking female can buy $500,000 of life insurance for a 10-year term for about $275 per year. When that term expires and the woman is 40 years old, the next 10-year term policy for $500,000 in coverage would cost about $360 per year. Still, that's a lot of coverage for a modest premium.

Permanent insurance (the most prevalent type is called *whole life*) combines an investment feature with term coverage and will last for a person's entire life. Part of your premium covers the risk of death in any given year, and the insurance company invests the rest of your premium on your behalf. These insurance policies offer you coverage until your eventual death, not just a 10- or 20-year term. These policies are more complicated, as they build *cash value* after a period of years (the policy can be exchanged for cash while you're alive) and have other investment-like features. The annual premiums are much higher than for comparable face-value term policies, and the premiums don't always stay level. Whole-life policies are best used by more sophisticated consumers with complex financial needs, and variants of permanent insurance such as universal life or variable life should usually be avoided. For most people, term policies are the way to go.

Another form of life insurance is called a *variable annuity*. These policies are really stock market investments wrapped inside an insurance policy, to take advantage of the preferential tax treatment for insurance policies. When someone receives the proceeds from a life insurance policy there are no income taxes payable by the beneficiary, and if properly designed there are no estate taxes payable by the owner or insured, either. This favorable tax treatment is true of all forms of life insurance. The insurance industry created variable annuities to exploit this tax advantage using stock market investments. Since these are complicated policies, use risky investments, and carry high fees, they're inappropriate for most investors and certainly unnecessary for anyone seeking pure life insurance protection.

Most young people don't need any life insurance at all. Again, life insurance is needed to replace the lost income of someone who dies, in order to benefit people who depend on that income. If you're a single young person, there's nobody but yourself depending on your income. Even if you're married, your spouse probably has her own income and would be fine financially should you meet an untimely death. Once you have children, however, the entire picture changes: these young souls depend on their parents for everything, and the loss of one parent would create serious financial hardship for the surviving family members. It's at this point in your life that a term life insurance policy will become an important, even necessary purchase.

LIABILITY INSURANCE

Liability is what happens when you're successfully sued by someone else for something you did wrong, and you're required to pay money as damages to the person who sued you. Commercial enterprises face frequent liability risks from the products and services they offer in consumer and business transactions. Individuals, however, also need to consider liability risks. It's easy to become the subject of a lawsuit in the United States, even if you did nothing wrong. Regardless of fault, you'll be burdened with the expenses of hiring lawyers, investigations, use of experts, and other litigation costs. If you're found responsible, you'll have to pay money for damages as well. Liability insurance covers the costs of defending a lawsuit and potential damages that may result.

Fortunately, the primary forms of property insurance such as homeowner's, renter's, and automobile insurance policies all carry liability insurance to cover people against certain types of legal risks, primarily the risk of accidents. If someone injures another person in an accident, the person causing the accident may be legally responsible for financial damages to those who were injured. Because these policies aren't primarily for liability protection, however, they're ill-suited to provide broader protection against other forms of liability risk or to cover situations where the possible financial damages may be great (such as injuring a child).

Some people seek supplemental liability protection through an *umbrella policy*, the common name for excess liability insurance. These policies offer higher limits than typical property insurance (more financial protection) and cover risks that are excluded from other policies (broader liability protection). For example, homeowner's insurance often excludes coverage for libel and slander (injuring someone's reputation by making false statements in print or in word), whereas these risks will be covered by an umbrella policy. Most young people have no need for an umbrella policy.

SOCIAL MEDIA RISKS

A number of highly publicized cases of bullying, causing embarrassment, and shaming have involved social media or other electronic communications. Sometimes it's hard to tell you're doing something hurtful: sharing a little gossip, passing along the latest rumor, or posting a photograph of friends are common activities on social media. What if that gossip was malicious and caused someone deep pain? What if the rumor was absolutely false and ended up going viral? What if the photo embarrassed someone into losing her job? It certainly takes the fun out of social media to worry about these risks, but worry you must, because liability insurance won't cover you for intentional acts such as bullying on social media. Publishing false information about someone can get you sued, and posting on social media is an act of publishing. Bullying or shaming (for example, posting nude photos of an ex) can be considered wrongful harassment and can get you in trouble. As intentional acts, harassment and posting malicious content are excluded from liability coverage by most insurance policies, and therefore pose substantial financial risk to anyone who does this.

INSURANCE FOR OTHER RISKS

The insurance business may seem boring to outsiders, but it's an innovative and constantly evolving industry. You can buy insurance to cover the costs of completing the production of a movie, if the stars should walk off the set. If you're a professional athlete, you can insure against the risk of a career-ending injury. A well-known insurance broker, Lloyds of London, specializes in insuring unusual risks. Over the years, they've written policies that insured a restaurant critic's taste buds, the risk of laryngitis for rock stars, and the world's longest cigar (12 feet).

One new risk is that of identity theft, a crime where a person uses your personal data to commit fraud and profit at your expense. Victims have had funds taken out of their bank accounts or large debts run up under their names. A victim suffers not only out-of-pocket financial losses, but additional costs trying to restore her reputation with creditors. While insurance is available for identity theft, these policies generally cover only the "repair" costs from identity theft, and some experts recommend a credit monitoring service instead, that will alert you to any suspicious activity involving your accounts.

Another modern risk is data security and loss on your computers. These concerns are of major importance to businesses, especially those utilizing electronic commerce, but they affect everybody. Imagine if everything on your computer was wiped out, stolen, or destroyed. Replacing the computer itself would have a cost, maybe $1,000 or so, but the lost pictures, music, and documents would be almost impossible, and expensive, to replace. Rather than using insurance for these risks, the best defense is a data backup system. Cloud-based backups are available for under $50 per year, or you can use a separate storage drive to perform automated backups. If you don't back up your data, you're taking a huge risk that's easily avoidable.

NOTES

1. Kaiser Family Foundation, "Employer Health Benefits 2015 Annual Survey," September 2015.

2. U.S. Centers for Disease Control and Prevention, National Vital Statistics Report, "Deaths: Leading Causes for 2010," Table 1, all races, both sexes, December 20, 2013.

3. U.S Census Bureau, "Americans with Disabilities: 2010," Figure 2, July 2012.

4. Ibid.

5. U.S. Social Security Administration, Actuarial Life Table, "Period Life Table, 2011," average male and female death probabilities ages 40–43.

ELEVEN

Taxes

Taxes are the price we pay for government and the services it provides. It sounds simple, but taxes aren't always transparent, nor is it obvious what we get for them. Taxes have been around since ancient times, and resistance to paying them has been around just as long. People gripe a lot about taxes, usually complaining that taxes are too high, too numerous, too complicated, or that *somebody else* isn't paying enough of them. Nobody, it seems, is very happy about paying taxes. Still, without taxes it would be difficult for us to function as a society.

Many taxes are explicit. If you're a land owner in most parts of the United States, once or twice a year you'll get a local property tax bill. It's pretty clear from the bill how much you have to pay, and that you're the one who has to pay it. Other taxes aren't as obvious. Walmart, for example, pays about $8 billion in corporate income taxes on its pretax income of $25 billion every year to all levels of government.[1] Since Walmart writes the checks for these taxes, it sure looks as though they're paying them. However, some of the income tax that Walmart pays is embedded in the price of the products it sells, so it isn't just Walmart that pays corporate income tax—its customers also pay them. Perhaps this is why Albert Einstein reportedly said that there's nothing harder to understand than the income tax.

HOW TAXES WORK

A *tax* is a mandatory payment required by and paid to a governmental authority. A tax isn't a voluntary exchange between a taxpayer and the government, it's a duty imposed upon the taxpayer. A tax arises through the operation of law and is something that wouldn't be paid in the absence of such a law. In our society laws are passed by governments composed of representatives that we, as the governed, freely choose through elections. Governments—and only governments—have the authority to create, impose, and collect taxes, so it's impossible to separate taxes from laws and government.

There are three basic triggers for paying taxes. The first trigger is an *asset*: owning something of value can impose an obligation to pay a tax. For example, in some places you pay an annual tax based on the value of your automobile, in most places the owner of real estate must pay an annual tax based on its value, and when you die you may pay a tax based on the total value of everything you own. A second trigger for a tax is *income*: the act of earning money can impose an obligation to pay an income tax to local, state, and federal governments. A third trigger for a tax is a *transaction*: purchasing an item in a retail store, for example, usually requires the payment of sales tax. We now even have a tax for *failing* to make a transaction: if you don't have or purchase health insurance, you're subject to a federal tax under the Affordable Care Act.

Each tax requires elaborate rules, procedures, and collection mechanisms to make sure that all the taxes due are paid on a timely basis by the party owing them. Every level of government in the United States has created tax authorities employing trained staff to carry out their missions. Taxes are involuntary payments, so authorities spend a lot of their resources on compliance to make sure people pay what they owe. It's illegal not to pay a tax that's due, resulting in fines and criminal penalties.

Some people distinguish a tax from a user fee, which is a payment made to government for the use of a government service. The gasoline tax is an example: state and federal taxes on the sale of gasoline and diesel fuel go to highway departments across the country to build and maintain roads, bridges, and tunnels. The people who use the roads are in effect paying for them through the fuel taxes. These are still taxes, because they're mandatory payments made to a governmental authority. The fact that there's a large overlap between the people who pay the taxes and the people who benefit from them is a feature of how the tax revenues are spent, not the tax itself.

WHAT TAXES SUPPORT

Taxes pay for services the government provides directly, like operating a local fire department, or by paying a portion of the cost of that service, called a *subsidy*. If you live in public housing, use Section 8 vouchers, or rent an apartment built with tax credits, you're using government services provided by taxes. If you use food stamps to buy groceries, that's another government service funded by taxes. Governments at all levels use tax revenues to support these kinds of housing and food programs.

A lot of tax dollars pay for health care. Virtually all health care services in this country receive a government subsidy, whether that care is provided directly by government (such as VA hospitals, local health clinics, or county-run hospitals) or through private insurance indirectly supported by the tax system. The two public insurance programs—Medicaid and Medicare—both use tax dollars to fund or subsidize their insurance premiums. Government also provides research grants to universities and other organizations to pay scientists to investigate diseases, develop treatments, and improve public health.

Another large recipient of tax dollars is the education system. Government pays for compulsory education through eighth grade and funds free schools through high school graduation. Many localities provide for free kindergarten, and some communities fund early childhood education before entry into the public schools. Taxes also pay for our libraries. School districts use different forms of taxation to pay the costs of K-12 schools, usually relying on a combination of local property taxes, state and local income taxes, and federal grants (which themselves are largely funded by federal income taxes). State governments also use tax dollars to support colleges, reducing the tuition costs that students would otherwise have to pay. The federal government provides grants to universities (not just for health care) and also supports student loan programs using tax dollars.

Governments throughout history have funded infrastructure, from building roads and canals to harbors and tunnels, then airports and communications networks (the Internet was created so government researchers could exchange data files). A lot of infrastructure spending takes place through the private sector, of course: communications networks are now almost entirely private, most railroads and utility companies are privately owned, and even some highways are privately funded. Still, governments at all levels remain active in paying for infrastructure. These publicly funded projects include Internet access for underserved areas, rural electrification, public transportation systems, port facilities, and roadways.

Perhaps the first order of government, above all else, is to provide for the common security and defense of its citizens. The federal government spends our tax dollars on the army, navy, air force, and coast guard to protect our borders, defend our overseas interests, and support our allies. The state governments fund the National Guard and state police, and local governments pay for municipal police, county sheriffs, and fire departments. All levels of government also run court systems and pay for prisons.

Governments spend our tax dollars on myriad other activities. Taxes fund economic development projects; protect our environment; provide disaster relief to the afflicted; aid our farmers; and operate our parks and recreation programs. Taxes also fund the operations of government itself. When governments borrow money they must also use taxes to pay interest on the debt and pay off the principal. Vigorous political debates arise over the extent of the services that government should provide, because everything that government pays for must ultimately be funded by taxes.

SALES TAXES

In almost every location in the United States, if you make a retail purchase of any product you'll pay a *sales tax*. If you buy a pack of chewing gum at the 7-11 priced at $0.89, you'll pay another 7 or 8 percent as sales tax. This tax arises as a result of the transaction: if you don't make a purchase, you don't pay the tax. The sales tax is calculated separately and added to the purchase price. It's up to the retailer to *remit* the sales tax to the government, and technically it's the retailer who's legally liable to pay the tax. However, the consumer ultimately pays this tax since it's added to the purchase price at the point of sale.

Sales taxes vary by location, and there can be multiple levels of sales taxes on a single retail purchase. The state, county, and city can each levy a sales tax, and it's possible that another taxing authority such as a school district, transportation authority, or other special taxing entity will add another tax. The consumer sees just one combined tax rate, and it's the retailer who divides it up to the various authorities. A few states have no sales taxes at all: Montana, New Hampshire, and Oregon (don't worry, they have other taxes). Most of the combined local sales taxes are in the 5 to 10 percent range.[2]

Not every product is subject to a sales tax, as many states offer *exemptions* for food and medicine, as examples. Most states don't tax prescription drugs, and some states also exempt non-prescription drugs. Most states also exempt food items or reduce the applicable sales tax rate. The state has to determine what's food and what's not (Gatorade and popsicles give states some trouble). Other products are exempted from sales taxes at the behest of interest groups or because lawmakers think that's in the public interest.

Internet commerce has caused tax authorities great consternation. Until 2015, a federal law prohibited new state taxes on Internet transactions, but sales were always subject to state sales taxes if the retailer had a physical presence in that state, such as a warehouse or sales office. Many online retailers are now collecting sales taxes and remitting them to the states. Even where there's no retailer presence, consumers are required by state law to pay a *use tax* on any out-of-state purchases that avoided a sales tax. Since retailers don't collect the use tax, consumers are supposed to report it on their tax returns. Most consumers ignore their duty to pay use taxes, and states tend to enforce this only for big-ticket purchases.

Historically, sales taxes applied to the sale of products and not to the sale of services. The purchase of a haircut, lawn care, going to a doctor, or having your car washed have all been exempt from sales taxes. In the last decade, as states and localities have struggled with their finances, tax authorities have attempted to apply sales taxes to some services. This has largely been a failure. A few states now tax some services, but the vast majority of services remain outside the sales tax system. Since about 80 percent of what the U.S. economy produces is a service, it's reasonable to question whether the historical practice of taxing products and exempting services continues to make sense.

The U.S. government doesn't have a sales tax. Instead, it uses income and payroll taxes as its primary revenue base. In contrast, many developed countries in the rest of the world have imposed a form of national sales tax called a *value-added tax* (VAT). A VAT charges a tax at each level of production or supply, applying the tax only to the difference between the selling price and the input costs of the seller. At the end of the supply chain the consumer pays the entire amount of the tax when she buys the product or service, while each business along the way collects and remits a portion of the total tax. In theory a VAT applies to all goods and services, but in practice there are many exceptions. The VAT is an economically efficient form of tax. However, when used in conjunction with an income tax, instead of as a replacement, the VAT results in high levels of government taxation that can distort incentives, inhibit commerce, and lead to poor economic performance.

INCOME TAXES

When a person earns wages from a job, interest from a bank account, or retirement pay from a pension, this presents an opportunity to collect *income taxes*. Income taxes are a relatively new phenomenon in the United States: there were no sustained national income taxes until 1913. More than half of all federal government revenues comes from the income tax today. At the state and local level, about 25 percent of all revenues comes from income taxes, with 35 percent coming from sales taxes and 35 percent coming from property taxes.[3] Income taxes are a big source of revenue for our governments.

Defining income can be challenging; this is the complexity Einstein was complaining about. We could say that income is any money that comes into a household or business, but that would lead to taxing many transactions that don't have any element of increase, benefit, or profit. For example, if you buy a computer for $1,000 and sell it a year later to someone for $500, you've received $500 (so that's "income") but only because you parted with something of value. If you're in business, all the revenues you receive are incoming money, but only after you pay your expenses do you have any profit left over. So for income tax purposes, the system taxes income from wages, investments, and business profits.

Whenever you tax income, it creates a deterrent to creating that income. Low taxes tend not to influence behavior, but high taxes cause people to avoid creating income or to find ways to avoid taxation, legal or otherwise. Tax authorities carefully define different kinds of income and apply different tax rates to that income to create the right incentives. For example, many people think that long-term investments are good for the economy, so income from these investments (called *capital gains*) is taxed at a lower rate than wage income. Gifts of money or objects of value aren't considered income to the recipient. The expenses that businesses can deduct in calculating their profits are also carefully defined.

Federal income taxes are paid on *taxable income*, calculated from the entire income of a taxpayer after making adjustments and deductions. Certain items are excluded from taxable income, such as money paid as alimony or contributed to a retirement plan, since the tax is paid elsewhere (by the alimony recipient or when the retirement money is withdrawn). You also deduct certain costs of living that the government has decided to treat favorably, lowering taxable income and ultimately the amount of tax. These deductions include interest on mortgages, taxes paid to state and local governments, charitable contributions, uninsured casualty losses, and unusually high medical expenses. The process of determining taxable income is repeated for state and city income taxes, although most state and city tax authorities use the federal taxable income calculation as a starting point, simplifying the determination of state and local income taxes.

Tax authorities use a system of *withholding* to deduct your estimated income taxes from your wages, or require estimated payments from taxpayers for other income, so there may be no tax bill due at the end of the year. You pay your taxes "as you go." For wage earners, a portion of your regular paycheck will pay your city, state, and federal income taxes in advance; at the end of the year you file a tax return and either pay additional taxes or get a refund from the government. The tax authorities keep track of your payments during the year as does your employer's payroll system. You'll see these taxes detailed on a statement accompanying each paycheck or direct deposit acknowledgment.

Once you determine taxable income, you calculate the income tax due by applying the applicable *tax rate* to the taxable income. Most income tax systems throughout the world, including in the United States, are *progressive*. This means applying higher tax rates to higher incomes. The United States achieves this by using *tax brackets*, a range of income to which the tax rate applies. A few examples using 2015 federal tax rates will illustrate this (brackets change every year for inflation, or if Congress passes a new law).

Table 11.1 first considers a single person with a taxable income of $20,000 (after adjusting your income for any retirement plan contributions and taking allowable deductions). On your first $9,225 of income, you'll pay a 10 percent tax rate (the 10 percent bracket is $0 to $9,225), and on the $10,775 remainder of your taxable income you'll pay a higher rate, 15 percent (the 15 percent bracket is $9,226 to $37,450). So your total federal income tax is $922.50 + $1,616.25 = $2,538.75, producing an average federal tax rate of 12.7 percent. (You'll still have state income tax to pay, and maybe even a city income tax, too.)

Table 11.1 next considers a married couple with both spouses employed, together earning $160,000 per year in taxable income (again, after all adjustments and deductions). The tax brackets are different for married people than for single people, so your 10 percent bracket goes up to $18,450 and your 15 percent bracket goes up to $74,900. For joint income between $74,901 and $151,200 the tax bracket is 25 percent, and for joint income between $151,201 and $230,450 it's 28 percent. Your federal income tax is $1,845.00 + $8,467.50 + $19,075.00 + $2,464.00 = $31,851.50, producing an average federal tax rate of 19.9 percent. So you can see that the more income you make, the higher share of it you'll pay in federal taxes under our progressive tax rate system. The highest federal tax bracket is 39.6 percent for individual annual incomes over $413,200 or joint annual incomes over $464,850.

Because of the progressive rate structure, adjustments, and deductions to income, it turns out that a lot of people in the United States actually pay no federal income tax at all (and if they pay no federal income tax, they probably pay no state income tax, either). This doesn't mean they pay no taxes, but that they pay no *income* taxes. The numbers vary each year, but somewhere between 45 percent and 50 percent of all U.S. households pay no federal income taxes. *Zero.* Furthermore, the progressivity built into the rate structure described above results in high-income households

Table 11.1 Illustration of Progressive Tax Rates (Federal Tax Brackets 2015)

	Taxable Income From	Taxable Income Up To	Amount Subject To Tax	Tax Rate	Tax Amount
Single Person with Taxable Income of $20,000					
10% Bracket	$0	$9,225	$9,225	10%	$922.50
15% Bracket	$9,226	$37,450	$10,775	15%	$1616.25
Total Tax					$2,538.75
Average Tax Rate				12.7%	
Married Couple with Taxable Income of $160,000					
10% Bracket	$0	$18,450	$18,450	10%	$1,845.00
15% Bracket	$18,451	$74,900	$56,450	15%	$8,467.50
25% Bracket	$74,901	$151,200	$76,300	25%	$19,075.00
28% Bracket	$151,201	$230,450	$8,800	28%	$2,464.00
Total Tax					$31,851.50
Average Tax Rate				19.9%	

Source: Tax Foundation, "2015 Tax Brackets" (October 2, 2014); Author's analysis.

paying the bulk of total federal income taxes. For example, the top 1 percent of households by income pay around 38 percent of total federal income taxes, and the top 10 percent together pay about 70 percent of all the federal income taxes collected in the United States each year.[4]

EMPLOYMENT TAXES

You might be surprised the first time you receive a paycheck and discover how little money is left after all the taxes and deductions are taken out. A *pay stub* details the income you make; in the case of hourly wages, it's the product of an hourly rate multiplied by the hours worked during the pay period. The pay stub shows all the income tax withholding—city, state, and federal. It also shows other deductions for what are collectively called *employment taxes*. Finally, the pay stub details deductions for the employee's share of benefits such as contributions to a retirement plan, health insurance premiums, and life insurance. Even though it's not a deduction, pay stubs will also show the *employer's* share of your health insurance premium, so you'll be aware of its total cost.

The Federal Insurance Contributions Act (FICA) requires payment of *payroll taxes* to fund the Social Security and Medicare programs described in the next chapter. Employees pay the Social Security tax of 6.2 percent on every dollar they earn up to $118,500 (this limit for 2015 changes every year based on inflation); if you're lucky enough to make more than that, you won't pay additional Social Security taxes. Unlike income taxes, there's no progressivity in the rate, and no adjustments or deductions. The second payroll tax is the Medicare tax of 1.45 percent. Unlike the Social Security tax, the Medicare tax applies to *all* your wages without limit, so you pay the tax from the first dollar you earn to the last. For all wages over $200,000 there's an *additional* 0.9 percent Medicare tax, making this a progressive tax.[5]

Employers pay a matching payroll tax as well: the employer pays a Social Security tax of 6.2 percent and a Medicare tax of 1.45 percent of every employee's wages (the additional 0.9 percent Medicare tax on wages over $200,000 is *not* matched by the employer). The employee doesn't see these tax payments on her pay stub, but it's important for her to understand that her employer also pays the FICA tax. In theory, if the employer didn't have to pay the FICA tax, this money would be available to pay higher wages. The total FICA tax on the first $118,500 of wages, then, is 15.3 percent, used to fund the Medicare and Social Security programs.

Another employment tax funds *unemployment benefits*, primarily paid to the state, but there's also a tax at the federal level. These taxes vary by state and are usually paid only by the employer, not the employee, at a rate around 1–2 percent of wages. These taxes fund unemployment benefits to those people who lose their jobs, and because these benefits are actually a form of insurance, it's proper to consider these taxes a form of insurance premiums. They're collected through the tax system because the payments are mandatory and based on employees' wages: it's a tax to pay for unemployment insurance.

Employment taxes apply only to the income of employees, so you have to define "employee" and also "income." Most benefits like health insurance are excluded from income, but other forms of compensation such as personal use of a company vehicle will count just like cash. Not every person who does work for someone else is an employee. For example, if you work for your neighbor shoveling snow off her steps in the winter, you're not an employee, you're an *independent contractor*. People also use the term *freelancer* to describe independent workers. Independent contractors and people who work for themselves (called *self-employed*) also must pay employment taxes, in fact they have to pay *both sides* of the taxes, the entire 15.3 percent. There are sometimes disputes about whether a person is an employee or a contractor, and the government has published extensive guidelines to help employers make the correct determination.

The government collects employment taxes through the withholding system, just as it collects employee income taxes. For the employee's share of payroll taxes, the employer retains this money from your earnings and pays it to the tax authorities on your behalf, usually every month or quarter. The employer also makes payments to the tax authorities for the employer's share of FICA and unemployment taxes, as well as any income and sales taxes due from operating the business. Unfortunately, some employers fail to make all the tax payments they owe, especially when the employer has financial problems. Not paying withholding or income taxes to the government is a serious crime, and those who commit it risk prosecution. Fortunately, in the rare cases where an employer fails to make withholding tax payments due on behalf of an employee, the government holds the employer responsible for this money, and treats it as if paid with respect to the employee.

PROPERTY TAXES

The most common form of property tax in the United States is a local real estate tax on land and buildings. The taxing authority—typically a town, city, or county—determines the value of a property and applies a tax rate to the valuation. These valuations are updated periodically (usually by professional *appraisers*) and can be influenced by recent sales, general market conditions, and any improvements made to the buildings. Sometimes there are other taxes embedded in the property tax rate to reflect where the money is used: for local government, for schools, for libraries, and for other government programs. The taxpayer usually sees just one total tax rate.

Even if you don't own any real estate yourself, the property tax concerns you. If you live in a home that your parents or guardians own, they'll be paying the property tax, which affects how much money is left over to spend on other things. If you live in a property you rent, your landlord must pay property taxes, so your rent will include a share of the property taxes, even if it's not explicitly shown on the lease. Even as a college student renting housing from a nonprofit owner (such as a tax-exempt college or university), you may be paying property taxes indirectly: some colleges and universities make payments in lieu of property taxes to localities in order to be good citizens and help support the operations of local government. Those payments, too, will be part of your rent.

For individuals, taxes on personal property have been virtually eliminated throughout the United States. In just a few places there are taxes on business personal property or property used to generate income by individuals. The types of property subject to this kind of tax include business inventory, farm equipment, and machinery. The same principles apply: the tax authority determines a valuation, applies the property tax rate (often the same as the real estate tax rate), and determines the resulting tax. Not surprisingly, there are numerous exclusions, credits, and limits making this kind of tax just as complex as others. The total share of local taxes generated by personal property taxes is relatively low.

OTHER TAXES

The four major types of taxes described above constitute the vast majority of all taxes collected in the United States. Still, there are numerous other taxes that consumers will pay. An *excise tax* is a form of sales tax that applies to specific products, usually on a per-unit basis rather than based on value. The primary goods subject to federal and state excise taxes are fuel, alcohol, and tobacco. Sometimes these taxes are called "sin taxes," since alcohol and tobacco are considered dangerous to the user, and using fuel pollutes the environment. These taxes are usually included in the stated price of the product, unlike a sales tax which is added explicitly. Because an excise tax is already like a sales tax, most states—but not all— don't charge a sales tax on goods that already include an excise tax.

But we're just getting started with the excise taxes. You pay a tax when you transfer property, which is an excise tax. You pay many travel-related excise taxes, including on airline tickets, hotels, rental cars, and taxi fares. There's an excise tax on gambling, indoor tanning, cruises, local telephone service, and cable TV. There are producer excise taxes on almost every form of fuel in addition to the excise taxes consumers pay at the pump. There are excise taxes on health insurance policies and any insurance issued by a foreign company. There's an excise tax on the sale of new heavy trucks and on new cars that are considered "gas guzzlers." There are excise taxes applied to certain manufactured goods, including medical devices, vaccines, tires, bows and arrows, sport fishing equipment, ozone-depleting chemicals, and coal.[6] Many states and localities also impose annual excise taxes based on the value of aircraft, motor vehicles, and personal watercraft (and which decline with the value of the property). Sometimes you see these taxes explicitly, and sometimes they're included in the cost of what you buy, directly or indirectly.

When someone receives money or something of value as a gift, it's not considered income to the recipient, and therefore there's no income tax due. Under some circumstances the person making the gift—called a *donor*—must pay a *gift tax*. Many people make gifts at the time they die from the property they've accumulated at the time of death, called an *estate*. The United States uses a unified gift and estate tax system, where all gifts made by someone during her lifetime and after death from her estate are considered together. A donor can give away $14,000 each year to as many people as she wishes that doesn't count toward any gift tax, and any gifts over $5.5 million (combined gifts during life or after death) will ultimately be subject to a federal gift and estate tax of 40 percent.[7] Many states also have similar taxes in the 15 to 20 percent range and often with a lower exemption, so the total tax bite can be substantial. The trend in states has been to eliminate or reduce estate taxes so people won't relocate as they get older to avoid these taxes.

TAX EXPENDITURES

Even if you've never filed an income tax return, you can probably tell already that taxation is complicated. The obligation to file a tax return results from earning income, and earning income is a good thing—that's how we pay for the things we need and want. With that obligation comes a duty to properly maintain records, report your income, and file the proper tax returns when they're due. The Internal Revenue Service (IRS) estimates that the average non-business taxpayer spends 5 hours and $40 filling out its easiest form (for those people with only wage income) or 8 hours and $110 completing more complicated tax returns. This is just for the federal government: a typical taxpayer may have to file income tax returns with the city and state governments each year, as well.

Tax complexity has become a very real concern in the United States—and not just because of the time and cost to file income tax returns. By making the tax code complicated, it can mask or hide where the government spends our tax dollars. The federal government can spend $100 million on a new program, and when it does so we can see clearly where the money is going. If the federal government changes the tax law to reduce taxes on a certain activity by $100 million, that's much harder to see. The government isn't spending any money; instead it's giving up tax revenues through a change in the tax law. Some people call these loopholes; economists call them *tax expenditures.*

Tax expenditures are the lost tax revenues from special provisions in the tax code that benefit certain groups, activities, or forms of income. It's as if in the absence of the special tax provision, all the tax money is received, then immediately spent again as a direct expenditure of cash. The total amount of tax expenditures at the federal level is nearly $1.2 trillion each year.[8] Wow. This means a "neutral" tax code without all those loopholes would generate $1.2 trillion more each year in federal taxes (and the same thing happens with each state's tax code). To put that number in perspective, it's more than one-third of all the revenue the federal government collects each year. Unfortunately, it has proven difficult to eliminate these special provisions, because they include popular items: excluding from income the value of employer health insurance benefits, allowing home mortgage interest deductions, offering lower taxes on capital gains, permitting deductions for contributions to retirement plans, excluding income from Social Security and veteran's benefits, and allowing charitable deductions. All these "loopholes" have their fans, but they're still tax expenditures resulting in lost tax revenue.

TAXES AND BEHAVIOR

In some cases, who pays the tax is obvious: the retail purchaser pays the sales tax, the driver pays the fuel tax at the pump, and the employer pays her half of the Social Security tax. But if the retailer has to lower the selling price because of the sales tax, or the gas station charges less because of the gasoline tax, or the employer pays lower wages because of the Social Security tax, then the cost of the tax is actually shared. Where the burden of a tax *really* falls is called its *tax incidence.* For example, a corporation may compute its profits each year, file a corporate income tax return, and remit the tax payments to the government. Does that mean the "corporation" pays the entire corporate income tax? Maybe not: the corporate income tax can be passed onto consumers in the form of higher prices, can be borne by the corporation's workers in the form of lower wages, or can be absorbed by the business owners in the form of lower profits. Only if this last possibility takes place does the "corporation" actually bear the cost of this tax. Economists and public policy leaders hotly debate the question of tax incidence.

Another useful tax concept to understand is the marginal tax rate, particularly when considering the income tax. The *marginal tax rate* applies to the next dollar earned: it determines how much you keep of each additional dollar you make. Recall the single person earning $20,000 in adjusted gross income each year, and suppose she receives a $1,000 raise. Since she's in the 15 percent bracket, she'll pay an additional $150 in federal income tax; perhaps an additional $50 in state and local income taxes; and another $76.50 in FICA taxes. She'll pay total taxes of $276.50 on her additional $1,000 of earnings, meaning she faces a marginal tax rate of 27.7 percent. Very high earners in the 39.6 percent federal income tax bracket can face a marginal tax rate over 55 percent on their income after adding city, state, and Medicare taxes. If you know that you're going to keep less than half of your additional income, how hard will you work to generate that extra income?

Taxes influence behavior. In the case of taxes on business, an increase in the corporate income tax can cause corporations to reduce wages or increase prices. The increase of a sales tax can cause shoppers to reduce their spending, or an increase in the income tax may encourage workers to stay home or work fewer hours. Public health officials have encouraged governments to raise the tax on tobacco because they think people will smoke less if cigarettes cost more, and experience has shown them to be right. How consumers and businesses respond to changes in taxes will depend on many factors, and it's difficult to predict accurately what will happen as a result of every change in tax policy. It's certainly true that "if you tax something, then you get less of it." But government must tax some things, or there would be no way to pay for government services.

In your own decision making, keep in mind that taxes matter, and it's *only* after-tax money that counts. For example, if you're considering two different jobs, both of which are in places you'd be happy to live, you should consider not just the jobs themselves and the cost of living in each place, but also the taxes levied in each location. In some areas, take-out food is exempt from sales tax, while eating the same food dining in is taxable—will that change your behavior? If you buy something on the Internet from some vendors today you won't pay a sales tax, but if you buy the same item at a local retailer you will. The government gives you a tax deduction to save for retirement through a 401(k) plan because it wants people to save for retirement, and you'll save taxes if you do. Taxes are everywhere, and so are the incentives to reduce and avoid them.

TAX CONSIDERATIONS FOR BUSINESS

Taxes also create important incentives for behavior and decision making when considering what form of organization a business will choose. Like individuals, businesses must also pay income taxes, sometimes through a separate tax return or sometimes by including the business income on individual tax returns. The primary tax consideration for choosing what form of business to operate is double-taxation, since in some cases the profits from a business can be subject to two levels of taxation. Profits may be taxed first to the business, and then when those remaining profits are distributed to the business's owners, they can be taxed a second time as income to the owners.

Some forms of business organization aren't typically subject to a second level of taxation, while other forms of business almost always are. Because of this, business promoters and organizers (or more accurately, their accountants and lawyers) will help choose the proper business form, or take other actions, that may avoid this second level of taxation. Of the four basic forms of business organization—sole proprietorship, partnership, corporation, and LLC—all but corporations are treated as *pass-through* entities for tax purposes. Pass-through entities don't directly pay taxes on their income. A sole proprietorship completes a Schedule C as part of the individual income tax form, while partnerships and LLCs file their own income tax returns to the IRS for *informational* purposes. The income that these entities generate will "pass through" to the owners of the entity in proportion to their owner-ship, whether it's to the single owner of a sole proprietorship, the multiple partners in a partnership, or the one-to-many members of an LLC. Partnerships and LLCs send a form each year to their owners that indicates how much income they them-selves need to report on their individual income tax returns.

Table 11.2 shows an example of a partnership with 10 equal partners that earns $1,000,000 of profits for the year. Because it's a pass-through entity for tax purposes, each partner reports $100,000 of income on her tax return, and pays income tax at a combined marginal tax rate of about 45 percent, leaving a total of $55,000 each after taxes, or a total of $550,000 in *after-tax profit* for all ten partners. Organized as a corporation, Table 11.2 shows that same business with $1,000,000 of profits will pay $410,000 total in federal and state taxes (using New York's tax rate). That leaves $590,000 potentially available for the shareholders, which, if entirely dis-tributed, would be taxed as dividends at combined marginal tax rates of 31 percent (state and federal), leaving $407,100 in after-tax profit when we're all done. Corpo-rate business profits go through two levels of taxation: first at the corporate level, then any distributions of those profits are taxed again at the individual level. If the profits aren't distributed to the owners, they're not taxed at that second level. You can also see the total tax bite is larger for a corporation than what all the partners in the partnership together pay for the same amount of business income.

A corporation can choose to be treated as a pass-through entity only if it meets certain conditions, including that all the shareholders agree. This is called mak-ing an "S" corporation election; otherwise it's considered a "C" corporation and subject to the two levels of taxation on its profits and distributions (the letters refer to sections in the corporate tax code). S corporations can have no more than

Table 11.2   Double Taxation of Business Income

	Partnership	Corporation
Business Income	$1,000,000	$1,000,000
Partner Combined Tax Rate	45%	
Total Partner Taxes	$450,000	
Corporate Combined Tax Rate		41%
Total Corporate Taxes		$410,000
Income Subject to Dividend Tax	$550,000	$590,000
Dividend Combined Tax Rate	0%	31%
Dividend Taxes	$0	$182,900
Owners' Income after Taxes	$550,000	$407,100

Source: Author's analysis.

100 shareholders, so if the business is a large publicly traded corporation, it will necessarily remain a C corporation. If a corporation meets all the qualifying conditions and chooses S corporation taxation, then its profits will pass through to the individual shareholders. Because of the lower total taxes of pass-through businesses, they tend to be preferred by organizers, which is one reason the LLC has become so popular. The LLC also provides limited-liability protection that sole proprietorships and general partnerships don't. The LLC doesn't have its own tax status: a single-person LLC files taxes like a sole proprietorship, a multiple-person LLC files taxes like a partnership, and in some cases an LLC can even file taxes like a corporation.

Some businesses operate as nonprofit organizations, meaning they're not seeking to make a profit on investor capital, but instead they exist to serve another social purpose. For example, nonprofit organizations can be charities, churches, educational institutions, foundations, social associations, and hospitals. Sometimes these organizations are called "501(c)(3)" entities, after the applicable tax code section. The Internal Revenue Service publishes detailed guidelines that determine which organizations qualify for tax exempt status, and if they qualify, these organizations don't have to pay any federal or state income taxes. They're often also exempt from other taxes such as local real estate taxes. Some organizations may have both taxable and tax-exempt activities, in which case they'll pay income tax on the nonexempt income. In most cases, a nonprofit organization will organize itself as a corporation, because tax rules make it difficult for the other business forms to qualify for tax-exempt status.

NOTES

1. Wal-Mart Stores, Inc., "Walmart 2015 Annual Report," p. 36, fiscal years ending January 31, 2013–2015.

2. Scott Drenkard and Jared Walczak, "State and Local Sales Tax Rates in 2015," *The Tax Foundation,* April 8, 2015.

3. Liz Malm and Ellen Kant, "The Sources of State and Local Tax Revenues," *The Tax Foundation,* January 28, 2013.

4. Scott Greenberg, "Summary of the Latest Federal Income Tax Data, 2015 Update," *The Tax Foundation,* November 19, 2015.

5. U.S. Department of the Treasury, Internal Revenue Service, Publication 15, "(Circular E), Employer's Tax Guide for Use in 2015," December 22, 2014.

6. U.S. Department of the Treasury, Internal Revenue Service, Publication 510, "Excise Taxes (Including Fuel Tax Credits and Refunds)," February 27, 2015.

7. U.S. Department of the Treasury, Internal Revenue Service, Publication 559, "Survivors, Executors, and Administrators," March 3, 2015

8. Center on Budget and Policy Priorities, "Policy Basics: Federal Tax Expenditures," data for 2014, August 5, 2015.

TWELVE

Government Benefits

Government programs provide money and financial support for many purposes. For example, the federal government provides generous support to farmers in the form of price supports and crop insurance subsidies. If you live on a farm or aspire to become a farmer, these programs are providing government benefits to you. Many state governments pay for special education teachers in schools, so if you or a family members use these teachers, you're receiving a government benefit. Governments offer thousands of programs each aiding small numbers of people, and major programs that offer benefits to everybody.

A person must meet certain conditions to receive government benefits. Once eligible, the person continues to receive those benefits for a specified period or, in some cases, indefinitely, unless something changes. These benefits are often called *entitlements* because once a person qualifies, they're entitled—have a guaranteed right—to receive the benefit. Historically, governments at all levels have been reluctant to eliminate or reduce benefits to someone who currently receives them, limiting changes in entitlements to affect only future recipients.

Government benefits are designed to achieve social policy objectives, whether alleviation of poverty in old age, assistance for injured people, or providing income to the unemployed. Many of these programs are need-based and assist people who would otherwise suffer. There used to be shame associated with accepting government benefits, but today the benefits are so widespread that the stigma has largely disappeared. Still, it's a source of pride for many people that they can provide for themselves and their families without need for government aid.

SOCIAL SECURITY

The *Social Security* program administered by the federal government provides payments to retired people, those with disabilities, and their surviving

children and spouses. It operates as two different programs, one for retired workers (Social Security), and another for disabilities and income support (Supplemental
Security Income or SSI). This is a large program, providing $860 billion in pay-
ments to around 60 million people out of our 320 million total population. The
vast majority of today's recipients are retired workers, about 40 million people
receiving an average of $16,000 per year. Roughly 10 million people receive disabil-
ity benefits, and the rest of the recipients are the spouses and children of deceased
beneficiaries.[1]

Social Security is primarily a work-based system, but not all U.S. workers are
fully covered: many state and federal government workers have their own separate
retirement systems as an alternative to the retirement portion of Social Security.
Every person born in this country or who becomes a naturalized citizen qualifies
for Social Security. You can also get a Social Security number if you're a noncitizen
with a work visa. If you were born here, your parents probably applied for a Social
Security number for you. You may have used this number already to get a driver's
license, passport, credit card, or to take a standardized educational test. The original card issued by the Social Security Administration (SSA) is important, so keep
it in a safe place at home; never keep it with you on a regular basis. Your Social
Security number is the most valuable piece of identifying information you'll ever
have.

Social Security grew out of the Great Depression to prevent the aged from living
in poverty when they couldn't work to provide for themselves. When it started in
1937 the qualifying retirement age was 65, but not many people lived that long: the
life expectancy for men was under 62 (men were the primary wage earners then)
and almost 66 for women.[2] The program planned to serve only the small number
of people who would substantially outlive their expected lifespans. For everyone
born after 1960 the current retirement age is 67, but a lot more people are expected
to significantly surpass that milestone: if you're 22 today, a man can expect to live
to age 77 and a woman to age 82.[3] So unlike when the program started, today most
people collect Social Security benefits for many years.

The Social Security system has also expanded its beneficiaries over the years,
paying surviving spouses and children, the disabled, and people who didn't work
long enough to qualify for retirement benefits (you or your spouse must pay taxes
into the system for ten years to receive full retirement benefits). To achieve this,
Social Security has increased the taxes and wage base that fund the system (the total
tax rate on wages for the first 13 years of the system was 2 percent, versus 12.4 percent
today) and, to a lesser extent, by increasing the retirement age. In theory, the SSA
collects all the taxes, invests the proceeds in safe but low-yielding U.S. government
securities, and uses the proceeds to pay benefits at a future date. In practice, current taxpayers are largely funding current retirees.

Because workers make tax payments to fund the retirement part of the system,
they feel like the benefits they receive are earned, akin to a private-sector pension
or retirement plan. There's some truth to this, but it depends on your age, marital
status, and income. Beneficiaries today as a group are receiving substantially more

in total payments than the invested value of the contributions they and their employers paid as taxes on their behalf over the years. In effect, they're receiving partial transfer payments from other taxpayers. The first Social Security recipient, for example, paid under $25 in taxes and received almost $23,000 in benefits.[4] Young people as a group today, except for the very poor, can expect to pay far more in Social Security taxes than they'll ever receive back in benefits.

This imbalance between funding and benefits has prompted concern about the stability of the Social Security system. Unlike private sector retirement programs such as 401(k) plans or defined-benefit pensions, the government doesn't hold an investment portfolio of assets to fund future payments. Current tax payments aren't being held and invested until retirement; they're immediately paid out to current retirees and other beneficiaries. Social Security's receipts today are less than its expenditures, and the accumulated reserves from previous tax payments are held as Treasury securities, debts that have to be paid by future taxes. Like most policy problems involving money, this will be resolved by some combination of reduced future benefits (perhaps limited to affluent beneficiaries), higher retirement ages, and increased taxes.

MEDICARE

Medicare is the federal government's health insurance program for older Americans. While it's a distinct program from the retirement and disability benefits of Social Security and is administered by a separate agency, it's commonly and *mistakenly* considered part of the Social Security system. While you won't be using the services of Medicare for many years, your family members will be; and you'll be paying taxes into the system from the very first day you start working.

Medicare started in 1966 and offers health insurance to people 65 and older. Like commercially available health insurance, Medicare participants pay a monthly premium (if they buy more than basic hospitalization coverage, which is free), co-payments, and deductibles. There are several optional components to Medicare, so beneficiaries have control over how much insurance they buy. Once reaching age 65, eligibility is essentially the same as for Social Security: citizenship or qualified work status. State government workers with their own retirement systems who have paid the Medicare taxes through their payroll deductions are also covered

As people age their health problems usually increase. Not every older person has serious health conditions, of course, and exercise, good nutrition, avoiding tobacco and drugs, getting sufficient rest, managing stress, and having regular checkups can greatly increase your odds of living a long and healthy life. Ultimately, however, your health in old age is a lottery: some people will "win" and escape major issues, many will have a handful of problems to deal with, and some will suffer severe and chronic health conditions. Our national social policy is to assist older people with the higher costs of health care as they age by providing generous support with government subsidies. Medicare is an intergenerational transfer program, where younger, healthier people help to pay for the medical costs of their elders.

Medicare has expanded over the years because of the bulging population of older Americans, by increasing the services it pays for, and by adding coverage for some people under age 65 (those with disabilities and certain rare diseases). It now covers hospitalization, nursing, and physician costs; short-term nursing home, home health care, and hospice services; and prescription drugs. Medicare doesn't pay for long-term nursing home, assisted living, and home health care services, or routine dental, vision, and hearing services.

Many beneficiaries buy commercial health insurance plans to supplement Medicare. The Medicare Advantage program, for example, allows beneficiaries to enroll in a private insurance plan to receive their Medicare benefits. While these plans vary, they typically cover more services than Medicare and reduce the co-payments and deductibles. Beneficiaries pay supplemental premiums for these plans, which also receive direct payments from the Medicare system. Insurers that offer these plans typically control costs by limiting the provider network that beneficiaries can use. Private plans also provide insurance for high levels of out-of-pocket expenditures.

Medicare is the largest single source of payments to health care providers in the United States, giving it great power to set reimbursement rates and terms. Not every hospital and doctor must accept Medicare patients, but if they do they must accept the Medicare fee schedule for services. The reimbursement schedule is complex, as are the requirements for health care providers to participate in the system. The Medicare reimbursement rate for most health care services is substantially lower than rates paid by private health insurance companies. Despite this, most beneficiaries don't have trouble finding a provider who accepts Medicare, but as Medicare lowers its payments to control costs, fewer health care providers will be able to accept new Medicare patients. Critics assert that some providers order unnecessary tests and treatments to increase their revenues because of the low payment schedule, and studies support this claim.

Nearly 60 million people in this country participate in Medicare today, about 95 percent of the aged population.[5] This gives it an enormous constituency beyond its sheer financial impact. Beneficiaries as a group pay only a small portion of their health care costs. Premiums cover only about 15 percent of Medicare spending, with the balance paid by the Medicare payroll taxes (some of which were paid by current beneficiaries) and from general tax revenues of the federal government. A diminishing surplus of receipts over expenses is set aside in Treasury securities, but at the end of the day the federal government as a whole retains the obligation to fund Medicare.

Medicare spending is approaching $550 billion of the more than $3 trillion total spent annually on health care in the U.S.[6] Health care costs in this country have increased dramatically over the last 50 years, increasing at a much higher rate than most other goods and services or the general rate of inflation. We spend more than 17 percent of our total GDP on health care, compared to roughly 8 percent of GDP for our peer countries across the world such as Germany, France, and Japan.[7] As baby boomers continue to enter the pool of beneficiaries, and as health care costs keep increasing, the pressures on the Medicare system will build. There's a vigorous debate about the long-term stability of Medicare financing, a debate that will necessarily confront young people, who today are a lifetime away from receiving these benefits.

POVERTY

Social Security and Medicare serve all Americans regardless of whether they're rich or poor. Many state and federal assistance programs serve only those with lower incomes. The federal government has defined the term *poverty* to mean a very specific level of income, and many government benefits use that definition to determine eligibility. For example, eligibility for Medicaid, CHIP, and the subsidies for the exchanges under the Affordable Care Act (all discussed below) are based on the poverty level. So are eligibility for Head Start (an early education program), food stamps, school lunches, and free legal services. The precise income limit varies by family size but not by state (except for Alaska and Hawaii), despite wide differences in the cost of living across the country.

The federal government issues its poverty guidelines every year based on household size, as shown in Table 12.1. It doesn't matter if people in the household are related by blood, they just need to live together and share expenses. It's estimated that 46.7 million people in the United States live in households with incomes below the poverty limits.[8]

The annual income limits for Hawaii are 15 percent higher at each household size, and for Alaska they're 25 percent higher. The programs using poverty levels for eligibility often use multiples of the poverty level itself. For example, a pregnant woman living alone in California qualifies for Medicaid there at 208 percent of the federal poverty level, so if her income is below $24,482, she'll be able to receive Medicaid benefits there. The basic poverty measure includes all forms of cash income such as wages, Social Security and disability benefits, pensions, and child support. Poverty measures *don't* take into account non-cash benefits such as food stamps, housing subsidies, and health insurance. The poverty income limits are before taxes, although poverty-level incomes typically have no income tax burden.

Table 12.1   Poverty Guidelines for 2015

Number of People in Household	Annual Income
1	$11,770
2	$15,930
3	$20,090
4	$24,250
5	$28,410
6	$32,570
Each additional person:	Add $4,160 per person

Source: U.S. Department of Health and Human Services, "2015 Poverty Guidelines" (September 3, 2015).

But where did these numbers come from? The U.S. Census Bureau made its first determination of the poverty level in 1963, based on the amount of money a family of three would have to spend to feed itself properly. If a family had to spend more than one-third of its income on food, it was deemed to be in poverty. From there the Census Bureau made adjustments for family size and, over time, increases in the cost of food. Today the Department of Health and Human Services simplifies the poverty figures for use by government agencies, but over fifty years later we're still using the same basic methodology, simply adjusted for food costs.

There are many criticisms of the Census Bureau poverty figures. Using the same income limits for urban and rural areas, and for every state except two, is certainly an administrative convenience, but it doesn't reflect the reality of vastly different costs of living. Considering only the cost of food, and ignoring housing, health care, and transportation, reflects only a narrow part of household spending. Excluding the value of non-cash benefits is another obvious concern. In fact, studies that measure poverty based on consumption—looking at how much people spend, what they own, and the quality of their homes—tell a story of substantially improved conditions for most poor Americans over the last few decades. Measures of poverty that just use cash income generally show a worsening of poverty over the same period.

MEDICAID AND THE AFFORDABLE CARE ACT

Medicaid is a health insurance program for the poor. Unlike Social Security and Medicare, which are national programs, Medicaid is funded and run by each state, aided by substantial contributions from the federal government. It's also a need-based program: low income is the primary requirement, and in most states eligibility is set at 138 percent of the federal poverty level. Each state develops its own program terms, including eligibility, scope of coverage, reimbursement rates, provider networks, and method of administration, subject to federal rules and guidelines. Many states operate under a *waiver* from the federal government, allowing them more flexibility in their Medicaid programs.

The Medicaid program provides benefits alongside the Children's Health Insurance Program (CHIP), under which the federal government funds states to provide health insurance to children who might not otherwise be eligible for Medicaid. Almost half of Medicaid beneficiaries are, in fact, children; about one-quarter of beneficiaries are the elderly and disabled; and the rest are poor adults. In total, the Medicaid system provides health insurance coverage to more people than any other health insurance in the United States. Some 70 million people receive Medicaid / CHIP benefits every year, and with expansion under the Affordable Care Act (ACA) passed in 2010 even more people will become eligible.[9]

The health care services covered by Medicaid are similar to those covered by Medicare, although each state's plan will vary. One important benefit provided under Medicaid (and not available under Medicare) is long-term nursing care: Medicaid collectively pays for almost half of all nursing home care in the United States today. Beneficiaries may be asked to contribute some level of cost sharing in the form of premiums, co-payments, and deductibles, but federal law limits this cost sharing and permits it from only certain categories of beneficiaries.

About half of all Medicaid beneficiaries receive their care through managed care organizations under contract with the state Medicaid programs, which pay these organizations per-capita premiums. For most of the rest, states reimburse providers according to set fee schedules. Medicaid reimbursement rates are generally below those paid by private insurers and Medicare, and as a result the network of available providers is limited. Still, surveys show that Medicaid beneficiaries have access to health care services at about the same rates as those covered by private insurance.

With Medicaid covering the poor, Medicare covering the elderly, and employer provided health insurance covering the workforce, it would seem that health insurance would be available for just about everyone. Unfortunately, that's not the case. Some people can't afford, or choose not to buy, health insurance in the commercial marketplace. Not only does the ACA require large employers to offer affordable health insurance to their workers, the ACA also imposes a duty on every person without health insurance to buy it or pay a fine. To help people buy their own insurance policies the ACA created a system of income-based subsidies offered through state-based health-insurance exchanges, creating a marketplace where people can shop for affordable health insurance. People who use the ACA exchanges can buy individual health insurance policies at a sliding discount based on their financial need.

Like Medicare, concern about the long-term financial stability of Medicaid has provoked vigorous debate. Current spending on Medicaid (with CHIP) is $550 billion and will approach $1 trillion by 2020.[10] The expansion of Medicaid in 2010 included a promise by the federal government to pay for most of the increased costs, but that promise may not last. Medicaid is already one of the largest categories of spending at the state level, and increases in the number of beneficiaries, continued health care inflation, and strained state budgets from other spending commitments may force states to rein in these programs. The federal government, already providing 60 percent of total Medicaid spending, may be in no better position to increase funding to this program providing critical services to the needy. The long-term financial impact of the ACA remains subject to debate, but most observers acknowledge that maintaining the subsidies of the ACA exchanges will require substantial federal spending.

FOOD STAMPS

The food stamp program, now officially called the Supplemental Nutrition Assistance Program (SNAP), provides money that people can use to buy groceries. Like many aid programs, the federal government provides the money, while state social service agencies distribute the benefits. In early days, beneficiaries would purchase books of stamps with indicated values on them (like postage stamps) and receive additional stamps for free; then they'd redeem the stamps for food at participating grocers. These stamps evolved into cash-like coupons and finally, today, electronic benefit transfer cards (EBT, just like prepaid debit cards) that are charged and reloaded each month with additional funds. Beneficiaries today make no payments to receive these benefits.

The U.S. Department of Agriculture started the food stamp program in 1939 to help farmers by creating more demand for their crops. Today, its emphasis is to help the poor buy their groceries. The federal government generally sets the eligibility criteria: you must be a citizen or legal resident with income below the poverty level, and not own certain assets above a specified limit. Most able-bodied food stamp recipients must be working, looking for work, or in a training program to maintain their benefits. Students, with some exceptions, aren't eligible for SNAP benefits.

Recipients of SNAP benefits can use the money to purchase most grocery items, but certain products can't be bought with these benefits. The program pays for groceries, so prepared foods (restaurant meals and the like) and even hot foods aren't allowed. Non-food items are also excluded from the program, such as pet food, health and beauty aids, cleaning supplies, paper products, and household items. You can't buy tobacco or alcohol with SNAP benefits. While these restrictions may seem paternalistic, the program's goal is to support the food needs of the poor, not to provide general assistance for routine household purchases. But the program doesn't make value judgments about nutritional quality: ice cream, donuts, and potato chips are just as legitimate under SNAP as vegetables, yogurt, and eggs.

Today about 45 million people use SNAP benefits each year, about the same number of people who live below the poverty line. There was a surge in participation after the recession of 2008–2009, and spending has kept rising since then. In recent years SNAP spending has been $70–75 billion annually, providing the average beneficiary household about $3,100 per year in food money. The federal government sets SNAP funding as part of the annual budget process, so benefit levels can change based on budget and political priorities, unlike entitlement programs that continue their spending on auto-pilot.[11]

There are other food assistance programs for people with low incomes. The federal government funds two programs for meals at schools, providing free or reduced-cost lunches and, in some places, breakfasts as well. There's also a program providing food benefits to certain day-care facilities for children and adults. Another important program benefits women, infants, and children (WIC) who are nutritionally at risk, such as pregnant and breast-feeding women and their young children. The WIC program, through state agencies administering federal funds, serves around 8 million people below 185 percent of the poverty level by giving them vouchers or EBT cards to buy food.[12] Unlike SNAP, WIC benefits must be used to purchase specific high-nutrition food such as infant formula, baby food, fruits and vegetables, and foods high in protein.

STUDENT LOANS

Recall from Chapter 5 that the average student who borrows money for college will have about $35,000 in debt upon graduation. The federal government today is the primary source of funding for college loans in the United States. Several different federal loan programs, administered by the educational institutions in partnership with the U.S. Department of Education, provide the funding. These funds can be used for private and public colleges, universities, vocational schools, and community colleges.

The U.S. government also runs several grant programs, including Pell Grants, a need-based program that provides up to $5,775 per year, and TEACH grants, a program open to everyone that provides up to $4,000 per year for people who will become teachers in certain high-need fields such as foreign languages, math, science, and special education.[13] Unlike student loans, grant aid doesn't have to be paid back. State governments provide some college financial aid; the amount and program will vary by state. Private organizations also offer financial aid usually in the form of scholarships, both need and merit based. Finally, banks and other private market lenders offer college loans, but these are usually more expensive and typically require a guarantor (like your parents) to sign on the loan with you and assume responsibility for payment. Private-sector loans should be considered a last resort for college funding.

The loan process begins with the Free Application for Federal Student Aid form (FAFSA), which compiles personal and financial information about a student and her family. The vast majority of funds provided by the federal government are to students who demonstrate financial need, although some grant and loan aid is available even for those students who don't meet the need criteria. The determination of how much aid a student is offered results from a comprehensive analysis of a student's and her family's income, savings, and expenses as reported on the FAFSA form. The federal aid application process results in a combination of aid through any eligible grants, loans, and work-study funds (a subsidized program where a student works part time to earn money). The FAFSA is the gateway for almost all college financial aid, whether based on need or not, from the government or elsewhere.

Colleges themselves are another major source of financial aid to students, providing scholarships (another name for grant aid, either need or merit based) and sometimes also direct loans, in addition to administering federal aid money. The educational institutions have their own versions of the FAFSA form in order to calculate financial need, but both calculations determine an expected family contribution (EFC): the amount of money a family will pay each year toward the total cost of college, after aid of all kinds has been factored in. Because of all the financial aid available from various sources, schools have developed a "net price calculator" available on their websites (and on other websites as well) that uses personalized information about each applicant and the college's own costs to estimate how much of the total cost of college will be borne by the student and her family. Use this information carefully, as schools don't always distinguish grant aid from loans and work-study awards, all of which are considered financial aid.

Some colleges are even experimenting with income-share arrangements, where students receive a cash grant for college costs, and in exchange they pledge a small percentage of their income for a period of years (for example, 3 percent of income for seven years). If you earn very little, you pay back very little. As these programs are new, if available at your school, you should consider them with care.

The problem with loans is that you must pay them back. Most of the government student loans suspend the obligation to make any payments until six months after you finish college. Then, like with all other loans, you'll have to pay interest and repay the principal over the term of the loan. For need-based loans the interest rate is subsidized by the federal government, meaning they offer you a lower rate than a bank or private lender typically would. The government also bears the costs of loans that are never repaid, which is why even the federal unsubsidized loans (not need-based) are less costly than private bank loans. For most borrowers the subsidized loans max out at $12,500 per year, and the unsubsidized loans are capped at $20,500 per year (for graduate students).

The government offers a lot of flexibility in determining how long you can take to pay back the loans, generally between 10 and 25 years. Keep in mind that as with all loans, any outstanding principal is charged interest, so the longer you take to repay the loan, the more total interest you'll end up paying. With an average debt of $35,000 paid back over 10 years at 5 percent interest, the payment will be $370 per month; not insignificant, but entirely manageable on typical college-graduate incomes (paying that back over 20 years lowers the monthly payment to $230). But many borrowers will have higher debt, other obligations, or low incomes, so the government allows you to elect repayment plans where payments are tied to your income. In cases of permanent disability or death you don't have to repay the loan at all; it's very hard to use bankruptcy, however, to avoid paying back a student loan.

Some borrowers never have to repay the entire amount of their loans. The government allows the loan to be forgiven (cancelled) if there's still a loan balance at the end of the term, usually 20 or 25 years. This is a great opportunity for borrowers whose incomes are insufficient to repay the entire debt. A federal program implemented in 2015 called "REPAYE" (Revised Pay As You Earn) now consolidates several earlier loan forgiveness programs into one plan and allows forgiveness for *all* direct federal student loans after 20 (undergraduate loans) or 25 years (graduate school debt). The program limits monthly payments to 10 percent of discretionary income while the loans are outstanding. Another program offers loan forgiveness after just 10 years (and limits monthly payments) for borrowers who work in public interest jobs, defined broadly to include government, education, and other nonprofit entities. Teachers at schools serving low-income students also have a special loan-forgiveness option.

All these programs the government offers add up to a lot of opportunity for student borrowers. However, it's a complex system and requires good planning to maximize the available benefits. College financial aid counselors are great resources, and many borrowers resort to private advisors. It's worth the effort to learn about all the financial aid programs offered by the government and educational institutions, and seek out every source of college financial aid. There's enough aid available so that every capable student can have a college education.

HOME LOAN PROGRAMS

Besides student loans, the federal government funds and administers over 50 major loan programs in the United States. These loans support business, agriculture, disaster relief, and aid for veterans. The majority of the loans offered by the federal government, however, support housing.

For housing aid, the government doesn't usually lend any money to a borrower. Instead, a private lender makes the loan and administers it, subject to government rules. The benefit arises through *insurance* of the loan to the private lender: if the loan meets the criteria established by the government, the government will bear the loss if the loan goes into default. Other programs style the benefit as a *guarantee* for a portion of the loan amount, but in either case the result is the same: the federal government bears some or all of the risk that a loan won't be repaid. This makes these loans attractive to lenders and results in a robust supply of capital for home mortgages.

The Federal Housing Administration (FHA) insures a variety of loan programs. FHA loans aren't targeted at low-income people. However, because they have a low down-payment requirement, FHA loans are popular with people who don't have much savings. Still, borrowers must have good credit, steady employment, and sufficient income to support the loan payments. If you're a veteran of the armed forces there are home loan guarantee programs from the U.S. Department of Veteran's Affairs (VA), and several programs make loans to Native Americans. The U.S. Department of Agriculture (USDA) actually offers some direct loans and grants to support home purchase and rehabilitation in rural parts of the United States.

In addition to directly-insured loans, by far the largest support the government gives to housing is through two government-sponsored enterprises (GSEs), which have become a dominant influence in the home mortgage market. The federal government created the Federal National Mortgage Corporation (Fannie Mae) and the Federal Home Loan Mortgage Corporation (Freddie Mac) to provide secondary markets for mortgages, to increase home lending and lower loan costs. These GSEs later became publicly traded companies with an implicit federal guarantee: the U.S. government would step in and support either company in the event of a financial catastrophe, which is exactly what happened in 2008. The government placed both of these entities into a "conservatorship" with direct financial oversight that continues to this day.

These GSEs purchase loans originated by private lending institutions, package them into bundles containing thousands of individual loans totaling hundreds of millions of dollars, and sell them to investors as *mortgage-backed securities*. This packaging is called *securitizing* a loan. These packaged loans are popular with investors because they generate regular cash flow, offer diversification from the large number of loans, and provide safety with the implicit guarantee of the federal government. It's a popular mechanism for lenders because they make money originating the loan and then get their capital back quickly when the loan is securitized. And they're popular with consumers, since the vast majority of loans will qualify for purchase by the GSEs (there's a maximum loan size), making mortgages readily available and at lower cost than otherwise would be the case. The federal government also securitizes the loans it insures or guarantees under the FHA, VA, and USDA loan programs.

OTHER HOUSING SUPPORT

Besides programs that increase the availability and lower the cost of home loans, there are also programs aiding renters for whom home ownership isn't feasible. Most cities provide *public housing* through an agency that owns and operates free-standing homes and apartment buildings. The money for these homes comes largely from the U.S. Department of Housing and Urban Development (HUD), which provides financial support for these local public housing agencies (PHAs). Over one million households live in public housing today. Eligibility is need-based, focused on low-income, the elderly, and the disabled. You must also be a citizen or legal resident of the country to obtain public housing benefits; in some places there are long waiting lists. Public housing tenants sign a lease and pay low rent based on their income, and must exhibit good conduct or lose the right to stay in public housing.

Another option for low-income renters is the Housing Choice Voucher program, also known as "Section 8" for the law that created it. PHAs provide cash-like vouchers for low-income, elderly, and disabled tenants who are citizens or legal residents, putting them into private rental units of their choice. The landlord charges a market level rent, and tenants pay using a combination of these vouchers and their own money. The rental units must meet quality standards set by the government, and the local PHA inspects these properties to make sure they comply. Because of the flexibility these vouchers provide to low-income tenants, it's a very popular program, with demand far exceeding the available funding. HUD programs also provide direct financial support to owners of multi-family rental properties if they rent to low-income residents.

Another federal subsidy for affordable housing operates through the tax system as the Low Income Housing Tax Credit (LIHTC). As a tax expenditure the cost of the LIHTC is largely hidden, although some direct funding was provided after the financial collapse in 2008, bringing the annual cost of the program to almost $10 billion. A private housing developer designs a multi-family housing project and promises to rent a certain percentage of the units at reduced costs to low-income tenants. The government issues *tax credits* to the developer (a refund or reduction of taxes) in exchange for this promise to rent to low-income tenants. The developer sells the credits for cash to investors such as banks that use these credits to reduce their federal income taxes. In this way the project developer gets equity, the low-income population gets more affordable housing, the investors buying the credits have a lower tax bill, and the cost of the program is largely shielded from public scrutiny. Some states supplement the LIHTC with their own forms of low-income housing tax credits.

DIRECT FINANCIAL ASSISTANCE

There are few federal programs that provide direct cash assistance to low-income people. The primary general assistance program is called Temporary Assistance for Needy Families (TANF). There must be a minor child or pregnant woman in the household for an adult to qualify for this assistance. Each state runs its own TANF program with federal funding that supplements state money, and states can customize their programs subject to the national rules. There are usually work requirements and time limits for TANF assistance, with a maximum of five years. This is the closest we have to a general welfare program, in recent years supporting about 2 million recipients monthly at a cost of $32 billion annually in combined federal and state funds.[14]

The *earned income tax credit* (EITC) gives a cash "refund" to low-income wage earners through the annual income tax return process. The EITC varies depending on family composition and income level, but you must have earned income and file a tax return to get the credit, even if you have no federal income tax liability (recall that only about half of all U.S. households owe a federal income tax). This program gives about $66 billion each year to 28 million people.[15] Many analysts consider the EITC one of the best anti-poverty measures from government, because it encourages work and doesn't distort the labor market like a minimum wage does.

JOB-RELATED ASSISTANCE

Each state provides an *unemployment insurance* fund to make payments to unemployed workers. This is a program funded jointly by state and federal taxes on employers' payrolls. Each state has some flexibility, subject to federal rules, to determine eligibility, payment amounts, and length of benefits. Generally, unemployment payments are paid up to six months, but the federal government often passes special legislation to extend jobless benefits during periods of high unemployment. The average benefit is $300 per week but varies widely by state, with the objective to replace about half of a worker's income. People receiving benefits must seek work, and those who are terminated for cause (or who quit on their own) aren't eligible for payments. In 2014 over 7 million people received in excess of $40 billion in unemployment insurance benefits.[16]

A state-level program with no federal funding is the *workers' compensation* system, providing lost wages and medical payments to injured workers (a separate federal system provides benefits to injured employees of the U.S. government). This is an insurance program, with premiums paid by employers and benefits administered through an insurance company (a few states run their own insurance programs). State law determines eligibility, and state agencies administer the programs. These programs originated in the early twentieth century to take workplace injury disputes outside the legal system, so the expensive, lengthy, and uncertain outcomes of a court battle would be avoided. Unfortunately, the system today requires lawyers for all parties and is rife with abuse, often serving as a supplement to unemployment insurance for lightly-injured workers who can't find a job. Employers pay over $80 billion each year in premiums to provide in excess of $60 billion in lost wages and medical benefits (the excess adds to insurance reserves for future claims).[17]

OTHER BENEFIT PROGRAMS

Scores of additional programs target specific groups of people for assistance. In particular, if you're a veteran of the armed forces, or a family member of one, there are numerous benefits available through the VA. There are also aid programs for Native Americans, but you don't have to be in a special group to enjoy some of the smaller federal programs. Federal money provides funds to help the poor obtain legal services, early education, job training, expensive medicines, birth control, pay utility bills, and insulate their homes. The U.S. government's *benefits.gov* website lists almost 1,400 benefits including over 600 joint federal-state programs, so there are a lot of opportunities to find a financial benefit you might qualify for.

Many government programs are partnerships between the federal and state governments, with jointly-provided funds administered by the states under national guidelines. Each state, however, also provides its own benefits to residents, funding and administering the programs without federal money or oversight. States have their own programs for college funding, buying homes, caring for children, getting a job, and learning a new skill. Because we operate in a federal system, where each state is its own sovereign, states have great leeway in determining what programs are right for its residents. Not all of these programs offer cash benefits—some simply offer guidance and information—but if you need assistance with your financial life, investigate all the programs offered by your state and local governments.

NOTES

1. U.S. Social Security Administration, "The 2015 Annual Report of the Board of Trustees of the Federal Old-Age and Survivors Insurance and Federal Disability Insurance Trust Funds," July 22, 2015.

2. U.S. Centers for Disease Control and Prevention, United States Life Tables, "United States Life Tables and Actuarial Tables 1939–1941," Table B, all races, 1947.

3. U.S. Social Security Administration, Actuarial Life Table, "Period Life Table, 2011," age 22.

4. U.S. Social Security Administration, Research Notes & Special Studies by the Historian's Office, "Research Note Number 3: Details of Ida May Fuller's Payroll Tax Contributions," July 1996.

5. U.S. Centers for Medicare & Medicaid Services, "CMS Financial Report, Fiscal Year 2015," November 9, 2015.

6. Ibid.

7. Andrew O. Smith, *Sand in the Gears: How Public Policy Has Crippled American Manufacturing*, Chapter 3 (Dulles, VA: Potomac Books, 2013).

8. U.S. Census Bureau, "Income and Poverty in the United States: 2014," Table 3, September 2015.

9. U.S. Centers for Medicare & Medicaid Services, "CMS Financial Report, Fiscal Year 2015," November 9, 2015.

10. Ibid.

11. U.S. Department of Agriculture, Food and Nutrition Service, "Supplemental Nutrition Assistance Program (SNAP), Monthly Data—National Level," 2012–2014 data, November 6, 2015.

12. U.S. Department of Agriculture, Food and Nutrition Service, "WIC Program, Monthly Data—National Level," August 2015 data, November 6, 2015.

13. See generally the U.S. Department of Education's financial aid website, https://studentaid.ed.gov/sa/.

14. Congressional Budget Office, "Temporary Assistance for Needy Families: Spending and Policy Options," January 2015.

15. Jessica Hathaway, "Tax Credits for Working Families: Earned Income Tax Credit (EITC)," National Conference of State Legislatures, data for 2013, September 22, 2015.

16. U.S. Department of Labor, Office of Unemployment Insurance, Division of Fiscal and Actuarial Services, "President's Budget FY 2016," February 2, 2015.

17. National Academy of Social Insurance, "Workers' Compensation: Benefits, Coverage, and Costs, 2012," August 2014

THIRTEEN

Legal Issues

You're surrounded by legal issues. The apartment you live in is governed by a legal contract called a lease. The car you own was purchased with borrowed money, requiring a loan agreement and security interest, both of which are legal documents. The part-time job you have during the summer requires that your employer follow numerous legal rules about how to pay and treat you in the workplace. The song you just illegally downloaded from the Internet is protected by federal copyright laws and might subject you to a lawsuit for damages by the song's owner. Law intersects with money all the time, so you need to manage the legal risks in your financial life and avoid the perils of our legal system.

CONTRACTS

Contracts are everywhere. Each time you buy something at a store you've actually created and fulfilled a contract for purchase. Your smartphone is governed by a very lengthy (and one-sided) contract with your cell phone company. Your enrollment papers at college are a contract. So are the terms and conditions of your health insurance. Even using your credit card or debit card is subject to a lengthy contract. Just about every type of consumer transaction that takes place in the United States is controlled by a contract that has the force of law behind it. But what *is* a contract, anyway?

A contract is simply an agreement between two or more parties. Your landlord agrees to let you live in an apartment, you agree to pay rent. BlueCross agrees to pay for your medical care, you agree to pay the insurance premium and follow their procedures. MBNA agrees to let you use its Visa card to make purchases, you agree to pay the bills it sends you. A contract imposes obligations, and there must be something of value exchanged between the parties to make a contract enforceable (this is called *consideration*). A promise to do something in the future, for example, is something of value. So is money. If you promise to babysit for the neighbors next week and they promise to pay you, those promises form a contract. If your brother pays you $10 not to tell your parents about something he did wrong and you accept the money, that's also a contract, and you're obligated to keep his secret.

Besides consideration (the exchange of something of value), you need an agreement to make a contract enforceable. This means both an offer to do something and an acceptance of that offer, with both parties having the same basic understanding about what the agreement requires. There also has to be sufficient specificity about the terms of a contract to make it binding. For example, if you agree to sell your friend your apartment furniture when you move out, but there's no discussion of price, you don't have a contract. Price is almost always a critical term of a contract. Most contracts *don't* have to be in writing to be enforceable, but it's a good idea because *oral contracts* are very difficult to prove, and in some places the law allows only a short period of time to resolve oral contract disputes. Some types of contracts always have to be in writing to be valid, such as those involving real estate.

Let's say you have a cell phone contract that offers a reduced price on a new smartphone in exchange for a two-year commitment to buy the monthly service, and you decide to change providers. Or you have a simple written agreement with your roommates about your lease, and one of them decides to move out early. In these cases, if the contractual obligations aren't met, the person violating the terms is said to have *breached* the contract. The injured party has the right, but not the obligation, to initiate a lawsuit to get compensation for any damages the breach of contract caused. The concept of damages is important: if a breach of contract hasn't caused any loss, there's no point in suing somebody. In the roommate example, if another acceptable roommate is quickly found to take over the rental obligation, there are no damages: no harm, no foul, as they say.

Whenever you're a party to a contract you should take it seriously. As a consumer you'll often be presented with a lengthy contract in tiny print you'd rather not read, but by ignoring the terms you're taking a risk. If you don't meet your obligations under the contract, and the other party sues you, you'll probably lose: courts generally enforce the terms of contracts, even when they're one-sided and seem unfair. These one-sided contracts—where you don't realistically have a chance to negotiate terms (for example, a cell phone contract, bank account forms, or most leases)—are called *contracts of adhesion,* and ambiguous terms are usually interpreted against the parties that wrote these contracts. Still, that's little comfort: if you get sued you've already lost, because you need to pay your lawyer. Many consumer contracts require *arbitration* to settle any disputes, instead of lawsuits. Arbitration is like an informal trial, resolving disputes more quickly and at lower cost than using courts; it also tends to favor business interests over the consumer, and large damage awards almost never result.

PRENUPTIAL AGREEMENTS

A special form of contract that fascinates young people is a prenuptial agreement, perhaps because they're common among celebrities and featured in the media. A *prenuptial agreement* is a contract entered into before marriage by the couple that describes the financial and other arrangements that would take place in the event of divorce. Unfortunately, divorce is the outcome of many marriages: it's estimated that between 40 percent and 50 percent will eventually end in divorce. The divorce rate varies substantially depending on education and age: older and more educated couples have lower divorce rates, with perhaps only one-third ending in divorce. So that's a pretty good success rate.[1]

For most young people contemplating their first marriage, with no children, little accumulated wealth, and no unusual assets they're bringing to the marriage, a prenuptial agreement is unnecessary. As couples wait longer to get married, they accumulate more assets. If one spouse is wealthy, has a family business, a second marriage is involved, or there are children from previous relationships, then a prenuptial agreement makes more sense. These agreements identify the property each spouse brings into the marriage and determine how those assets and personal items will be divided in a divorce. They can address how future income from a business or wealth from a bequest will be handled. They can determine in advance any support payments (alimony) that one spouse might receive from the other. These agreements can even protect one spouse from the preexisting debts of the other. The one thing prenuptial agreements typically can't do is predetermine child custody and support, since courts always consider the best interests of the children regardless of what a prenuptial agreement says.

Like all contracts a prenuptial agreement needs to be taken seriously, because a properly written agreement will be enforced by the courts. Both spouses should have separate lawyers review the agreement well before the actual marriage. There must be full and accurate disclosure of all premarital assets. The parties should be of sound mind and body when signing the agreement, and some states even require a minimum waiting period before it can be signed. If a couple chooses not to have a prenuptial agreement, state law will govern the financial arrangements in a divorce. Absent a prenuptial agreement, spouses usually have the right to share in all the property acquired during the marriage, are jointly responsible for any debts, and will share in the control and disposition of marital property.

LIABILITY

Liability arises when a person becomes responsible to pay for something she did, or is responsible for, that causes another person some damage. Without the law, a loss remains where it falls. The law uses liability to shift a loss from the party that suffers it, to another party deemed responsible or who caused it. In almost all cases of liability we're talking about money: money pays for harms that people suffer, even if they're not obviously economic. For example, if someone injures another person in an accident, she might be responsible for the medical costs of the injured person as well as the pain and suffering the injured person endured. Both types of harm must be reduced to a monetary figure, because that's how the system works.

A party who breaks (breaches) a contract will be responsible to the other party—liable—for the harm resulting because of the breach (also called *damages*). A court determines the amount of damages, attempting to compensate for *economic loss* and make it as if the breach hadn't occurred. Where a person suffers physical and emotional harm, courts can also award money for *pain and suffering*. In unusual circumstances where someone engages in atrocious conduct, the court may award *punitive damages* as well, to punish the bad conduct and set an example for other people to deter them from similar wrongdoing. All forms of damages are determined as a dollar amount. In certain disputes, particularly those involving real estate contracts, a court can award *specific performance* as a remedy: the parties must complete the contract as intended, and not rely on money damages. In the U.S. court system, each side usually pays its own legal bills, although in unusual circumstances, and under some laws, the losing party may have to pay the legal bills of both sides.

There are certain areas of the law where wrongdoing isn't required for a party to be liable for losses, called *strict liability*. Strict liability is in contrast to "negligence," where someone's carelessness caused a harm. If you're injured by a defective product, the manufacturer is strictly liable for any harm you suffer, regardless of how reckless you may be in using that product. Other areas where strict liability applies are for damages from unusually dangerous activities (such as using explosives or working with dangerous chemicals), harm from keeping wild animals, and damage to someone else's property.

PROPERTY

Property is valuable, whether it's a financial asset, your home, or personal belongings. Property can also be *intangible*, such as a business trademark (iPhone, Kleenex, Toyota) or rights under a contract. All of these things are property under the law. If you own property it's yours, and nobody can take it from you unless there's a legal basis. You can give away or even destroy your own property if you like (it's just usually not a good idea to do so). Many people don't stop to think about it, but the protection of property rights in the United States is one of our country's most important values. Experts who study the success and failure of economies across the world have shown that countries with strong property rights have greater economic success. It's such an important right that the U.S. Constitution protects property in several different ways, prohibiting the taking of property by government without due process and fair compensation, and limiting laws that interfere with contracts, for example.

The law distinguishes between *real property* (real estate and buildings), *personal property* (anything you can touch or hold that isn't attached to land), and *intangible property* (things that have no physical form). The basic rule of property ownership applies regardless of the form of property: you can't use property owned by another without permission. Taking someone else's property without consent is theft, which is punishable as a crime and can also make you financially liable for the value of the property you took. Nor can you damage the property of another without being held liable: strict liability applies here, so even if you didn't intend to cause damage, or caused damage despite acting with great care, you're still responsible. Any interference with another person's property is a *trespass*, regardless of what type of property is involved, and you can be liable for this, as well. You may see a person's land posted with "No Trespassing" signs, but even without the posting, you can't legally come onto someone else's land without permission.

INTELLECTUAL PROPERTY

Property that comes from the expression of ideas is called *intellectual property* (IP). These ideas can be represented as words, music, images, inventions, software code, formulas, and other works resulting from creative effort. The three primary forms of IP are copyrights, trademarks, and patents, and although each is quite different, they share the same fundamental protection. In order to promote the formation of these creative works, the law grants the owner *exclusive ownership* rights in the IP she created—a legal monopoly. Without this protection of intellectual property, there would be less incentive to create these works. The legal monopoly lasts for a fixed period of time (except a trademark, which can last indefinitely), but as long as you own the IP, nobody else can use it without your permission.

Copyright applies to anything written such as poems and novels, and also to music, photographs, paintings, movies, videos, radio broadcasts, television programs, live performances, and the like, whether they're published or not. The law prohibits copying any of these artistic works without permission, and owners of these works also control any performance, adaptation (called a *derivative work*), public display, electronic transmission, or sale. In the United States, a copyright begins the moment a creative expression is made: when the video is filmed, the book is written, the photograph is taken. No further action is required to create the copyright, but completing the registration process with the U.S. Copyright Office, and marking the work with a copyright symbol, grants certain legal advantages in a dispute. But your copyright exists as an inherent part of the creative work itself. For works created after 1978, the copyright lasts for the life of the author plus 70 years (it lasts for a different term if the work was anonymous, made before 1978, or made under a contract). When the copyright expires, the work enters the *public domain*, and anyone can copy or use it as she wishes. Not everything can be copyrighted, however: we don't permit titles, recipes, or geographic names to have copyrights.

The entertainment industry has gone after people who illegally downloaded music and movies, saddling them with thousands of dollars of fines and threatened jail time in the hope of deterring illegal downloading. That doesn't seem to have worked. Still, it takes money, time, and talent to create music and films, and when someone downloads those works without permission or payment, that's stealing. It's wrong and illegal, even if it's largely tolerated. If producers of music and film (for example) don't get paid, they won't be able to keep making their art for long. In the world of music, a longstanding method of paying the owners of copyright for their works has been the use of intermediary organizations to collect payments from broadcasters and send money to the owners as royalties. The American Society of Composers, Authors, and Publishers (ASCAP) and Broadcast Music, Inc. (BMI), are the two leading collectives that almost every business, restaurant, bar, radio station, TV network, website, and mobile app deals with so they can play music legally. These "broadcasters" pay various fees to ASCAP and BMI, which track how often each song is played and send royalties to the composers, songwriters, lyricists, and music publishers that own the music. The rates for some of these royalties (including the rates for Internet radio) are set by a government body called the Copyright Royalty Board.

An important limit on copyright is *fair use*. It would be impossible, and bad for creativity and free expression, if an owner of a copyrighted work could limit commentary about it such as criticism and parody. The concept of fair use allows the public certain access to copyrighted works. For example, making a single copy of a magazine article, inviting a few friends over to watch a movie you rented, recording a television program to watch later, and posting a few brief quotes from another publication on your Facebook page are all examples of fair use. What they have in common is that none of these uses makes money for the user. Unfortunately there's no clear-cut definition of what's permitted, but there are four factors to consider: the purpose of the use (non-commercial is better); the nature of the work (non-fiction has less copyright protection); how much you use (less is better); and its effect (whether it really interferes with the owner's value). One thing that's *not* fair use is the incorporation of one work into another: any adaptations, modifications, or derivatives of an original work must get permission from the original owner.

A *trademark* is any image, symbol, word, or combination that businesses use as a brand name or other identifier. A trademark (or a service mark) distinguishes one product, service, or business from another. The goal of trademarks is to prevent consumer confusion: trademarks distinguish one company from another, one brand from another, one service from another. The iPad is a trademark of Apple; the bitten apple symbol is another of its trademarks. The brand Hollister, the embroidered moose symbol, and the A&F logo are all trademarks of Abercrombie & Fitch Co. An owner develops a trademark right by using the mark in commerce; you can protect a clever trademark without using it in commerce only for a short period of time. Firms often invest a lot of money to develop and build a brand represented by a trademark, thereby creating substantial value. Normally a trademark lasts as long as it's in use, potentially forever. You can register a trademark with the federal government through the U.S. Patent and Trademark Office (USPTO) and gain additional legal protections in the event of a dispute; the registration lasts ten years and can be renewed indefinitely, so long as the mark remains in use. Each state also has laws that grant state-level trademark protections.

Patents are the most complicated form of intellectual property. A *patent* is an invention that can take one of three forms: a new plant (a biological organism that uses photosynthesis), a new design (of something that can be manufactured), or offering new utility (a new or improved process, machine, material, or object). Novelty is the key to a patent, but a patent will be issued only if the invention is also useful (actually works) and non-obvious (changing a color is obvious). These requirements are sometimes very difficult to interpret, and the initial determination is made by over 7,500 highly-trained patent examiners who work for the USPTO and review the history of similar inventions. You can't patent an idea: you must have a complete description of the invention to seek a patent. Sometimes a patent is issued for something that many people think is obvious or even trivial. An important example is the one-click ordering system developed by Amazon and patented as a business process. The USPTO issued Amazon a patent, and despite much criticism and legal challenge, it has been upheld in this country. In Europe, however, this patent has been repeatedly denied (the European Union has its own patent laws). Once issued, a U.S. patent lasts for 20 years and can't be renewed, although many companies modify their inventions and seek additional patents on the improvements, thereby extending the practical length of their original patents.

Not everybody protects their intellectual property with a copyright or patent. A patent requires that a complete description of the invention be published for the whole world to see, and after 20 years anybody can use it. Secrecy is another way to protect your inventions: Coca Cola guards its recipe for cola instead of using a patent, and many food companies keep their recipes confidential. We call valuable business information that companies protect by secrecy a *trade secret*. This can include customer names, product or service prices, designs, and formulas. Each state has laws that protect trade secrets, and employees can't use this information for their own benefit or disclose it to new employers when they change jobs. You may be asked to sign a *confidentiality agreement* when you get a new job (sometimes called a *non-disclosure agreement* or NDA), promising to maintain the secrecy of your employer's confidential information. These agreements are generally enforceable and should be taken seriously by anyone who signs them.

It's often said that obtaining a patent, copyright, or trademark is simply a "license to sue." This means that an owner of IP must take affirmative steps to enforce its rights, typically by filing a lawsuit. Lawsuits are costly, time consuming, and inherently risky. In some cases the winning party can collect its attorneys' fees from the losing side, but that's rare. There aren't many lawsuits over small infractions of copyright or trademark law, and patent owners know that litigation includes the risk that the original patent can be challenged and possibly overturned. If you're the creator of IP, you'll want the greatest protection; if you're a user of IP, you'll want it to be in the public domain. Whatever side you'll be on, remember that IP is valuable; it takes time and money to develop; its ownership should be respected; and it's expensive to protect.

ACCIDENTS

Accidents happen all the time. Injuries from serious accidents can lead to lost income (the injured person can't work), medical expenses, emotional trauma, and problems with daily living. Our legal system searches for the person at fault; after all, if there was an accident, it must have been someone's fault, right? If you're responsible for your own accident (you tripped over a bag you left on the floor inside your house), the law stays out of it. But if another party causes the accident—an inattentive driver rolls through a stop sign and clips your bumper—then the law of *torts* might intervene. (The word is from the Latin *tortum*, meaning "injustice.") Otherwise, the losses from an accident remain where they fall.

Tort law covers injuries to property and people, and requires four elements to shift liability from one party to another. The first element is *duty*: you must have some duty to the party harmed. For example, absent a special relationship, a person generally has no obligation under the law to help another person who's injured. It might be mean or selfish not to help, but there's no legal duty to provide aid. The second element of a tort is *breach*: once a duty is established, did someone violate that duty? In general, each person has a duty toward another not to act in a careless manner. If your careless act leads to an accident, you'll have breached your duty to act with care. The third element is *causation*: did your breach of a duty lead to an injury? Suppose you get food poisoning from a restaurant and your doctor misdiagnoses you, sending you home untreated. Is the doctor liable for your suffering? No: the cause of your suffering was the food poisoning. The law excuses a remote causation: an injury that results from an unlikely combination of events won't usually meet the standard. (The concept of causation in the law can be very complicated, and is often decided on a case-by-case basis.) Finally, the last element of a tort is *damages*: even if all the other elements are met, you must have suffered actual harm to bring a successful legal action. Let's say you bump into an unoccupied car while trying to park: if the other car is fine, no tort action will succeed.

The heart of most tort cases is *negligence*, whether the defendant acted with sufficient care under the circumstances in order to be liable. The law applies a fictitious "reasonable person" standard and asks how that person *should have* behaved under the circumstances, a determination often made by juries. Without negligence the law doesn't typically find liability. It's possible for an accident to happen where everyone is blameless, or where both parties are equally at fault: someone has an allergic reaction to a medicine, or two people rushing somewhere both collide on a sidewalk. Our society has become so lawsuit oriented (*litigious*), however, that we always expect someone else to pay for an accident. Even reckless victims can prevail in lawsuits today.

Certain intentional harms are also torts, such as libel, slander, and trespass to property. *Libel* is a published falsehood that injures a person's reputation; *slander* is the same thing done by spoken word (both are forms of *defamation*). The statement must be false: truth is an absolute defense to libel or slander. These actions are rare because they're so difficult to win under our legal system, where we value freedom of the media. Public figures (such as politicians or celebrities) have an even harder time winning defamation cases, because the law requires that the statement was made *knowing* it was false, or with a "reckless indifference to the truth." Not every country reveres free speech the way we do: libel cases in the United Kingdom, for example, require the *publisher* to prove that the statement is *true*, not like the U.S. where the subject must prove the allegation is false. In the age of social media and online bullying, beware: libel law still applies. Even worse, basic liability insurance doesn't cover these actions.

CIVIL LITIGATION

Our legal system separates civil disputes (disagreements involving people or businesses) from criminal matters (violations of law that are prosecuted by the government). A criminal prosecution is expensive: you'll need a lawyer (although if you're poor the court will hire one for you at no charge), and if you're convicted of a crime you may pay a fine or go to jail, during which time you'll be unable to work or attend school, and after which you'll find it harder to get a good job. Moral of the story: don't break the law. This section, however, is focused on civil litigation, carrying out a lawsuit involving individuals or businesses. Parties that lose in a civil matter don't go to jail, instead they pay money to the winning party.

The state and federal governments each operate their own court systems. The federal courts have the power to hear only certain types of cases; otherwise the cases must go through the state courts. Each system has several levels of courts. In the federal system, the lowest court is called District Court, also called a trial court, where disputes originate. After a District Court decision, an unhappy party may appeal to the Court of Appeals, and after that to the Supreme Court, although that court hears few appeals each year. (The federal government also operates specialized court systems for bankruptcy, taxes, military justice, and federal agencies.)

States use trial courts such as *municipal courts* and *county courts*, depending on the type of dispute or amount of money involved. Most places also have a *small claims court* for low-dollar disputes where you don't need a lawyer and the procedures are informal. Like the federal system, each state has an *appellate court system* as well as a court for final appeals, usually called some variation of "Supreme Court" such as the Supreme Judicial Court (Massachusetts) or the Supreme Court (California). Oddly enough, in the New York the trial courts are called Supreme Court and the highest court is called the Court of Appeals. The state systems also operate courts for special matters, dealing with probate (for wills and estates), family law, the environment, and landlord-tenant disputes.

Instituting a lawsuit must follow a formal process. A civil action begins with a *complaint*, where a *plaintiff* explains what the other party did wrong, how they've been harmed, and what remedy they want the court to provide. Importantly, every complaint must have a basis in the law; it's not enough to be harmed or unhappy about something. The *defendant* has a certain amount of time to respond, through a formal document called an *answer*. (If the defendant doesn't respond, the plaintiff can seek a *default judgment*, and the case is over.) After the answer the parties enter into *discovery*, where they seek information from each other following a structured process. Once discovery has been completed the parties have a *trial*, where each side presents its evidence and arguments, after which a judge or a jury determines what facts are true (often the facts are disputed), applies the law, and decides who wins. An unhappy party can appeal, but it must identify specific errors made by the trial court and meet strict deadlines for submitting the proper forms. The winner of a lawsuit has to enforce whatever judgment the court awarded, which usually involves collecting money from the other party. If the losing party is unwilling to pay, the court can order law enforcement officials to *garnish* the wages or seize the property of the losing party.

The U.S. Constitution grants the right to a jury trial for all criminal matters and larger civil matters, and this right applies in state courts as well. A *jury* is a group of citizens (usually chosen from a list of registered voters) who come together temporarily to participate in the trial. They hear evidence and arguments from both parties, listen to the judge explain the law, and take everything they've heard into account to make a decision. In a *bench trial*, the judge alone hears all the evidence and makes the final decision about who wins and how much. In rare cases a judge can overturn a jury decision in a civil trial about who won or the amount of damages, but never in a criminal case. In federal courts for civil matters there can be 6 to 12 jurors, and the decision must be unanimous. In state courts the number of jurors can vary, and some states allow majority or super-majority verdicts (always, and everywhere in the United States, jury decisions in criminal trials must be unanimous). If a jury fails to get enough votes for a decision it's said to be *hung*, and a *mistrial* is declared. The parties may start over if they wish.

Every type of claim has a *statute of limitations* setting a time limit to file a lawsuit, or lose the opportunity forever. If an action for breach of contract must be brought within 6 years of the contract's violation, any lawsuit brought after that time will be dismissed, no matter how strong the case. Each state has its own statute of limitations: for written contracts in most states it's between 3 and 10 years, for torts in most states it's between 2 and 6 years.[2] The party initiating the lawsuit almost always has the *burden of proof*: the plaintiff must convince the judge or jury that more evidence favors her case than the defendant's. The defendant may mount a defense but is under no obligation to do so, and in fact the case can be dismissed at an early stage of the trial if the judge concludes the plaintiff hasn't made its case. In a *class action*, a large number of people suffering a similar harm combine together to bring the case as a single lawsuit, instead of initiating numerous individual cases about the same thing. Class actions are often used by consumers against large companies.

LAW IN THE WORKPLACE

The federal government through the Occupational Safety and Health Administration (*OSHA*) protects the health and safety of workers on the job. It has issued voluminous regulations governing safety in the workplace, from specific rules by industry (for example, safety equipment to be used at construction sites, proper maintenance of electrical equipment) to general standards for every business (for example, access to information about chemicals used in the workplace, the required use of safety glasses, boots, and gloves). Businesses must record and report any workplace accident. OSHA officials make regular, unannounced inspections and often fine businesses for rule violations. The Family Medical Leave Act (*FMLA*) requires employers to offer unpaid leave so workers can address their own medical conditions (including childbirth), or aid a close family member, and be able to return to their jobs following the leave.

Federal law prevents *employment discrimination* based on race, gender, religion, national origin, physical or mental disability, and age through enforcement by the Equal Employment Opportunity Commission (*EEOC*). Employees and job applicants with these characteristics are referred to as members of a *protected class*. Workplace discrimination means treating someone unfairly because of these characteristics, such as denying a promotion or requiring longer work hours. Except in a few cases these laws apply only to employers with 15 or more employees. The age discrimination rules protect people age 40 and over, so this law won't necessarily help you—yet. Provisions protecting disabled people require employers to make *reasonable accommodations* in the workplace (even if it costs money) so disabled employees can do their jobs. It's illegal for an employer to retaliate against an employee who makes a complaint under one of these anti-discrimination laws. Simply being in a protected class and suffering a disappointment at work (not getting a raise, receiving workplace discipline, losing your job) isn't enough to win a case: the employer just needs to show it had some legitimate basis for its action. In practice, these cases are hard to win.

Sex discrimination is one of the most frequently contested areas in all of employment law. Special rules protect pregnant women, and other laws require equal pay for equal work by employees of different genders. Laws also prevent *sexual harassment* in the workplace, such as unwelcome sexual advances or conditioning job progress on sexual activity. A *hostile work environment*, such as nude pictures on the walls or frequent use of sexually explicit language, can also constitute sexual harassment. An employee experiencing harassment is required to notify her employer, who must take action to stop the harassment. Although the sex discrimination rules were designed to protect women, they can also be used by men: the law requires equal treatment regardless of gender. There's no federal law that prevents discrimination based on sexual orientation, although current law has been interpreted to provide protection to gay and transgendered employees, and some states and localities have passed these types of nondiscrimination laws.

Labor unions are organizations that represent groups of workers collectively to bargain over wages and working conditions. Unions negotiate contracts with individual employers or on an industry-wide basis (such as in the automobile industry). If unions are unhappy with an employer, their members can strike against that employer, which means they stop working until the dispute is resolved. The union movement began in earnest in the early 1900s in the manufacturing sector and with skilled trades (electricians, plumbers, welders), and grew rapidly under federal labor laws passed in the 1930s. However, union membership in the private sector has been falling for decades, and today fewer than 7 percent of private-sector workers are in labor unions. In the government sector, however, union membership has been steady for decades at around 35 percent of workers (teachers, fireman, police).[3] Whether unions are a positive force in our economy has been hotly debated. Union membership is usually voluntary, so if you become employed by an organization where workers are in a union, it will be your own decision whether to join.

Many young people care about workplace privacy, especially for electronic communication (Is there any other kind?), and government has been regulating only around the edges here. Despite the value our culture and law place on privacy, there are few privacy protections in the workplace. The good news: your life outside of work is generally off-limits to your employer, you can't usually be forced to take a lie detector test, your medical records are private, and so are your personal phone calls. That's about it. All property owned by your employer, including computers and phones, can be monitored and searched, so your work e-mail account, for example, is fair game. Employers can require drug tests, block websites, prohibit the use of social media at work, monitor you with video cameras, listen in on business calls, search you for good cause, and require you to follow numerous policies as a condition of employment. Most businesses have lengthy employee policy manuals that include provisions about workplace privacy: if your employer has a manual, read it carefully.

Many businesses invest in training and rely on a quality workforce to build competitive advantage, and they also want to protect their intellectual property. Because of this, employers increasingly require their staff to sign *non-compete agreements*. Non-compete agreements limit the future jobs you can take, by prohibiting a former employee from working for a competitor. Because working is such a fundamental right, courts have taken a dim view of these agreements, and in a few states they're simply not enforceable. Where non-compete agreements are allowed, they must be narrowly written to protect a legitimate interest of the employer, such as a trade secret or confidential information. Also, they generally won't be enforced if they go too far in geographic scope, the job activity prevented, or time limit. For example, a worldwide ban for ten years from working in any capacity in the electronics industry won't be enforced, but a prohibition for six months from working in New England as a programmer for a direct competitor in the software industry probably will be. If you're asked to sign a non-compete at your workplace, you should consult an attorney first.

USING LAWYERS

Unless you're very lucky, you'll need a personal lawyer several times in your life. How do you find the right attorney? Many local bar associations (a professional association of attorneys) run a referral service, and often employer's benefit plans provide for free phone consultations with lawyers to get you started. Asking your friends and business associates can also be a good resource. Large international law firms with thousands of lawyers are great for businesses but typically don't provide the services you'll need for personal matters. Individuals should use local and regional law firms, including solo practitioners. Not every legal matter requires a lawyer—you can form a corporation, take a matter to small claims court, prepare a health care proxy, even write a will (or get it ready for a lawyer's review) without hiring a lawyer.

Lawyers are bound by a strict code of ethics requiring them (among other things) to disclose their fees up front. For some matters, especially personal injury cases, lawyers use a *contingency fee*, where they take as their fee 30 to 40 percent of any award you win as a plaintiff, and they even pay the up-front costs of the lawsuit (court filing fees, compiling evidence, travel expenses). With a contingency fee you only pay the lawyer if you win. Otherwise lawyers usually charge an hourly rate, and often they won't charge you for an initial consultation (ask about that before your first meeting). Meeting with a lawyer can be intimidating, but ask as many questions as you want about the attorney's background and experience. Any information you share with an attorney is a secret and protected by the *attorney-client privilege* (unless you're planning a crime); tell your attorney everything about your legal problem, otherwise you'll impede her ability to help you. Legal matters can be complex and emotionally demanding, so you want an attorney with whom you feel comfortable, who has experience with problems like yours, and who has a track record of success.

NOTES

1. Claire Cain Miller, "The Divorce Surge Is Over, but the Myth Lives On," *New York Times*, December 2, 2014.

2. Matthiesen, Wickert & Lehrer, S.C., "Statutes of Limitations for All 50 States," November 9, 2015.

3. Andrew O. Smith, *Sand in the Gears: How Public Policy Has Crippled American Manufacturing*, Chapter 8 (Dulles, VA: Potomac Books, 2013).

FOURTEEN

Growing Older

As you get older, your financial needs and interests change. If you're lucky to have two parents in your life today, that will eventually change—both of your parents will probably be gone while you're still of working age. Deaths impact the financial lives of families, sometimes dramatically. And at any time you may confront health problems, yours or your family's. Finally, far down the road is retirement, when you stop working in your main career or occupation. Retirement planning should start early. It's never too late to make changes in your life to get ready for retirement, but the earlier you start, the more comfortable your retirement will be.

RETIREMENT PLANS

Older workers possess useful experience, valuable human capital, and skills that are often difficult to replace. By the time some people reach their mid-60s, however, their energy levels, memories, physical stamina, and interest in work start to decline. Most people don't want to work forever. They eventually enter *retirement*, finding other activities to occupy their golden years. Financially, retirement means your work income is eliminated or reduced dramatically, so you rely on other income sources to maintain your standard of living. Retirement is a relatively recent phenomenon: until the middle of the twentieth century, most people worked until they died. When the Social Security system started in 1937, there was little need for it. Today, however, retirement planning is central to your long-term financial security.

If you go to a four-year college after high school and then enter the workforce on a full-time basis, you'll work 45 years or more before you retire. That seems far away, but since you can expect to live into your late 70s or early 80s, a retirement plan needs to provide income for about 20 years. If you start planning for retirement early in your career, those 20 years can be financially secure, otherwise your later years might be fraught with uncertainty and money worries. Even with poor planning, it's unlikely you'll spend retirement in poverty, as Social Security provides a safety net. But you'd like to do better than the bare minimum, wouldn't you?

Many employers sponsor workplace retirement plans, where the employee saves a portion of her earnings and controls the investment of the money. These retirement plans offer investment options from insured bank CDs to stock index mutual funds, and the employee owns all the money she contributes to the account forever. Most employers also contribute money on your behalf, for example, matching a portion of what you yourself put in. These are called *defined-contribution* plans because the employee determines the contribution; the most common type is called a 401(k) plan, after the section of the tax code that covers it. Workers in nonprofits have similar plans called 403(b) plans, and federal government workers have Thrift Savings Plans (TSPs). These retirement plans offer two forms of tax advantage: none of the money you or your employer contributes is subject to income tax when you receive it, and earnings inside the retirement account (like dividends or interest) aren't taxed until later. When you retire and start spending the money, everything you take out of the plan becomes taxable income. You've *deferred* paying taxes for many years, allowing the money to grow inside your retirement plan. That's why these plans are considered tax advantaged.

For people without workplace retirement plans, commercial banks and mutual fund companies offer individual retirement accounts (IRAs) that provide similar tax advantages. By investing a portion of your earnings in an IRA, you receive the same immediate tax benefit (wage earnings you contribute aren't taxed) and the same continuing tax benefit (earnings inside your IRA plan aren't taxed until later). When you reach retirement and withdraw the funds, you pay income tax on everything you withdraw. The IRA plan sponsor determines what investment options are available, similar to most 401(k) plans, from government-issued securities to individual stocks. The big difference is that there's no employer contribution to an IRA. All the money comes from you.

One form of retirement plan doesn't offer an immediate tax deduction but does allow all the income to accumulate tax-free. These plans all feature the name "Roth" in their descriptions, after Senator William V. Roth, Jr. of Delaware, who championed the legislation that created these plans. For Roth plans, you contribute your money *after* you've paid the income taxes on your earnings. For example, if you start with $3,000 to put into an IRA and pay 20 percent in income taxes to local, state, and federal governments, you'll have $2,400 left to put into a Roth IRA, versus the full $3,000 available for a non-Roth IRA. The difference is at retirement: you'll *never* pay any income tax on any money you pull out of the Roth retirement plan, whereas every penny you withdraw from a non-Roth plan is subject to income tax. So you lose one tax advantage but gain another: none of the accumulated investment earnings is *ever* taxed. It's not a deferral, but a permanent tax avoidance. Roth retirement plans aren't always the better choice, but they've become very popular.

You don't need a tax advantage to save for retirement. Tax rules limit how much money you can contribute to any tax-advantaged plan, depending on your age and income, and there's always uncertainty about future tax rates. If tax rates are higher when you retire than while you're working, the tax advantages of these plans will decrease or disappear. Still, financial advisors recommend that you put as much money into tax-advantaged retirement plans as the tax laws permit. Beyond that you can use any investment you want to save for retirement. As one example, your home can be a large retirement asset. Most people have paid off their mortgage debt by the time they retire, and their home may have appreciated in value for many years. If you decide to relocate or downsize, there's an opportunity to recover some equity in your home and use that as retirement income. *Reverse mortgages* allow a homeowner to remain in her principal residence and borrow against the home equity to receive regular payments. Unfortunately, reverse mortgages have been associated with fraud and abuse, so if you or a loved one ever considers such an option, seek third-party advice and proceed very cautiously.

PENSIONS

Another type of retirement plan is a *pension*. While the term *pension* can refer to many forms of retirement payments, its proper use describes a fixed retirement payment (that may adjust for inflation) made by a third party that ceases upon death. The pension plan itself relies for funding on a large pool of assets managed by professional advisors. To create this pool of assets employers contribute to the plan for many years. The plan invests the funds for long-term returns, so when those workers retire there will be money available to pay retirement benefits. The amount of the retirement payment is usually determined by the salary of the person when they were working. For example, a pension might pay two-thirds of a person's annual income at the time she retires, or it might be a percentage of the worker's average wages over the most recent five years before retirement. The recipient of the pension doesn't own a fund or have any rights to the assets that generate the retirement income. When the pension recipient dies (or in some cases when the surviving spouse dies), the pension payment ceases.

Pensions are called *defined-benefit* plans because of the commitment to make specific payments to the retiree. The pension plan itself must make sure there are enough assets in the plan to pay all the future retirement benefits, regardless of economic circumstances. The pension plan bears the risk of investment losses, unlike a defined-contribution retirement plan, where the owner of the account bears the risk of investment losses. On the other hand, if the investments perform well and someone dies owning a large defined-contribution retirement fund like a 401(k) or IRA, that money can pass to surviving family members. Pension plans are regulated by the government to make sure they have enough money to pay the benefits they promised, but as people live longer and companies struggle to make the payments necessary to fully fund the obligations, these plans have fallen out of favor.

Pensions are still used widely for retirement in state and local government, and the federal government offers a pension under the Federal Employee Retirement System.

Every pension plan has a sponsor that's responsible for the financial health of the plan. Sometimes the beneficiaries make payments to help fund the plan, but sponsors make the vast majority of pension fund contributions. Each year, *actuaries* make complicated calculations to estimate how the investments will perform many years into the future, how long beneficiaries will live, what benefits they'll receive, and whether new funding is required to make it all balance. If the plan doesn't have enough money to pay all the promised benefits, the plan sponsor—usually a private corporation, labor union, or government agency—is supposed to add even more money. If plan sponsors get into financial distress and can't make sufficient payments to keep the pension plan solvent, a federal insurance fund run by the Pension Benefit Guarantee Corporation will bail it out. When this happens, the beneficiaries almost always receive lower benefits than they were promised.

HOW MUCH DO YOU NEED?

If you follow all the advice in this book, it seems you're supposed to take most of the money you earn and save it. Save for a home. Save for starting a family or for sending your children to college. Save for vacations and for an emergency fund. You have to "save" to pay back your college loans. And now you're being told to save for retirement, and you've barely started your financial life. If you do all this saving, how can you spend a little and enjoy life? Unfortunately, you *do* have to save for all these financial goals in life, and there's no way to avoid it. Saving, after all, is simply delayed spending: you can spend it now or spend it later, after you've invested it and allowed your savings to grow. You should save during your productive work years, because once you reach retirement age, you'll have much less ability to keep earning money.

There's no one-size-fits-all answer to how much you should save for retirement. Financial advisors recommend you generate sufficient retirement income to provide a percentage of your pre-retirement income, say 60 or 70 percent, to last well beyond your expected lifespan. You don't want to run out of money at the end of your life, but it's not a simple analysis. In retirement you can expect large medical bills, even with Medicare's generous benefits to older Americans; estimates run at over $120,000 in total out-of-pocket expenses for the average individual retiree over her post-retirement lifetime.[1] On the other hand, you won't have to save out of your retirement income or, likely, pay off much debt. Most financial advisors suggest making your retirement a priority over other savings goals such as college funds for children, since they'll have time to take care of their own finances. Put yourself first.

A *fixed annuity* is a financial instrument that pays a predetermined amount of money for a period of years: the owner makes a payment up front and in return gets regular income from the annuity. The annuity can make payments for a set term, such as 10 or 15 years, or it can last for the life of the retiree (*life annuity*), in which case an insurance company assumes the financial risk of a beneficiary living a long time. On the other hand, someone *buying* a life annuity risks paying for the annuity up front and not living long enough to collect many payments. A pension payment is a form of life annuity. Each monthly payment from an annuity returns part of your principal and earnings on the remaining principal. You're spending down your assets, but if you plan well, you won't spend all your money during your lifetime. Where you control your own retirement funds such as in an IRA or 401(k) plan, you can create your own monthly payments that resemble a fixed annuity. Here's an example:

Let's say you're a 68-year-old woman about to retire. According to mortality tables, your expected lifespan is another 18 years, and since half of all 68-year-old women will live more than 18 additional years, you need a cushion.[2] Table 14.1 shows that if you have $500,000 in retirement savings earning 6 percent on average, you'll be able to generate $40,000 per year in retirement income for 24 years before running out of money, not counting your Social Security payments. That's not long enough: about one-quarter of women retiring at 68 will live past age 92, so you should plan to get lucky. If you're able to live on $35,000 per year in retirement (before Social Security benefits), that same $500,000 should last until you're over 101 years old (only a 1.5 percent chance of that). These annuity calculations are sensitive to the rate of return on your investments. If you make only 4 percent on your retirement assets, you'll need $610,000 to generate that same $40,000 per year for 24 years, or $640,000 to pay you $35,000 for 33 years. Using your retirement assets as an annuity can provide a reliable income stream in retirement, but you're spending down your savings, so be careful not to spend it all.

By starting your retirement savings early, you can make compounding a powerful tool. Table 14.2 illustrates how a small difference during your first 10 years of working can mean hundreds of thousands of dollars extra in retirement. Let's say you start working full-time at age 22 and save for retirement by putting $3,000 per year into an IRA. Alternatively, you enjoy yourself a bit more in your 20s and spend that money instead of saving it. Then, at age 32, you recognize the need for retirement savings and begin making your $3,000 annual contributions. How much of a difference will that 10-year delay make if you retire at age 70? At an average annual

Table 14.1   Annuity Payments

	Earning 6% Per Year	Earning 4% Per Year
Required Initial Value	$502,100	$610,000
Annual Payment	$40,007	$40,008
Number of Years	24	24
Required Initial Value	$502,100	$640,300
Annual Payment	$35,284	$35,283
Number of Years	33	33

Source: Author's analysis.

Table 14.2   Impact of 10 Years Extra Retirement Savings

Begin Savings	22 years old	32 years old
Retirement Age	70 years old	70 years old
Annual Savings	$3,000	$3,000
Annual Return	6%	6%
Value at Retirement	$769,694	$407,713

Source: Author's analysis.

investment return of 6 percent, our "early saver" will have nearly $770,000 at retirement, whereas our "late saver" will have just under $408,000. That $362,000 difference comes from the extra 10 years of saving just $3,000 per year in your early working years compounded during the later years; so start saving for retirement *now*.

WILLS AND ESTATES

Of every 100,000 20-year-old women living today, 99,499 of them will reach age 30, and 98,632 of those women will reach age 40.[3] So the chance of a young person dying is remote. When young people die it's usually from traffic accidents, poisoning, and suicide (in that order).[4] Besides the painful emotions among friends, family, and colleagues, there are important financial considerations associated with death, whether it's your own early demise or, as the natural order of things, when you lose your parents and grandparents. A *will* (also called a *last testament*) gives directions to survivors about how a person's property should be handled after they're gone. Wills can also provide other important instructions such as appointing guardians for minor children and identifying a final resting place.

Do you love your parents? Let's hope so, because if you're like most unmarried young people, you don't have a will, and if you die everything you own will go to your parents. This is called dying *intestate*, which is a fancy word that means you didn't have a will, and each state has rules that transfer your property to your family members when there's no will. In most states, your property goes to living family members in order of priority: first to any spouse; if no spouse, then to any children; if no children, then to any parents; if no parents, then to any siblings. So, if that's how you want your family to get your property, no need for a will. There are other good reasons to have a will, however. You can choose who receives your personal effects, such as your music collection or car. You can leave money to charity or to a special friend, perhaps a caregiver in later years (a *bequest*). The transfer of property under a will is subject to the tax treatment on lifetime gifts described in Chapter 11 (fewer than 1 percent of all deaths trigger any estate taxes). Having a will also simplifies legal proceedings, lowering the total cost and time of the whole process.

Most of your assets and debts at the time of death are part of your *estate*. Unfortunately, a debt doesn't die with you (although any obligation to perform a service is automatically extinguished). Some forms of property won't be part of your estate: joint bank accounts and real estate owned as a *joint tenancy*, for example, automatically become the property of the surviving owner after death. A will appoints an *executor* to administer your estate: to locate and manage property while the estate is being settled, pay off any taxes and other debts, file tax returns, communicate with government agencies and anyone having had business with you, identify and find all beneficiaries, resolve any uncertainties or disputes, transfer the property to the beneficiaries at the appropriate time, and carry out any other of the will's instructions including funeral arrangements. The executor also deals with the *probate court*, a specialized state court that handles all matters involving a person's will and estate, usually with assistance from an attorney.

An executor is often a beneficiary or close family member, such as a spouse, parent, or adult child, since it's helpful to have familiarity with the person who died (the *decedent*) and family members. A good executor will be trustworthy, organized, detail-oriented, and patient. There are many practical considerations, as well: you'll probably want someone living nearby who has the time available to do considerable work. It's an honor to serve as executor, but also a burden, as it can take 6 to 12 months to settle a typical estate. Executors receive payment for their services as set by state law. Most wills identify several alternative executors who will serve in the absence of the person ahead of them, so you have a backup if your first choice declines or is unavailable.

When should you make a will? Here are the triggers: acquiring substantial assets, having a child, or getting married. As soon as one of these things happens, make a will. It can't hurt to have a will before these trigger events, but it's an absolute necessity after them. You can do it yourself: online resources, books in libraries, and low-cost software can help. Because wills are perhaps the most important legal document any person ever signs, state laws require formalized procedures to properly *execute* a will. Typically, the person signing the will does so with a notary public present who verifies identity and places an official stamp on the signature page. Most states also require that multiple witnesses observe the signing of a will and sign the document at the same time. Many states recognize a will if it's completely handwritten and signed by the person who wrote it, called a *holographic will*, without a notarized signature or formal witnessing. Often these types of wills result from accidents or emergencies when death is imminent.

TRUSTS

A *trust* is a form of property ownership where the owner gives property away but creates restrictions on how it can be used. A *grantor* establishes a trust by transferring property, identifying the people she wants to use it (*beneficiaries*), and describing any conditions. Often, grantors create a trust in their wills (*testamentary trusts*), so after their death the specified property becomes the assets that the trust will then hold and manage. Grantors can also establish a trust while they're alive (*living trusts*). All it takes to establish a trust is simply a written document—a will or a trust agreement—that transfers the property to a *trustee*, who technically, and legally, owns all the property in the trust. A trustee has a duty to manage and distribute that property to the beneficiaries according to the grantor's instructions.

Grantors use trusts to give assets away but make sure they're handled wisely and carefully by the beneficiaries. Imagine a young couple who perish in a car accident, leaving behind an infant daughter and life insurance of $100,000. The couple's will might name a guardian for the orphan and establish a trust to hold and manage the life insurance money, since the child is too young to do this herself. Or consider a family business where the founder wants one child to control the business but other children to share in the wealth. Putting the shares of the business in a trust allows a single trustee to control the company, but all the beneficiaries can share the money it makes. A common thread in many trusts is giving substantial property to future generations, although many trusts have charitable purposes to support the grantors' favorite philanthropies. Trusts are often complex and require skilled legal and accounting advice to establish and administer.

There are also potential tax advantages in using trusts to transfer property to a next generation. The uniform gift and estate tax in the United States imposes a tax of up to 40 percent at the federal level and another 15 to 20 percent in some states. You can't avoid these taxes altogether using trusts, but you can reduce them. For example, if you transfer property that you expect to increase in value, the tax is calculated on the value when it's transferred to the trust, not years later when the beneficiaries might get the money. Certain trusts allow assets to benefit grandchildren, allowing one generation's worth of gift tax to be avoided, subject to limits. In order to receive tax advantages a trust must be *irrevocable*, meaning the trust arrangement can't be rescinded, otherwise the trust assets are considered part of the grantor's estate for tax purposes. Assets in a *revocable trust* are subject to estate taxes.

Donors can maintain privacy by using trusts because trusts don't go through probate courts, where all documents are public records. Another benefit of using trusts is that the trustee immediately controls the assets upon death. Because there's no probate court or executor involved, beneficiaries receive gifts or distributions without delay. Having assets in a trust can decrease the total costs of settling an estate, since some probate costs are based on the total size of the estate. Many donors use a revocable trust to control and use the assets during their lifetimes. A revocable trust allows donors to change the terms and beneficiaries right up until they die. The downside of revocable trusts for large estates is the potential tax bite.

Because the trustee is the legal owner, a trust can protect assets from liability or reckless spending. In many trusts the trustee is prohibited from making distributions to pay any judgments from lawsuits against a beneficiary. This may seem unjust, but consider that the trust may also belong to other beneficiaries, not just the one being sued. Sometimes beneficiaries are reckless, living beyond their means or behaving self-destructively. A trustee usually has discretion to limit payments to beneficiaries who use the money inappropriately, funding a drug habit, for example. Unless they're set up for charity, trusts can't last forever. Ultimately, the assets have to be distributed outright to the beneficiaries. But a properly written trust can control and protect assets for several generations.

HEALTH ISSUES

As you age, the likelihood increases that something will damage your health. You can contract diseases, maim body parts, suffer genetic disorders, impair the brain or senses, and lose bodily functions. Some of these problems are mild, others prevent full engagement in life, and some require significant accommodation. Disability insurance only provides replacement income for wages during a typical working life—it doesn't usually cover past age 65. Disability increases dramatically with age: around 35 percent of 65- to 74-year-olds have a disability that impacts their ability to perform a major life activity, rising to 40 percent at 75 to 84 and 55 percent over age 85.[5] Whether it's your own old age—so far away—or the old age of family members, health and disability will be a central concern during retirement.

You already know that the average retired person will incur increased health care costs, including doctor's visits, medications, and procedures. If you need long-term care in a nursing home or similar medical facility, that can cost $80,000 to $100,000 per year for a good program, which isn't covered by Medicare. Insurance for this is available, but expensive; if you're poor, Medicaid will pay for nursing homes. Fortunately, the chances of landing in a nursing home for more than a year are actually pretty low. Special nursing homes called *hospice* provide comfort to the terminally ill during their last few weeks of life. Assistance with daily living in the home may be necessary as we age, to provide help with meals, bathing, or getting dressed. These personal care activities are typically provided at relatively low cost on a part-time basis by nonmedical workers.

Experts recommend that all older people should have two legal documents that are readily available online or in books at the library. The first is a *living will*, but it's not a will at all and has nothing to do with a person's estate: it provides an *advance directive* for health care providers in the event the patient can't make her wishes known. For example, a living will can tell doctors you don't want to be resuscitated if you stop breathing (Do Not Resuscitate or DNR), you don't want a feeding tube (Do Not Intubate or DNI), or whether artificial life support should be used. It can also identify any treatments that should or shouldn't be performed if the circumstances arise. A living will helps family members understand the wishes of the patient at a time of great emotion or when it may not be possible to communicate. It's a good practice for older people to discuss the contents of a living will with their children well before needing serious medical treatment. You should ask your parents if they have one.

The second important document for older people is a *health care power of attorney* (HCPOA), sometimes called a *health-care proxy*. Alzheimer's disease and dementia particularly afflict the old. While some loss of memory is simply part of the aging process, dementia ultimately renders a person unable to make decisions about her own health. Incapacitation can occur in other ways, such as suffering a stroke or going into a coma. The HCPOA gives authority to another person (called an *agent*) to make all medical decisions for the patient, once medical staff has concluded that the patient can't decide for herself. Thus, the agent should be chosen carefully. All HCPOAs must comply with federal rules governing patient privacy. Sometimes an older person grants a *durable power of attorney*, authorizing a trusted relative or close friend to handle all financial affairs on behalf of that person, such as banking, bill payment, and investment management.

FAMILY OBLIGATIONS

There are times in our lives, especially during illness or old age, when we can't take care of ourselves. We're blessed in the United States to have a safety net of social services provided by government and charitable organizations for those who have nowhere else to turn. But these are services as a last resort, and they can't provide the comfort and care that a family member can offer. Despite the occasional conflict in even the healthiest families, most people understand that they owe a duty to their older relatives, especially to their parents, to help them in their time of need. This is both natural and appropriate. On the other hand, certain medical conditions are beyond the capacity of even the most devoted relative to manage. Parents don't want their children laboring in misery to care for them, but feelings of love and compassion are powerful motivators. As a young adult, you must be prepared to assist your older relatives as much as you can, while keeping in mind your own needs, financial and otherwise. Initiating a candid discussion with your older loved ones about end-of-life issues while they're still mentally and physically strong can help avoid painful drama later.

NOTES

1. "Health Care Costs for Couples in Retirement Rise to an Estimated $245,000," Fidelity Investments, October 7, 2015.

2. For this paragraph, see U.S. Social Security Administration, Actuarial Life Table, "Period Life Table, 2011," average female death probabilities; Author's analysis.

3. Ibid.

4. U.S. Centers for Disease Control and Prevention, National Vital Statistics Report, "Deaths: Final Data for 2013" Table 10, age group 15 to 24.

5. U.S Census Bureau, "Americans with Disabilities: 2010," Figure 2, July 2012.

APPENDIX 1

Website Content

This book has a free companion website with additional financial literacy content, teaching aids, blog postings, and links to other useful resources.

Go to www.financialliteracyformillennials.com.

APPENDIX 2

Takeaway Tips

TOP TEN FINANCIAL TIPS

Here are some of the important personal finance lessons taught in this book:

1. **Keep it simple**. Your financial life doesn't need to be complicated. Complexity makes it difficult to track, manage, and understand your money.

2. **Live modestly**. You'll always have limited resources and face an uncertain future, so being careful about how you spend your money will give you greater financial security.

3. **Avoid debt**. Owing money is the primary source of financial distress for individuals and households: it can destroy lives. Debt can sometimes be helpful but must be used sparingly.

4. **Save relentlessly**. Try always to spend less than you earn, no matter at what level of income. This will allow you to enjoy the benefits of compounded returns later in life.

5. **Embrace skepticism**. If there's a financial opportunity you don't readily understand, avoid it and don't look back. Chances are it will be a bad deal.

6. **Diversify investments**. Maintaining a mix in the types of investments you make will protect you against unnecessary loss and position you for the highest returns with the lowest risk.

7. **Taxes matter**. Every financial decision should consider the impact of taxes on both income and expenses: it's not what you make that counts, but what you keep.

8. **Think long term**. Most young people today will live a long time—if you're 20 today you can expect to live to nearly 80—so your decisions should reflect financial planning for a long lifetime.

9. **Understand yourself.** Your financial life is as personal as your social life, so your financial plan needs to reflect your individuality, ambitions, and risk tolerance. One size doesn't fit all.

10. **Take it seriously.** Money is important, so take the time to learn about personal finance, do additional research when necessary, and discuss it with people who may know more.

FIRST JOB TIPS

Every career starts with a first job, whether a summer internship or your first full-time job. Following are a dozen tips that will serve you well as you launch yourself into the workplace:

1. **Present well.** Dress nicely, groom properly, and use good manners. Be polite and respectful at all times. Avoid looking at your cell phone during meetings. Once you know the culture of your workplace you can adjust, but start with careful attention to appearances and etiquette.

2. **Be on time, even a little early.** Each person who sets a time for you will have a different definition of punctuality, but better for you to wait than to keep someone else waiting.

3. **Do every task cheerfully and enthusiastically, no matter how menial.** This means getting coffee, filing papers, even cleaning up a bathroom if asked. Sometimes people are testing you; other times they just need a hand with something, and you're there to help.

4. **Pay attention to details.** Most jobs ultimately rely on words and numbers, and using the wrong word or making an error with a number has consequences. Take each task seriously and be diligent in performing your work, even if it seems unimportant.

5. **Take initiative.** Bosses love it when they can assign a general task and not have to itemize every step to accomplish it. This will be a little hard for you to do at first, but strive to get there.

6. **Ask questions.** When you're given an assignment and it's unclear to you, ask for clarification. If you're midway through and aren't sure what direction to take, better to ask at that point than to keep going the wrong way.

7. **Ask for work.** If you have nothing to do, make yourself available to others and ask if you can assist. No need to be a pest, but if you've finished something, better to solicit another task than to sit around waiting for something to happen.

8. **Listen more than you speak.** You'll learn a lot by observing, listening, and thinking about what you hear before offering your opinion or views. Once you're more comfortable around your coworkers, you can offer your views more freely.

9. **Bosses prioritize conflicts, not you.** Every so often you'll be presented with multiple tasks that all have to be done at the same time, and there's no possible way to do it. It's best to go to the people who have assigned the tasks and let *them* decide which one will get done first.

10. **Manage time.** Don't spend 10 hours doing detailed research on something that was supposed to be a 30-minute cursory review. In a new work environment it will be more difficult to estimate how long a task will take, so always ask how much time the person assigning a task thinks it should take and when it's due.

11. **Manage up.** Your boss is a human being, too, subject to emotions, irrationality, error, and distraction. Part of your challenge is to deal with that calmly and effectively. Most organizations have some sort of hierarchy that's routinely violated, so you may be asked to do things by more than just "your boss"—accept it.

12. **Offices are political.** When groups of people gather to work, you must inevitably contend with diverse personalities, style differences, ambition, tension, and conflict. Understand this reality and work hard to be nice, cheerful, and well-liked.

TIPS FOR COLLEGE

College is an exciting experience, but it can also present overwhelming options and social challenges. It goes by quickly and will never be repeated—there are no do-overs for college—so here are some tips to get the most out of your college years:

1. **Take road trips.** A great part of the college experience is to visit friends, or to go with friends to visit their friends, at other campuses. Get out and experience different colleges, cities, and towns.

2. **Devote energy to making friends.** Nobody is ever turned off by someone else being friendly, forthcoming, or simply making an introduction. Good friendships can only start after becoming acquainted, and you should give people the benefit of the doubt if your first impression of them isn't positive. Work at making friends.

3. **Don't miss classes.** Even in the Internet era with class notes, problem sets, and additional resources online, there's value in the personal interactions; live classroom learning is more effective than watching the same class on video. A big part of the value of college is what you learn from and contribute to your classmates. Plus, if you miss classes you'll get behind and make it worse on yourself.

4. **Experiment with activities.** You'll have hundreds of different clubs, organizations, sports, and activities to choose from, so try something new.

Eventually, you'll find the handful of activities that fit your interests, but don't limit yourself too early. Get involved.

5. **Easy on the partying**. Drinking and recreational drug use is common on some campuses, and there's often peer pressure to party. It's okay to say no; a true friend won't hold it against you. Learn how to enjoy yourself without drinking, and remember that binge drinking can kill you. Resist your natural curiosity about drugs: we know a lot more now than we did a few decades ago, and there are terrible health effects from drug use, some of which are permanent.

6. **They're not smarter than you are**. At whatever college you attend you'll be surrounded by some of the brightest kids you've ever met, and at times you'll feel inadequate or lose your confidence. Be assured, your insecurity will be temporary. They'll be as impressed with you as you are with them, and they'll discover you have many qualities that make you an interesting person.

7. **You're there to learn**. While there are many aspects of the college experience, don't lose sight of the primary objective: education. Sure, enjoy the social life, but don't squander the opportunity to gain useful knowledge and enrich your mind. Experiment by going outside your comfort zone to take intellectual risks.

8. **Stay healthy**. It will be easy to become consumed with interesting courses, never-ending activities, and new friendships. Unless you're on an intercollegiate sports team, you'll have to be disciplined and make the time to work out. Shoot for daily exercise, then missing one day is no big deal. Commit to be fit. Sleep is also critical for your physical well-being, so try to get your eight hours every night.

9. **Watch your weight**. The food at most colleges is pretty good—you'll indulge in many late-night pizzas, and your room will fill up with snack food. If you monitor your weight weekly and find you've put on a few pounds, a quick adjustment to eating habits in real time beats having to deal with 10–15 pounds all at once.

10. **Remember personal safety**. Most campuses are like a cocoon, familiar and safe, but this can be deceptive. Colleges in urban centers are open to visitors, some of whom may be looking to prey on college kids, and even rural campuses face risks. Women in particular must be wary of harassment and sexual violence, including date rape. Pay attention, trust your instincts, use the late-night ride service, travel in groups, and plan ahead. Guard your valuables, even in your dorm room.

11. **Go to campus events**. Your college will have an accomplished faculty and attract public figures, potentially from all over the world. These visitors will give presentations to students outside the classroom on their work or current events. Your college will also sponsor many special events of all kinds— go to them. If you're at a university, many lectures, concerts, or forums will

be offered by the graduate schools there, so don't be afraid of going to an event even if it's sponsored by another school or department.

12. **Explore the area**. Your life will be centered at your school, but be on the lookout for opportunities to explore the city or region around it. Most areas have many cultural and entertainment resources, so get out and enjoy them. Be on the lookout for excursions organized by your school. These can be great experiences and a way to make new friends.

TIPS FOR GRADUATING STUDENTS

What follows is a series of messages about the coming decades of your life. They're styled as pieces of advice, which is in abundant supply at graduation time, and almost always unwelcome. While conceived for college graduates, almost everything that follows can apply to the high school graduate as well. Add up all the best commencement speeches you'll ever hear; subtract the humor; synthesize what's left; and this is what you'll get.

Mistakes are a necessary part of growing into adulthood, and the purpose of this advice isn't to help you avoid them all, just some that you might not otherwise see coming. Making mistakes means you're probably doing something for the first time, leaving your comfort zone, taking a chance. It takes a well-prepared person to live a meaningful life, and yours is about to take off. Enjoy the ride.

1. **Character counts**. Develop a reputation for honesty, reliability, and integrity. Once you lose someone's respect, it's hard to win back. Don't excuse ethical lapses: own your mistakes and correct them. Be honest with yourself, show compassion, and give help without asking. Exhibit kindness, don't criticize in public, and forgive easily. Keep your word and meet your commitments.

2. **Stay positive**. People respond well to optimism, so keep a sunny disposition even in tough times. Resist negative thoughts. Whatever task, whatever project, give it your all, even if you think the job beneath you. Show passion for your work, and your enthusiasm will be rewarded. Treat each job like the most important in the world, and each day as a gift.

3. **Keep learning**. Read everything you can: newspapers, magazines, web pages, news feeds. Join a book club and use your libraries. Go to lectures, participate in discussion groups, and watch documentary films. Take adult education classes and travel widely. Your occupation may also have continuing education requirements, but remember to enrich your soul. Life-long learning helps you reach your full potential and gain self-knowledge.

4. **Good people matter**. Having high-quality people around you makes a big difference in your life. This is as true of your friends as it is of your business colleagues. Choose carefully. Good people will protect you from foolish

mistakes and bring out the best in you. Bad people will impede your success and hasten your failures.

5. **Work is hard.** Jobs are called "work" for a reason. Some of your work experiences will be painful, demoralizing, and unrewarding. You'll be asked to do things you don't want to do by people who aren't as smart as you are. Don't expect work to always be fun or enjoyable. You'll find that these difficult situations are important life experiences.

6. **Toot your horn.** But quietly and sparingly. Being modest is an outstanding personal virtue. In the workplace, however, humility must be balanced with appropriate recognition. It's a competitive world out there, so you'll need to assert yourself without being abrasive. Let people know you can do the job, be confident without boasting, and good things will happen.

7. **Create balance.** There's more to life than your career. While a lucky few will find in their careers the greatest source of their happiness, that's too high a bar for most. Like what you do for work, a lot, most of the time; then find enjoyment in the other aspects of your life such as family, faith, friendships, volunteering, travel, entertainment, hobbies, and culture.

8. **Stuff happens.** Be prepared for disappointments and for people who will let you down. Life presents many obstacles, most of which you can't control, so accept this reality and work to influence what's in your power. You can't change what happened yesterday, you can only change the future. React positively to adversity; lick your wounds and then get on with it. Show resilience, tenacity, and grit: don't give up. Use your support networks, they're an important factor in longevity and happiness.

9. **Marry well.** If you decide to marry, be careful whom you choose. This decision will contribute to your happiness more than any other you'll make. Look for friendship and respect before you commit. Make sure you have mutual interests and shared life goals to sustain you after the passion fades. A successful marriage or long-term partnership takes work, and there will be tough times even in the best relationships. The right life partner can be empowering, energizing, and inspiring.

10. **Plan a family.** If you want a family, plan for it. Biology dictates that time is an unyielding factor for women, but men also need to consider child-rearing in their life plans. It's easy to get caught up in your life and career as young adults, then wake up one day and find that time for building a family is running out.

11. **Keep fit.** Your physical health will affect your psychological health. Nutrition is as important as staying active. Make time in your busy life for good health as you age. This includes all aspects of your health, such as oral hygiene, mental health, weight control, sufficient sleep, stress management, and regular exercise.

12. **Give back**. You may have enjoyed some privileges, or beaten the odds to rise from poverty. You probably have a better life than most people in this country, certainly better than billions of people around the world. Learn to make charitable giving a habit. Give back to your schools and religious institutions; help the needy. Volunteer and serve on boards, become involved in the civic life of your community, and engage in the political process.

APPENDIX 3

Curriculum Planning

This book is designed for young people 15 to 30 years old, including high school students. The curriculum standards of nineteen states require courses in personal finance for high school graduation, often taught with other subjects, such as business, economics, social studies, or family and consumer sciences. Four of these states require standalone courses, and an additional three states require that personal finance education simply be offered. Every state incorporates economics education into its curriculum standards, and all but seven states (plus D.C.) also incorporate personal finance education into those standards. Unfortunately, with so many different state standards and requirements, there's no uniformity about what constitutes financial literacy for young people.

Several organizations have produced national standards or comprehensive programs for financial literacy education. Foremost among them are the JumpStart Coalition for Personal Financial Literacy, the Council for Economic Education, the American Financial Services Education Foundation, and the National Endowment for Financial Education. The Federal Deposit Insurance Corporation produced the MoneySmart program, which has been used by students and adults alike as a comprehensive source of personal finance education. New online resources such as NextGenVest, EverFi, and NerdWallet are also offering innovative and relevant content to educate young people and other consumers. State leaders, however, haven't adopted any national standards, instead favoring their own rules that often incorporate basic economics as well. As these standards continue to evolve, education professionals will need additional guidance on conforming personal finance education to these requirements.

None of these programs or resources offer the breadth of topics covered in this book, which takes a practical and comprehensive view of what financial literacy requires. Teachers at the high school level must be guided by their own state curriculum requirements, while those at other levels have greater discretion to enhance their financial literacy education using this book. The book's website has lesson plans and additional teacher resources than can be used in high school, college, and adult education courses.

Go to www.financialliteracyformillennials.com.

Index

About the Author

Andrew O. Smith, MBA, JD, has been advising about money, investments, and financial planning since he was a student and helped form the Pennsylvania Investment Alliance, one of the first college investment clubs in the country. As a trustee, financial advisor, and licensed attorney, he has counseled trust funds, estates, investment partnerships, limited-liability corporations, insurance trusts, real estate partnerships, and individuals. Earlier in his career, Smith was a Series 3 licensed Commodity Trading Advisor and served as the chief financial officer for a registered investment fund. Smith began his career as a management consultant for Booz Allen & Hamilton and currently serves as the chief operating officer of Yenkin-Majestic Paint Corporation, a specialty chemical manufacturer. He is the author of *Sand in the Gears: How Public Policy Has Crippled American Manufacturing*. Smith earned a finance degree from the Wharton School and an engineering degree from the School of Engineering and Applied Science, both at the University of Pennsylvania. He also holds an MBA from the Booth School of Business and a JD from the Law School, both at the University of Chicago. In 1988, he was awarded the Olin Prize as the outstanding graduate in law and economics. Smith is a native of Bath, Maine.